Multimedia Cloud Computing Systems

Mohsen Amini Salehi • Xiangbo Li

Multimedia Cloud Computing Systems

 Springer

Mohsen Amini Salehi
Computing and Informatics
University of Louisiana at Lafayette
Lafayette, LA, USA

Xiangbo Li
Twitch Interactive Inc.
San Francisco, CA, USA

ISBN 978-3-030-88453-6   ISBN 978-3-030-88451-2   (eBook)
https://doi.org/10.1007/978-3-030-88451-2

This Springer imprint is published by the registered company Springer Nature Switzerland AG
The registered company address is: Gewerbestrasse 11, 6330 Cham, Switzerland

To my parents, Naser Amini Salehi and Sedighe Afchangi, who taught me love to learn and learn to love! And to my wife, Bahar, who helped me practicing those.

Preface

From the emergence of Cloud technology in 2007–2010, the goal of cloud providers has been mitigating the burden of system administration and maintenance via consolidating servers and forming centralized datacenters. Since then, several progresses have been made in the computing world. Importantly, the sunset of Moore's law during the past decade has shifted the heterogeneous computing landscape from "consistently heterogeneous" systems that include different forms of CPU to "inconsistently heterogeneous" systems where domain-specific processors, a.k.a. Application-Specific Integrated Circuits (ASICs), are used. The emergence of GPU, TPU, FPGA, and most recently, Data Processing Unit (DPU) is an example of this shift in the heterogeneous computing landscape. Datacenters with inconsistently heterogeneous machines will be the bedrock of next-generation cloud computing systems. We foresee that the increasing desire for high-level services in certain areas, such as Machine Learning, data analytics, mapping, and multimedia streaming alongside with the ASIC technology in cloud datacenters will give rise to the idea of domain-specific cloud systems in the remaining years of the current decade. While first generation of cloud systems eased the job of system administrators, the second generation aims at mitigating the burden for programmers and solution architects by providing them with high-level abstractions, APIs, and services within a certain context.

With this vision in mind, we observe a shortage for a platform to enable the goals of a domain-specific cloud. Accordingly, the goal of authoring this book is to overcome this shortage and lay the foundation for the platform of domain-specific clouds. Throughout the book, we particularly concentrate on multimedia streaming as the context and develop the Multimedia Streaming Cloud (MSC) platform. The platform will be cloud native and based on the serverless computing paradigm that will provide an isolated and low-overhead framework for the next generation of cloud-scale computing in the particular domain of multimedia streaming. The reason that we concentrate on the multimedia cloud is the popularity of these services in the current and future of the computing and network industry. Moreover, Dr. Amini and his research team in the High Performance Cloud Computing (HPCC) research group (http://hpcclab.org) have accumulated more than 6 years of knowledge and experience in cloud-based multimedia streaming that provides us with the vision needed to develop such platform and author this book. The second author of this book, Dr. Xiangbo Li, is an experienced research scientist and practitioner in cloud-based multimedia streaming. He was the first graduate of the HPCC Lab in 2016, where he worked on on-demand video transcoding using Cloud Services and under Dr. Amini's supervision laid the foundation of this research track in the HPCC Lab. Dr. Li is now an experienced software engineer and researcher on video platforms at the Twitch Interactive, a subsidiary of Amazon.com, Inc., where he worked on projects such as Amazon Interactive Video Service (AWS IVS) and several other projects.

This book targets audience in both academia and industry. In particular, researchers and practitioners in the Cloud and multimedia areas, solution architects, cloud programmers, and college students can benefit from the content of this book. We hope that this book can push the boundaries of knowledge in computing, help democratizing multimedia streaming, and make multimedia content a more useful tool to improve the life of human beings.

Lafayette, LA, USA   Mohsen Amini Salehi
July 2021

The original version of this book was revised: Affiliation of Author Xiangbo Li has been corrected. The correction to this book is available at https://doi.org/10.1007/978-3-030-88451-2_11

Acknowledgments

This book is the result of more than 6 years of research and development in the High Performance Cloud Computing (HPCC) research laboratory. A postdoctoral associate, Dr. Chavit Denninnart, and multiple Ph.D. and Master's students have helped and contributed significantly in developing the vision needed for authoring this book. We like to particularly acknowledge the contributions of Dr. Mahmoud Darwich, Mr. Davood Ghatreh-Samani, Mr. Ali Mokhtari, Mr. Vaughan Veillon, Mr. James Gentry, Yamini Joshi, Brad Landreneau, and our research visitor Shangrui Wu.

Authoring this book and conducting its research projects is supported by the National Science Foundation CAREER award titled, "CAREER: Developing a Flexible Serverless Multimedia Streaming Cloud Platform" (Award No. CNS-2047144).

Contents

Chapter 1
Introduction

1.1 Overview

Over the past few years, the computing industry has entered the post-Moore's law
era and the increase on the speed of the general-purpose processors (CPUs) has
slowed down. Instead, accelerators and extreme heterogeneous systems that include
Application Specific Integrated Circuits (ASICs) (e.g., special-purpose processors
for video encoding) are gaining popularity. This shift in the hardware evolution has
coincided with the need for specialized hardware that can offer real-time processing
as well as optimality that leads to cost-efficient processing. On another front,
serverless and Function-as-a-Service (FaaS) computing paradigms are emerging as
the next phase of cloud computing that eases cloud-based programming and democ-
ratizes developing new services. Moreover, the serverless paradigm has brought
about the true pay-as-you-go and transparent scalability. These developments in
the computing and cloud technology have paved the way for the new generation
of cloud systems, known as domain-specific clouds.

The essence of this book is to provide insights on the challenges, opportunities,
and characteristics of domain-specific cloud systems. In fact, these systems operate
in the edge-to-cloud continuum with heterogeneous resources and take advantage
of the serverless computing paradigm that enables their developers to rapidly
develop high-level services for their applications. That is, the special-purpose clouds
enable the developers to become solution-oriented and let them focus on developing
advanced services and integrate them to their applications.

This book particularly deals with the development of a platform for domain-
specific Multimedia Streaming Cloud (MSC). We desire that similar special-purpose
clouds will emerge in other widely-used contexts, such as data analytics, machine
learning, genomics processing, and map services. The insights provided in this book
can be instrumental for developing other types of domain-specific clouds as well.

In the rest of this chapter, we provide a bird-eye view of the MSC platform.
In Chap. 2, we explain the way multimedia streaming operates and elaborate on

© Springer Nature Switzerland AG 2021
M. A. Salehi, X. Li, *Multimedia Cloud Computing Systems*,
https://doi.org/10.1007/978-3-030-88451-2_1

each process involved in it. Then, in Chap. 3, we provide a holistic view of the challenges and components of the MSC. Next, in Chap. 4, we describe the potential applications of MSC and the ways it can help stream providers by providing them high-level programming abstractions and APIs. In Chap. 5, we discuss the computing component of MSC where heterogeneous machines and ASICs can expedite processing of the streaming services. As in a serverless platform the processing is carried out behind the scene, MSC offers the opportunity to aggregate function calls and reuse computation. Accordingly, Chap. 6 deals with the potential of reusing in this context and details of how to efficiently performing it. Latency is one of the main factors in evaluating the Quality of Experience (QoE) that users of a streaming service perceive. Details of the latency issue and how it can be reduced is discussed in Chap. 7. Those aspects of multimedia streaming and MSC that were not covered in the other chapters are discussed in Chap. 8. Next, Chap. 9 explains a prototype implementation and evaluation of the MSC platform. Finally, Chap. 10 projects emerging research areas in the intersection of multimedia streaming and cloud computing.

1.2   Multimedia Streaming and Cloud Computing

Multimedia streaming is not anymore limited to conventional video streaming such as those offered by YouTube and Netflix. It is, in fact, an integral part of an increasingly wide range of applications, often operating across a multi-tier edge-to-cloud environments. In smart cities, as just one context where multimedia streaming is used, the video-based infrastructure is an indispensable part of traffic control, healthcare, city planning, hospitals, entertainment, disaster management, maintenance, and manufacturing, among many other city services. Other widely used applications are in e-learning [8], remote surgery [14], video conferencing [12], network-based TVs [24], personal broadcasting (e.g., Facebook Live [30]), situational awareness via video surveillance [5, 15], and movie industry (e.g., Netflix [26] and Hulu).

Beyond all these, the pandemic brought about by COVID-19 acted as a milestone for the multimedia streaming industry. What prior to the pandemic was only *a solution* for many businesses (e.g., education, patient-care, commerce, etc.), had now become *the only* solution. In fact, the pandemic was a turning point for multimedia streaming: it turned multimedia streaming from an *option* to a critical *pillar* making the future-looking societies robust against unforeseen phenomena. Multimedia is an active and innovative industry with a promising future. There are already numerous new types of multimedia services that are finding their ways to our lives. Just a few notable mentions are virtual and augmented reality (VR/AR) [31, 33], 360° streaming, and holographic video [22]. Currently, these multimedia streaming applications constitute more than 75% of the whole Internet traffic and that is projected to grow by up to 82% [11, 16, 32] in the near future.

As multimedia streaming services grow in popularity and diversity, their demand for specialized hardware and software resources increases. Due to the burden and cost of purchasing, upgrading, and maintaining these resources, making use of cloud services has become a common practice for the stream providers. Currently, stream providers extensively (and often entirely) rely on cloud services (e.g., Amazon cloud [2]) to offer their streaming services in a robust and reliable manner and the costs of using clouds has become the main source of expenditure for them. Netflix, as an example, is estimated to spend more than $25 Million on Amazon cloud every month [23].

The businesses relying on the streaming services increasingly require specific services to serve the particular demands of their users. For instance, consider a business (streaming service provider) whose plan is to offer online education to disabled people via live streaming. To enhance visual recognition of color-blind students, this business needs low-latency services to increase the contrast of frames' colors. For deaf students, they need a service for dynamic multilingual subtitle generation. For blind students, they need a service to provide additional audio description [17]. Another child entertainment business requires a service for their application to dynamically extract harmful and illicit content from the multimedia contents and make them child-safe. A healthcare company needs to develop AI-based service in their application that monitors certain metrics in premature birth cases and inform the medical crew upon detecting important signs [13]. A situational-awareness application operating based on edge and cloud computing needs a face detection service to track suspects across multiple security cameras. A repair company needs a smart service that can enhance the quality of the stream captured by the smart glass, before sending it to an expert mechanic. A video/audio conferencing application (e.g., Zoom and Clubhouse) needs to develop real-time language translation services to enable multilingual meetings. An e-learning application may be added with a function to dynamically summarize educational videos; And a 360° streaming application can be equipped with a function to adapt streaming bit-rate to the available network bandwidth.

Offering the aforementioned services on the current general-purpose cloud systems is costly and slow. This is because they do not provide any high-level abstractions and/or programming support that helps offering these services or expedite their development. That is why the existing streaming services are inflexible and their offered services are often limited to the conventional ones (e.g., fast forwarding and rewinding). In retrospect, the emergence of cloud computing technology over the past decade (since 2010) has mainly mitigated the burden of system administration and maintenance without making major changes in the job of programmers and service developers. However, the aforementioned scenarios reveal that the businesses desire a custom-designed (a.k.a. domain-specific) cloud platform that can reap the benefits of the underlying edge-to-cloud environment and provide them with: (a) high-level programming abstractions that hide the complexity of working with different underlying infrastructures and enable them to rapidly develop new streaming services; (b) robust Quality of Experience (in terms of meeting the real-time constraints) via transparent scalability of the developed services without the user involvement in the resource allocation, monitoring, elasticity management, and content delivery; and (c) cost-efficient deployment of the services and paying just for the times underlying heterogeneous resources were utilized.

Accordingly, throughout this book, we explain the structure of a domain-specific cloud platform, called Multimedia Streaming Cloud (MSC), that satisfies the aforementioned desires. MSC will democratize streaming and enables the stream providers (and even viewers) to develop new stream processing services, much like the way people develop extensions for Google Chrome web browser nowadays. The marriage of multimedia streaming and cloud computing gives birth to the notion of *domain-specific cloud systems* and implies dealing with a set of new challenges, techniques, and technologies in distributed computing. Addressing these challenges and providing the MSC platform will mitigate the burden that stream providers have to currently overcome by their own. Instead, MSC will pave the way of stream providers to become solution-oriented and let them focus on developing advanced streaming services and integrate them to their applications.

1.3   The Essence of This Book

Scientists foresee that serverless special-purpose cloud platforms will be the next generation of the cloud computing industry [4]. Accordingly, this book aims at laying the foundations to build such a platform for multimedia streaming. The platform will offer high-level abstractions to hide the details of both resource and data management from stream providers in the edge-to-cloud continuum and let them focus on developing advanced streaming services and integrate them to their applications. Even though this book considers multimedia clouds, the identified challenges and solutions can be adapted and applied to a wider range, in building other domain-specific cloud platforms, e.g., for smart cities [25] and for data analytics [3].

Although numerous research works have been undertaken on cloud-based multimedia streaming, there is no comprehensive study that shed lights on challenges, techniques, and technologies in developing a special-purpose cloud platform for multimedia streaming. As such, the essence of authoring this book is to *first*, shed light on the sophisticated processes required for cloud-based multimedia streaming; *second*, provide a holistic view on the ways domain-specific clouds can aid multimedia stream providers; *third*, provide a comprehensive survey on the potential applications of multimedia streaming and cloud computing; and *fourth* discuss the future of multimedia streaming cloud and other domain-specific cloud technologies and identify possible avenues that require further research efforts from industry and academia.

1.4   Characteristics of the Multimedia Streaming Cloud (MSC)

1.4.1   Quality of Experience (QoE) in the MSC Platform

At high-level, stream providers and viewers expect a fast and uninterruptible streaming service. To interpret these expectations in low-level and measurable metrics, we first need to know the structure of a multimedia stream. In practice, streaming of a multimedia content occurs via partitioning the content into segments that are often of the same length (time-span). To have a high streaming QoE, certain QoE metrics both at the segment level and at the stream level must be fulfilled.

First and the foremost is the *latency* metric for each segment that guarantees the uninterruptiblity of the stream. In on-demand streaming, this metric is determined based on the presentation time of each segment in the stream and is considered in form of a soft deadline constraint for the segment. Conversely, in live-streaming, we have a hard deadline for each captured segment and it is measured based on a fixed time interval after the capturing time.

In addition to the latency, the *startup delay* is another factor the determines the quality of streaming. It is defined as the time between the viewer requests a content until the first segment is played on the screen. It is proven that if the startup delay is high, the viewers cancel the entire stream and choose another one. *Fairness* across users is another QoE factor in multimedia streaming. That is, for the same viewer subscription type, the streaming engine should be bias and miss the deadlines of some viewers in favor of some others.

1.4.2   Robustness of the MSC Platform

Processing multimedia segments is often time-consuming and uncertain that are detrimental to providing a robust streaming QoE. Therefore, to achieve robust QoE, currently, stream providers pre-process every single multimedia segment in numerous formats (between 90 and 270 versions) [6, 7]. However, pre-processing is not possible for live streams. Even for VOD, pre-processing of all services is cost-prohibitive, provided the long-tail access pattern to the content [7].

The lack of on-the-spot processing has been an impediment for offering flexible multimedia streaming services. To overcome this impediment, MSC's approach will be lazy (i.e., on-demand) and real-time processing of rarely-accessed contents on low-overhead containers. Note that the lazy processing cannot be outsourced to viewers' thin-clients (e.g., smartphones) with energy and compute limitations [21]. Besides, it raises compatibility issues, which is counterproductive.

1.4.3   Function-as-a-Service and Serverless Computing in the MSC Platform

Function-as-a-Service (FaaS) is gaining popularity as an on-demand and cost-efficient computing solution for cloud-based applications. Modern software engineering practices, such as DevOps [1] and Continuous Integration Continuous Delivery (CI/CD) [9], operate based on splitting an application into several stateless micro-services where each micro-service is essentially one (or more) functions. The user uploads the developed functions to the cloud and defines time-based or event-based triggers for them. While FaaS focuses on the front-end of micro-services via providing the ability for high-level programming in a wide-variety of languages, Backend-as-a-Service (BaaS) focuses on providing a virtualized (containerized) environment for executing the function in isolation from other functions and users. BaaS is also in charge of scheduling, execution, monitoring, and transparent elasticity of the function (micro-service). As shown in Fig. 1.1, in this paradigm, the serverless computing defined as the combination of FaaS and BaaS, i.e., Serverless=FaaS+BaaS.

Unlike Infrastructure-as-a-Service (IaaS) model where the user is in charge of managing the acquired resources and mapping arriving task requests to them, in the serverless paradigm, each function call (service request) is managed behind the scene. The function calls are submitted to a shared scheduling queue for execution, thus, in compare with the conventional IaaS paradigm, the resource idling is reduced and the cost-efficiency (for both provider and user) is potentially improved.

FaaS and Serverless computing are keys in achieving goals of the MSC platform. Importantly, the high-level programming ability for new multimedia services is provided by the FaaS solutions that enables stream providers or even viewers to develop their desired streaming services. Handling the arriving streaming requests

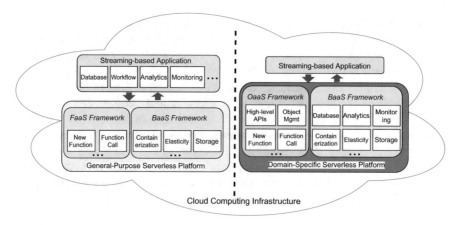

Fig. 1.1 The difference between a general-purpose serverless cloud platform versus a domain-specific one used for multimedia streaming

in a scalable and efficient manner is accomplished using BaaS that relieves the users from the burden of resource management and monitoring. Structure of the MSC platform itself is based on the serverless paradigm that makes its development and updating easier and faster.

Although general-purpose serverless computing relieves users from the burden of resource management, it is not truly transparent, because it falls short on abstracting data management. The users (developers) still have to engage with other services (e.g., Amazon DynamoDB [29] or AWS Serverless Application Model (SAM) [28]) to manage their processing data. The key to enable extreme transparency in MSC (and other domain-specific clouds) is to enable higher level abstractions that hides the details of data management as well as the resource management. Accordingly, as shown in Fig. 1.1, we introduce the **Object-as-a-Service (OaaS)** management abstraction in the special-purpose serverless cloud (and particularly MSC) as the first-class citizen. OaaS represents each streaming source (e.g., camera) as an object, hence, relieving users from the burden of *both data and resource management details*. The objects are natively aware of the edge-to-cloud continuum, resource heterogeneity, and users' QoE and cost preferences. Resource management of the objects can make the streaming robust against uncertainties in requests' execution times and arrival rate. The objects can capture the spatiotemporal property of streaming requests and reuse the function calls to the object to achieve cost-efficiency without compromising the viewers' QoE. The users can compose new objects and feature them with existing (built-in) or newly developed functions. The new domain-specific serverless platform has a richer BaaS framework too that includes modules for persistent (database) and monitoring.

Collectively, using these high-level abstractions mitigate the burden that stream providers currently have to overcome by their own in their streaming-based applications. Instead, domain-specific serverless cloud platforms (and MSC) pave the way of stream providers to become solution-oriented and let them quickly develop advanced streaming services and integrate them to their applications.

1.5   A Bird-Eye View of the Multimedia Streaming Cloud (MSC) Platform

A bird-eye view of the MSC platform and the edge-to-cloud environment it operates in is shown in Fig. 1.2. The MSC platform serves two types of users, namely *stream providers* and *viewers*. Stream providers desire MSC to enable them stream in various forms (e.g., live, recorded, AR/VR, etc.) with a low cost and the minimum administration and development efforts. In MSC, stream providers configure live (e.g., security camera) or recorded (e.g., VOD) multimedia sources in form of *streaming objects* with various real-time constraints (e.g., soft real-time for VOD and hard real-time for live-streaming) and then bind functions to them. The functions can be from the set of publicly available functions or be developed by

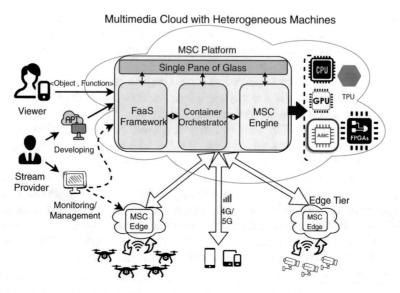

Fig. 1.2 Bird-eye view of the MSC streaming platform operating in the edge-to-cloud continuum

the stream provider to enable new services on the streaming objects. *Viewers* desire an uninterrupted and robust streaming experience with diverse services and fine-grain billing plans (e.g., pay-as-you-watch versus monthly subscription). A viewer of MSC uses an application (e.g., live streaming for disabled people) to issue requests in form of <object, function> to trigger a function call, defined for a particular streaming objects. It is as well possible that the stream provider and viewer be the same. For instance, in a home security system, the owner is both the stream provider and the viewer who triggers a specific function (e.g., face detection) on the camera object.

The computing resources available to MSC are highly heterogeneous, e.g., CPUs, GPUs, FPGAs, and ASICs. Prior studies [19, 20] show that stream processing can take advantage of heterogeneous computing machines offered by clouds to improve both their QoE and cost efficiency. In practice, cloud providers (e.g., Twitch [10]) are increasingly making use of such highly heterogeneous cloud datacenters to reduce their energy consumption and minimize their expenditure [19, 27].

To achieve its goals, MSC can be built upon and extends the currently available open-source frameworks and it is not needed to develop every tool from scratch. Forming new objects, monitoring their states, and managing their configurations can be carried out via a Single Pane of Glass (SPOG) framework that provides a unified access to the objects across the continuum. Developing new functions can be carried out via a FaaS framework that itself is connected to the SPOG to facilitate binding the functions to the streaming objects. Once the objects are formed, activating them is carried out in a lazy (on-demand) manner—upon calling a function of the object by an application. In this case, the containerized functions are provisioned and managed via a container orchestrator. A container that includes the MSC-engine acts as the object controller that can alter the object's state and allocating resources to manage the requests received by the object. The MSC platform that runs on the edge tier, called MSC-edge, essentially has the same architecture as the one runs on the cloud, except using a lightweight (edge-friendly) container orchestrator (e.g., lightweight Kubernetes, a.k.a. K3s [18]).

References

1. A systematic mapping study on microservices architecture in devops. *Journal of Systems and Software*, 170:110798, 2020.
2. Amazon EC2. http://aws.amazon.com/ec2. Accessed June 25, 2020.
3. Ekaba Bisong. Google bigquery. In *Building Machine Learning and Deep Learning Models on Google Cloud Platform*, pages 485–517. Springer, 2019.
4. Rajkumar Buyya, Satish Narayana Srirama, Giuliano Casale, Rodrigo Calheiros, Yogesh Simmhan, Blesson Varghese, Erol Gelenbe, Bahman Javadi, Luis Miguel Vaquero, Marco A. S. Netto, Adel Nadjaran Toosi, Maria Alejandra Rodriguez, Ignacio M. Llorente, Sabrina De Capitani Di Vimercati, Pierangela Samarati, Dejan Milojicic, Carlos Varela, Rami Bahsoon, Marcos Dias De Assuncao, Omer Rana, Wanlei Zhou, Hai Jin, Wolfgang Gentzsch, Albert Y. Zomaya, and Haiying Shen. A manifesto for future generation cloud computing: Research directions for the next decade. *ACM Computing Survey*, 51(5):105:1–105:38, Nov. 2018.
5. N. Chen, Y. Chen, Y. You, H. Ling, P. Liang, and R. Zimmermann. Dynamic urban surveillance video stream processing using fog computing. In *In Proceedings of the 2nd IEEE International Conference on Multimedia Big Data*, pages 105–112, Apr. 2016.
6. M. Darwich, E. Beyazit, M. A. Salehi, and M. Bayoumi. Cost efficient repository management for cloud-based on-demand video streaming. In *In Proceedings of 5th IEEE International Conference on Mobile Cloud Computing, Services, and Engineering*, pages 39–44, Apr. 2017.
7. Mahmoud Darwich, Mohsen Amini Salehi, Ege Beyazit, and Magdy Bayoumi. Cost-efficient cloud-based video streaming through measuring hotness. *The Computer Journal*, 2018.
8. Erhan Delen, Jeffrey Liew, and Victor Willson. Effects of interactivity and instructional scaffolding on learning: Self-regulation in online video-based environments. *Computers & Education*, 78:312–320, Sep. 2014.
9. Irfan Fadil, Asep Saeppani, Agun Guntara, and Fathoni Mahardika. Distributing parallel virtual image application using continuous integrity/continuous delivery based on cloud infrastructure. In *Proceedings of the 8th International Conference on Cyber and IT Service Management (CITSM)*, pages 1–4. IEEE, 2020.
10. Live Streaming Service for Gaming. https://www.twitch.tv/. Accessed May 5, 2020.
11. Cisco Visual Networking Index: Forecast and 2016–2021 Methodology. https://www.cisco.com/c/en/us/solutions/collateral/service-provider/visual-networking-index-vni/complete-white-paper-c11-481360.html. Accessed May 5, 2020.
12. Hisato Fukuda, Yoshinori Kobayashi, and Yoshinori Kuno. Teleoperation of a robot through audio-visual signal via video chat. In *Companion of the 2018 ACM/IEEE International Conference on Human-Robot Interaction*, HRI '18, pages 111–112, 2018.
13. Enhancing Healthcare and Eliminating Human Error in NICUs. https://www.wowza.com/wp-content/uploads/child-health-imprints-case-study.pdf. Accessed Jul. 5, 2020.
14. Takafumi Hiranaka, Yuta Nakanishi, Takaaki Fujishiro, Yuichi Hida, Masanori Tsubosaka, Yosaku Shibata, Kenjiro Okimura, and Harunobu Uemoto. The use of smart glasses for surgical video streaming. *Surgical Innovation*, 24(2):151–154, 2017.

15. Matin Hosseini, Mohsen Amini Salehi, and Raju Gottumukkala. Enabling interactive video streaming for public safety monitoring through batch scheduling. In *in proceedings of the 19th IEEE International Conference on High Performance Computing and Communications*, Dec. 2017.
16. Cisco Visual Networking Index. Forecast and methodology, 2014–2020. 2015.
17. Qin Jin and Junwei Liang. Video description generation using audio and visual cues. In *Proceedings of the ACM International Conference on Multimedia Retrieval*, pages 239–242, 2016.
18. Lightweight Kubernetes. https://k3s.io/. Accessed Aug. 7, 2020.
19. X. Li, M. A. Salehi, M. Bayoumi, N. Tzeng, and R. Buyya. Cost-efficient and robust on-demand video transcoding using heterogeneous cloud services. *IEEE Transactions on Parallel and Distributed Systems*, 29(3):556–571, Mar. 2018.
20. Xiangbo Li, Mohsen Amini Salehi, Yamini Joshi, Mahmoud Darwich, Landreneau Brad, and Magdi Bayoumi. Performance Analysis and Modelling of Video Stream Transcoding Using Heterogeneous Cloud Services. *IEEE Transactions on Parallel and Distributed Systems (TPDS)*, Sep. 2018.
21. Xiangbo Li, Mohsen Amini Salehi, and Magdy Bayoumi. Cloud-based video streaming for energy- and compute-limited thin clients. In *the Stream2015 Workshop at Indiana University*, Oct, 2015.
22. Jene W. Meulstee, Johan Nijsink, Ruud Schreurs, Luc M. Verhamme, Tong Xi, Hans H. K. Delye, Wilfred A. Borstlap, and Thomas J. J. Maal. Toward holographic-guided surgery. *Surgical Innovation*, 26(1):86–94, 2019.
23. Netflix Expenditure on AWS. https://www.cloudzero.com/blog/netflix-aws. Accessed June 25, 2021.
24. Jo Pierson and Joke Bauwens. *Digital Broadcasting: an introduction to new media*. Bloomsbury Publishing, 2015.
25. R. Polishetty, M. Roopaei, and P. Rad. A next-generation secure cloud-based deep learning license plate recognition for smart cities. In *Proceedings of the 15th IEEE International Conference on Machine Learning and Applications (ICMLA)*, pages 286–293, Dec. 2016.
26. Netflix Streaming Provider. https://www.netflix.com. Accessed May 5, 2020.
27. Z. Ruan and X. Ye. Cost-optimized video dissemination over heterogeneous cloud with slas support. *IEEE Access*, 7:42874–42888, 2019.
28. Amazon Serverless Application Model (SAM). https://aws.amazon.com/about-aws/whats-new/2020/07/announcing-aws-serverless-application-model-cli-generally-available-production-use/. Accessed Aug. 7, 2020.
29. Amazon DynamoDB Service. https://aws.amazon.com/dynamodb/. Accessed June 12, 2020.
30. Facebook Live Streaming Service. https://live.fb.com/. Accessed May 5, 2020.
31. Vibhu Saujanya Sharma, Rohit Mehra, Vikrant Kaulgud, and Sanjay Podder. An immersive future for software engineering: Avenues and approaches. In *Proceedings of the 40th International Conference on Software Engineering: New Ideas and Emerging Results*, ICSE-NIER '18, pages 105–108, 2018.
32. The Secrets to Massive Revenue Growth. https://www.square2marketing.com/blog/video-streaming-will-grow-to-70.05-billion-in-2021. Accessed June. 5, 2019.
33. M. Zink, R. Sitaraman, and K. Nahrstedt. Scalable 360 video stream delivery: Challenges, solutions, and opportunities. *Proceedings of the IEEE*, 107(4):639–650, April 2019.

Chapter 2
Demystifying Multimedia Streaming Workflow

2.1 Overview

The following calculation shows the storage space needed to persist only 1 s of a video with 720×1280 *pixels* resolution and 60 frames per second frame-rate where each pixel requires three 8-bit space for the RGB colors.

$$\frac{720 \times 1280 \; pixels}{frame} \cdot \frac{60 \; frames}{sec} \cdot \frac{3 \; colors}{pixel} \cdot \frac{8 \; bits}{color} = 1.3 \; Gb \qquad (2.1)$$

Unarguably, it is cost-prohibitive to store and impractical to stream this volume of raw video contents. This is where video compression techniques come into the play to compress the raw video based on some video compression (codec) standards (e.g., H.264 [23], HEVC [17] etc.). The goal of video compression is to remove the redundancy. It divides the frames into mainly three categories: I frame, P frame and B frame. I frame is an independent frame that can be encoded and decoded independently, video encoder only reduces the spatial redundancy inside the frame using intra prediction [15]. Both P and B frames are dependent on other frames to remove the temporal redundancy via inter-prediction [15]. Usually, one I frame and multiple P and B frames form a group, called Group of Picture (GOP), as shown in Fig. 2.1, that can be encoded and decoded independently. In fact, there are two types of GOPs: closed-GOP, in which the GOPs are entirely independent, and open-GOP [3], in which GOPs depend on each other. The notion of GOP is essential for splitting and streaming the multimedia (video) content.

Once the video is encoded, its contents are usually encrypted, so that unauthorized viewers cannot access them. There are mainly two ways to encrypt the video contents: common encryption (CENC) [7] and third party digital right management (DRM) [25]. For a given encrypted video, decoder needs to request the key first before being able to decode it. CENC is the commonly used encryption format, however, DRM is proven to be more secure than CENC, because CENC doesn't

© Springer Nature Switzerland AG 2021
M. A. Salehi, X. Li, *Multimedia Cloud Computing Systems*,
https://doi.org/10.1007/978-3-030-88451-2_2

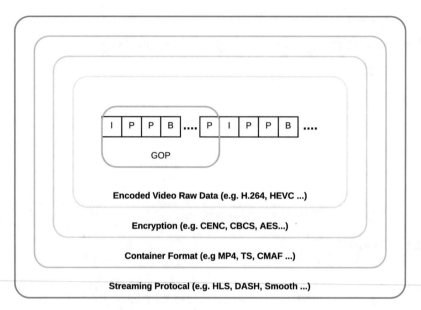

Fig. 2.1 The technologies involved in a streaming video content

encrypt the keys the way DRM does. It is needless to say that the higher security of
DRM comes with the higher processing cost.

An encoded and encrypted video content can be stored, however, to be streamed
and viewed on the player, it also has to be packaged into a container format (e.g.,
MP4 [2], TS [4], CMAF [12] etc.) with specific streaming protocol (e.g., HLS [19],
DASH [18], or Smooth [24]). Http Live Streaming (HLS) is a streaming protocol
used by the Apple devices, while DASH is another protocol supported by most of
the devices besides Apple. Thus, to support playback on different display devices,
streaming providers have to deliver both HLS and DASH formats, sometime even
the Smooth format for some Microsoft Silverlight devices. MP4 format is based on
ISOBFF [1], which is widely used in DASH streaming and latest version of HLS.
TS is another container format that is used for broadcasting and HLS streaming. The
advantage of the Mp4 format is its atom box structure that can provide decoding and
segment location at the beginning of the video, hence, achieving a fast startup time
and random access. On the other hand, this can become a bottleneck, since the rest
of the video segment cannot be decoded before parsing the movie box (*moov*). TS
container format is more widely used in broadcasting and live streaming, because
each TS segment can be decoded and viewed independently. CMAF is the latest
container format which aims to simplify the streaming by incorporating the features
for both HLS and DASH, so that streaming provider only needs to deliver one format
for all devices. Another advantage of CMAF is its chuck-based feature, which offers
a lower latency in compare with the HLS and DASH protocols.

As we briefly discussed, multimedia streaming is a complex process that includes several aspects—from the compression (encoding), packaging, and encryption to the content delivery and playback on the viewer's device. Various streaming techniques (e.g., 360-degree, virtual and augmented reality), streaming types (e.g., VOD and live streaming), display platforms (e.g., browsers and players), adapting streaming to the network conditions, etc. adds to this complexity. Accordingly, the goal of this section is to describe the basic processes involved in the streaming and provide a generic workflow for it (shown in Fig. 2.2). Moreover, we explain the basic solutions exist for each one these processes.

2.2   Video Streaming Types

Multimedia streaming can be categorized into two main types, namely video on demand (VOD) and live streaming. In VOD, the video contents are often pre-encoded and pre-packaged into one or multiple formats (e.g., mp4, ts) that are stored in a repository that is often in form of a cloud storage. By far, VOD is the most common type of video streaming and is offered by major video streaming providers, such as YouTube, Netflix, and Amazon Prime Video etc. Some VOD providers (e.g., Netflix and Hulu) offer professionally created videos and movies that are subscription-based and viewers are generally required to pay a monthly fee to access their service. Alternatively, other VOD services (e.g., YouTube) operate based user-provided videos. Such services are generally advertisement-based and free of charge. VODs have also applications in e-learning systems [14], Internet television [6], and in-flight entertainment systems [9]. Upon receiving a request to stream a video, it is *pulled* (downloaded) through HTTP or FTP protocols to the transcoder server that is discussed in the next sections.

In live video streaming, the video contents are streamed to the viewer(s), as they are captured by a camera. Live video streaming has numerous applications, such as event coverage and video calls. The live video streaming used in different applications have minor differences that are mainly attributed to the buffer size on the sender and receiver ends. In general, a larger buffer size causes a more stable streaming experience but imposes more delay. This delay can be tolerated in live broadcasting applications, however, delay-sensitive applications (e.g., video telephony) cannot bear the delay, thus need a shorter buffer size. Streaming live contents is different in the sense that the video contents are constantly generated by the camera and, instead of waiting for being pulled by the transcoder server, they should be *pushed* (via RTMP [8] protocol) to the transcoder server. Even though RTMP is an old protocol, it is still widely used in live video ingestion because of its low latency (in compare with HTTP) that is critical for live streaming. A newer protocol, known as SRT [21], that provides a lower latency and higher QoE than RTMP has been developed by Haivision for live streaming. Although this protocol has gained a lot of attention recently, it will take a long time to get device compliance and fight its way to the viewer's devices.

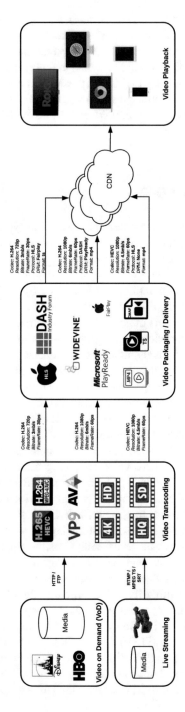

Fig. 2.2 A bird's-eye view to the workflow of processes performed on a video stream from the source to the viewer's device. The workflow includes compression, transcoding, packaging, and delivery processes

It is noteworthy that, there is another type of streaming, known as broadcasting, that can be considered as a hybrid of VOD and live streaming. In this type of streaming, the video contents can be either stored in the repository or be live. It uses RTMP or MPEGTS protocols to push the contents to the transcoder server. We will elaborate on different types of streaming in Chap. 4.

2.3   Video Transcoding

Video encoding is aimed to compress the video by reducing the spatial and temporal redundancy. In contrast, video transcoding is to aimed at making the video content compatible to the diverse playback devices, players, and network bandwidth of the viewer. That is, video transcoding is to re-encode the video into one or more other versions (e.g., in terms of codec, resolution, bitrate, framerate, etc.), so that the video can be played on heterogeneous display devices or fluctuating network conditions.

2.3.1   Bit Rate

Video bit rate is the number of bits used to encode a unit time of a video. Bit rate directly impacts on the video quality, i.e., a higher bit rate implies a better video quality. Unarguably, higher bit rates consume a larger network bandwidth and storage space. To stream videos to viewers with different network conditions, streaming service providers usually convert video with multiple bit rates, which is often known as adaptive bit rate.

2.3.2   Resolution

Resolution represents the dimensional size of a video, which indicates the number of pixels on each video frame. Therefore, a higher resolution contains more pixels and details, as results in a larger size. Video resolution usually needs to match with the screen size. Low resolution video plays on large screen will causes blurry after upsample, while high resolution plays on small screen is just a waste of bandwidth since viewer usually won't notice the difference due to the limited pixels on the screen. To adapt to the diverse screen size on the market, original videos have to be transcoded to multiple resolutions.

2.3.3 Frame Rate

Human vision system feels moving of the objects as a result of playing frames at a certain rate. Accordingly, frame rate is defined as the number of frames shown per second. Videos are usually recorded at high frame rate to produce smooth movement, while devices may not support such high frame rate. Therefore, in some cases, videos have to be reduced to a lower frame rate by removing some of the frames. However, increasing the frame rate is a more complicated process than reducing it, since it involves adding non-existent frames.

2.3.4 Codec

Video Compression standard is the key to compress a raw video, the encoding process mainly goes through four steps: prediction, transform, quantization, and entropy coding, while decoding is just the reverse of the encoding process. With different codecs manufactured on different devices (e.g., DVD player with MPEG-2 [5], BlueRay player with H.264 [23], 4K TV with HEVC [17]), an encoded video may have to be converted to the supported codec on that device. Changing codec is the most compute-intensive type of transcoding since it has to decode the bitstream with the old codec first and then encode it again with the new codec.

Table 2.1 shows a recommendation transcoding ladder for H.264 from Apple. Therefore, before streaming a video, having information about the viewers, such as the type of playback devices, the bandwidth statistics, etc. can help the streaming provider to make a better decision regarding the codec, resolution, bitrate, and other characteristics of the destination video to transcode it into, so that the viewer can have the best playback experience. In Fig. 2.2, as we can see, the transcoder server transcodes the ingested video into multiple versions that are usually stored in the repository waiting to be packaged and delivered to the viewers, whereas, live video streams are directly sent to packaging and delivery system.

Table 2.1 Apple HLS recommended encoding ladder for H.264

Resolution	Bitrate	Frame rate
416 × 234	145	≤30 fps
640 × 360	365	≤30 fps
768 × 432	730	≤30 fps
768 × 432	1100	≤30 fps
960 × 540	2000	≤ same as source
1280 × 720	3000	≤ same as source
1280 × 720	4500	≤ same as source
1920 × 1080	6000	≤ same as source
1920 × 1080	7800	≤ same as source

2.4   Video Delivery

2.4.1   Packaging

After video encoding and transcoding, the video contents are transformed into an elementary stream. However, this stream is not playable by most players and cannot even transmitted through the Internet. In order to play a video, the player needs to parse some decoding parameters (e.g., SPS, PPS etc.) first before being able to decode and render it. Container formats (e.g., MP4, TS, Flv etc.) is designed to provide the player those information by putting the decoding and random access information into some headers (e.g., 'moov' in MP4, 'PAT and PMT' in TS, etc.), so that the player can easily and quickly extract them and then begin to decode and render the video. This processing is called video packaging.

2.4.2   Encryption

In the video packaging process, video can be encrypted to avoid unauthorized access. As we mentioned before, there are mainly two ways of encryption: CENC and DRM. CENC delivers the key and the encrypted contents directly to authorized viewers, whereas, DRM usually uses a separate third party service. In this approach, the player has to first request the key from the third party server and then decode the video. Ideally, video contents are only needed to be encrypted by one encryption technology. However, in reality, Apple devices only support FairPlay [20], and some other devices only support Microsoft's PlayReady [16] or Google's Widewine [22]. Thus, to support all devices, video should be encrypted with different CENC or DRM technologies. More details about video security will be discussed in Chap. 8.3.

2.4.3   Streaming Protocols

The video content has been encoded, transcoded, packaged, and encrypted, which finally can be viewed on the playback devices. However, the next question is how to deliver this video from the server side to the client (viewer) side? The naive approach would be download the whole video, and then decode it and play it. This approach is called *progressive downloading* that was widely used in the early days of the Internet-based streaming. Nevertheless, this approach suffers from a high latency and it may take a few minutes or even a few hours to download the whole video before it can be watched on the viewer's device.

That was why the RTMP [8] streaming protocol with FLV video format (known as Adobe Flash-based streaming) became popular for a few years. In fact, the video contents have been segmented in the RTMP server and viewers did not have to wait for the whole video to be downloaded before watching it. In this manner, the video can be started on the viewer's device very quickly, and not to mention that the play finally can move backward or forward with RTMP. However, RTMP does have its own bottleneck. It can only deliver a single version of a video, and it also requires dedicated streaming servers which adds up the cost.

To address those drawbacks of RTMP, HTTP-based *Adaptive Bitrate Streaming (ABR)* has emerged and became the mainstream in the video streaming technology. Currently, ABR is predominantly used as the video delivery technology. It is capable of delivering multiple versions of the video at the same time, and also allow switching among them in real-time based on the viewer's network or device situation.

Among the common ABR streaming protocols, the HLS [19] and MPEG-DASH [18] are the most popular ones and widely used in the video streaming. Due to the protocol adaptability issue for different devices, in order to deliver video content to large variety of viewers, streaming service provider usually have to support both HLS and DASH delivery methods, and sometime even Smooth for Microsoft Silverlight [11] powered applications. Unfortunately, each streaming protocol has its own supported container format. DASH only supports the MP4 format, but HLS only allows TS format before. Until the version 7, HLS finally started to support MP4 format. Such diversity has added up a lot complexity and cost for delivering a video content.

Recently, the CMAF protocol [12] has been proposed to resolve such mess. As shown in Figs. 2.3 and 2.4, the stream service providers only need to deliver the video content with one container format which is supported by both DASH and

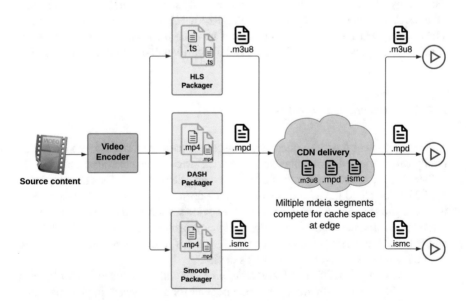

Fig. 2.3 Common video delivery system for multiple streaming protocols

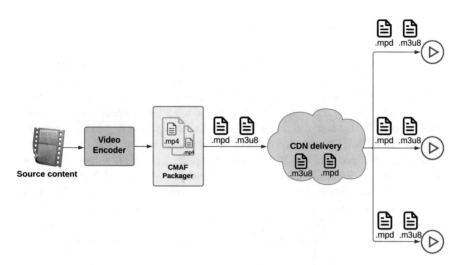

Fig. 2.4 Video delivery system using CMAF for both DASH and HLS

HLS protocol. CMAF not only reduces the complexity, but also lower the storage costs by half. Meanwhile, CMAF also opens another door for low latency streaming, which will be discussed more in Chap. 7.5.

2.5   Content Delivery Network (CDN)

When the video contents have been packaged and delivered to the viewers' device, they can be watched with a supported player. However, there are still a few more factors that need to be considered in order to provide good quality of services (QoS) of video stream. The first is network latency, since the viewers can be located far away from the streaming servers. Another one is popular videos, which can be frequently requested by different viewers, which gives the stream server large burden to handle such influx requests. Luckily such problems is not only for video stream, it happens to all web applications as well. The solution for these problems is to use a Content Delivery Network (CDN) [13]. CDN is essentially an edge server located near to the clients in different regions. It has a caching capability to store the latest request contents, so that the following same content requests can directly be pull from the cache instead of the origin streaming server. This largely reduces the playback latency and the workload burden at the origin servers. More details regarding CDN will be discussed in Sect. 7.2.

2.6   Video Playback

Once video contents have gone through encoding, transcoding, packaging, CDN and been delivered to the player. In order to successfully playback the video contents on the screen, the player needs to decode the video and then render it. Nonetheless, the player actually does more works than that. There are some cross-platform players that can play different types of video formats (e.g., VLC), however, most of the HTML5 player frameworks like dash.js,[1] hls.js,[2] flash, etc., can only request a certain protocol manifest and play a specific container format. Therefore, at the client side, it usually requires different web players under different operating systems or web browsers. Another essential work player has to perform is to select a right version of streams to play. As we mentioned earlier, streaming servers usually provides multiple versions of the same video, it is up to the player to choose the appropriate version based on the ABR algorithm [10] implemented inside it.

2.7   Summary

In this chapter, we unfolded the common practice for multimedia streaming. It involves a complicated workflow that begins with the content generation via camera in live streaming or via a repository in on-demand streaming. Then, it is followed by the transcoding, packaging, delivery, and finally playback processes. Each one of these processes include multiple protocols and technologies (e.g., CDN, codecs, etc.). To simplify this complicated workflow, in practice, on-demand stream providers pre-process and store several versions of the same multimedia content, whereas, live streamers have to skip some steps and compromise the quality of streaming. While this chapter elaborated on current practices in the streaming technology, the next chapter pushes the envelop and sheds light on the characteristics of forthcoming streaming technologies that allows users to interact with the multimedia content. Specifically, it deals with the complication of developing a serverless cloud platform dedicated to multimedia streaming that allows users to develop new services or customize the existing ones.

---

[1] https://github.com/Dash-Industry-Forum/dash.js.

[2] https://github.com/video-dev/hls.js/.

References

1. ISO/IEC 14496-12. Information technology — coding of audio-visual objects — part 12: Iso base media file format. *ISO/IEC 23001-7:2015*, 2, 2015.
2. ISO/IEC 14496-14. Information technology — coding of audio-visual objects — part 14: Mp4 file format, 2020.
3. Cheolhong An and Truong Q Nguyen. Iterative rate-distortion optimization of h. 264 with constant bit rate constraint. *IEEE Transactions on Image Processing*, 17(9):1605–1615, 2008.
4. Gun Bang, Hyun-cheol Kim, Myung-Seok Ki, Hui-Young Kim, Han-Kyu Lee, and Jin-Woo Hong. Storage/playback method and apparatus for mpeg-2 transport stream based on iso base media file format, June 3 2010. US Patent App. 12/594,307.
5. Barry G Haskell, Atul Puri, and Arun N Netravali. *Digital video: an introduction to MPEG-2.* Springer Science & Business Media, 1996.
6. Xiaojun Hei, Chao Liang, Jian Liang, Yong Liu, and Keith W Ross. A measurement study of a large-scale p2p IPTV system. *IEEE transactions on multimedia*, 9(8):1672–1687, 2007.
7. ZV Kilroy Hughes, David Singer, and Z Visharam. Iso/iec 23001-7 3rd edition-common encryption in iso base media file format files. *online at: http://mpeg.chiariglione.org/ standards/mpegb/common-encryption-iso-base-media-fileformat-files*, 2014.
8. Xiaohua Lei, Xiuhua Jiang, and Caihong Wang. Design and implementation of streaming media processing software based on RTMP. In *2012 5th International Congress on Image and Signal Processing*, pages 192–196. IEEE, 2012.
9. Hao Liu. In-flight entertainment system: state of the art and research directions. In *Second International Workshop on Semantic Media Adaptation and Personalization (SMAP 2007)*, pages 241–244. IEEE, 2007.
10. Zili Meng, Jing Chen, Yaning Guo, Chen Sun, Hongxin Hu, and Mingwei Xu. Pitree: Practical implementation of ABR algorithms using decision trees. In *Proceedings of the 27th ACM International Conference on Multimedia*, pages 2431–2439, 2019.
11. Laurence Moroney. *Microsoft Silverlight 4 Step by Step*. Microsoft Press, 2010.
12. Robert Peck, Jordi Cenzano, Xiangbo Li, and Yuriy Reznik. Towards mass deployment of CMAF.
13. Gang Peng. CDN: Content distribution network. *arXiv preprint cs/0411069*, 2004.
14. Lavanya Rajendran and Ramachandran Veilumuthu. A cost effective cloud service for e-learning video on demand. *European Journal of Scientific Research*, 55(4):569–579, 2011.
15. Iain E Richardson. *The H. 264 advanced video compression standard*. John Wiley & Sons, 2011.
16. Daniel Silhavy, Stefan Pham, Martin Lasak, Anita Chen, and Stefan Arbanowski. Low latency streaming and multi DRM with dash. js. In *Proceedings of the 11th ACM Multimedia Systems Conference*, pages 291–296, 2020.
17. Gary J Sullivan, Jens-Rainer Ohm, Woo-Jin Han, and Thomas Wiegand. Overview of the high efficiency video coding (HEVC) standard. *IEEE Transactions on circuits and systems for video technology*, 22(12):1649–1668, 2012.
18. Truong Cong Thang, Quang-Dung Ho, Jung Won Kang, and Anh T Pham. Adaptive streaming of audiovisual content using MPEG dash. *IEEE Transactions on Consumer Electronics*, 58(1):78–85, 2012.
19. Truong Cong Thang, Hung T Le, Anh T Pham, and Yong Man Ro. An evaluation of bitrate adaptation methods for http live streaming. *IEEE Journal on Selected Areas in Communications*, 32(4):693–705, 2014.
20. Ramya Venkataramu. Analysis and enhancement of apple's fairplay digital rights management. *Project report. The Faculty of The Department of Computer Science, San Jose State University*, 2007.
21. Mikael Wånggren and Love Thyresson. Live cloud ingest using open alternatives RIST & SRT. In *SMPTE 2019*, pages 1–25. SMPTE.
22. DRM Widevine. Architecture overview, 2017.

23. Thomas Wiegand, Gary J Sullivan, Gisle Bjontegaard, and Ajay Luthra. Overview of the H. 264/AVC video coding standard. *IEEE Transactions on circuits and systems for video technology*, 13(7):560–576, 2003.
24. Alex Zambelli. IIS smooth streaming technical overview. *Microsoft Corporation*, 3:40, 2009.
25. Yuanzhi Zou, Tiejun Huang, Wen Gao, and Longshe Huo. H. 264 video encryption scheme adaptive to DRM. *IEEE Transactions on Consumer Electronics*, 52(4):1289–1297, 2006.

Chapter 3
Multimedia Cloud: Designing a Special-Purpose Cloud Platform for Interactive Multimedia Streaming

3.1 Overview

The increasing prevalence of streaming-based applications in conjunction with the low-latency connectivity of 5G and 6G and artificial intelligence are creating endless opportunities and revolutionizing our world. In this context, the infrastructural support for a serverless cloud platform for multimedia streaming is a pressing priority. Major players, such as Twitch, Netflix, and Disney have started configuring their special-purpose and highly heterogeneous cloud platforms [13, 42]. Although in their current business model, their aim is to be able to operate at scale, recently AWS has launched the IVS service [39] that enables different live streamers to offer services to their users. This shows the trend towards the idea of democratizing streaming services via offering a multi-tenant special-purpose platform. We note that IVS service is only cloud-based and offers abstraction in the function-level. In contrast, MSC covers the whole edge-to-cloud continuum and offers higher level abstractions, known as Object-as-a-Service (OaaS), that eases the job of both users and developers.

Another motivation for a special-purpose cloud platform for streaming is to offer diverse streaming services, from VOD and live-streaming to 360° and holographic streaming and VR/AR services in a robust and flexible manner, with the minimum incurred cost and with custom-built facilities (e.g., hardware and platform). Accordingly, *special-purpose clouds* are to emerge in areas with high demand [3], such as multimedia streaming, vehicular networks, and big data analytics and natural language processing (NLP).

The ultimate goal of the special-purpose cloud for Multimedia Streaming, known as Multimedia Streaming Cloud (MSC), is to achieve interactivity in the streaming. That is, offering a wide variety of services to the stream viewers. This goal implies enabling stream providers to easily develop and deploy new services of their choice. For that purpose, the stream provider should concentrate on the services they are

© Springer Nature Switzerland AG 2021

M. A. Salehi, X. Li, *Multimedia Cloud Computing Systems*,

https://doi.org/10.1007/978-3-030-88451-2_3

going to offer, rather than the details of how to offer them. These features dictate the following objectives for the MSC platform:

- Extensibility for programmers (a.k.a. interactivity) via providing high-level programming abstractions (known as function-as-a-service and object-as-a-service) and APIs that ease the development and deployment of new services for programmers and solution architects.
- Enabling MSC users to focus on their business and leave technical details to the specialized cloud provider.
- Cost-efficiency for stream providers.
- Providing streaming QoE that is robust against uncertainties, such as request arrival rate and service execution time.
- Offering high-level programming end-points to customized and specialized hardware systems (ASICs) and accelerators (e.g., GPUs and TPUs) to users.
- Reducing the overhead of conventional cloud systems and increasing the resource utilization via employing lightweight virtualization platforms (containers) that are appropriate for serverless and micro-service-based solutions.
- Offering flexible pricing for the viewers. Particularly, allowing viewers to pay for exactly what they stream (a.k.a. pay-as-you-watch streaming).
- Unifying and ease the access to the resources in the Edge-to-Cloud continuum.

Although numerous research works have been undertaken to achieve all of these objectives via to cloud-assisted multimedia streaming (e.g., [1, 2, 4, 8, 16, 17, 34, 44]), their achievements have been limited, because their underlying cloud platform has not been designed for streaming services. In particular, existing open-source serverless platforms (e.g., OpenFaaS [33], Kubernetes [23], and Rancher [12]) are designed for general-purpose clouds. They do not support seamless transition across edge-to-cloud continuum and are not tailored based on the specific demands of multimedia streaming requests. They neither truly offer the notion of serverless and the user still has to be involved in data management (they do not offer Object-as-a-Service) nor they consider the heterogeneity of the underlying resources. *It is this infrastructural gap that this chapter aims to fill* by exploring the MSC platform and enabling OaaS in a truly serverless manner and by considering highly heterogeneous machines across the edge-to-cloud continuum.

3.2   Characterizing the Multimedia Streaming Cloud (MSC) Environment

In a multimedia cloud (MSC), desires of different *stakeholders* should be satisfied. The stakeholders are, namely *cloud providers, streaming service provider, application developers,* and *end-users* (i.e., viewers). The challenge is that the requirements of these stakeholders are often conflicting. For instance, cloud providers desire to maximize their resource utilization, whereas, streaming service providers are concerned about maximizing the QoS that its viewers perceive, while minimizing the incurred cost. Besides, these requirements should be met with respect to *streaming tasks' characteristics* and in the presence of various possible *uncertainties*. In fact, different stakeholders, characteristics of the streaming tasks, and uncertainties are three *aspects* that together form and characterize the MSC environment. In the next subsections, we elaborate on the details of each aspect.

3.2.1   Stakeholders of MSC

Stakeholders of the MSC platform are cloud providers, streaming service provider, application developers, and viewers.

Cloud providers' aim is to maximize their resource utilization and minimize their energy consumption and expenditure.

Stream providers' desire is to minimize their incurred costs of using cloud services while maximizing the QoE provided to their viewers. Earlier studies [24, 25] show that streaming tasks can take advantage of heterogeneous computing services offered by clouds with diverse prices to achieve cost efficiency. Specifically, making use of accelerators and ASICs have become increasingly popular to satisfy the desires.

Application programmers desire an extensible platform with high-level programming abstractions that ease the development of new streaming functionalities/services by abstracting management of the resource (e.g., edge, fog, and cloud) and its pertinent data. Cloud solution architects expect a high-level, stable (i.e., failure-aware), and low-latency streaming platform with resource virtualization platforms (e.g., containers) with customized modules that can handle streaming workloads. They expect that the platform relieves them from the system/resource management issues, such as those needed for load balancing, scaling up and down, scaling in and out, monitoring, data locality, caching, and heterogeneity.

Viewers desire an uninterrupted and robust streaming experience with versatile services and flexibility on the subscription plans (e.g., pay-as-you-watch versus monthly subscription).

3.2.2   Characteristics of Multimedia Streaming Tasks

Offering multimedia streaming services entails creating numerous task requests that should be mostly processed in a real-time manner. For instance, a video stream should be transcoded in real-time to match the display devices of viewers. Efficient processing of these task requests is a decisive factor and one of the main motivations of the MSC platform. As such, it is critical to know the characteristics of these tasks and design the MSC platform with respect to these characteristics. Below, we list the most prominent characteristics of the streaming tasks in the MSC platform:

- Streaming tasks have soft real-time nature and, in general, they should be processed and streamed to the viewer such that the viewer does not realize any delay in the streaming. This is interpreted as meeting the deadline constraint of streaming tasks and keeping the deadline-miss rate lower than what is agreed upon in the Service Level Agreement [28]. More specifically, there are different real-time constraints—soft real-time for on-demand streaming (e.g., VOD) and hard real-time for live-streaming [26]. In the former, the penalty of missing a task's deadline is just lowering the viewer's quality of experience (QoE) whereas in the latter, there is no value in processing streaming tasks that are outdated. That is, live streaming tasks that miss their deadlines have to be dropped to be able to keep up with the liveness of the stream. One more difference between on-demand and live streaming is the dynamism of the tasks' deadlines. In on-demand streaming, once processing a streaming task misses its deadline, the deadline of all tasks behind the missed tasks should be updated. This is not the case in live streaming and tasks' deadlines do not change.
- Not only streaming tasks should meet their deadline, but meeting the deadlines should be fair across concurrent streams. That is, the platform should not keep missing the tasks of one stream while other streams have a low deadline miss rate. To mitigate the impact of missing deadlines on viewers' QoE, it is suggested that the missed tasks are from streams of different viewers. Another factor that should be considered for the fairness is the viewer type. Subscribed viewers generally have more strict SLAs that free users and it is more important for the stream provider to keep them satisfied. As such maintaining fairness should be within the tasks of each viewer type.
- Different stream processing services have heterogeneous computing demands [25]. For instance, transcoding operations and object detection are compute-intensive that perform efficiently on high-end processors or accelerators. Alternatively, video transmuxing operation is not CPU intensive and can efficiently run on low-cost cloud resources (e.g., general-purpose instances in Amazon cloud). Another example is Application-Specific Integrated Circuits (ASIC) computers that can offer very high performance for certain services. For instance INF1 instances in Amazon cloud are custom designed for machine learning applications and FPGA-based resources that can be programmed to perform fast transcoding.
- The access pattern to streaming services is not uniform and generally follows a long-tail distribution [9, 10]. That is, only a small percentage of multimedia contents (approximately 5%) are requested very frequently and the rest of the contents are rarely streamed. This characteristic of the streaming services can be utilized to minimize cloud resource usages and reduce the cost. For instance, a video stream provider may choose to host the videos that are rarely streamed by users (the tail part of the distribution) to be hosted on low-cost and slow storage devices or even process them in a lazy (i.e., on-demand) manner, whereas, the hot videos that are frequently accessed by users are pre-processed in different

formats and maintained on expensive SSD units and cached on content delivery networks (CDNs).

- Processing multimedia services generally does not require the full-stack and high overhead operating system with a considerable boot time that are commonly provided in form of Virtual Machines (VMs) in general-purpose cloud systems. Instead, they require a fast and lightweight execution platforms, such as containers, unikernels, and AWS Firecracker, that can process each multimedia segment without interfering with other services.

3.2.3 Uncertainty

One definition of uncertainty is the difference between the available knowledge and the complete knowledge. Uncertainty is one of the main difficulties of computing systems, in particular, serverless cloud platforms such as MSC. It causes problems in fulfilling QoS desires of both stream providers and viewers. In spite of substantial exploration of uncertainty in different areas, ranging from biology to economics, it has not yet been sufficiently explored in the cloud literature.

Majority of the current solutions for cloud platforms assume a deterministic execution environment [6, 30, 32] or consider a predictable and stable performance for the virtualized environments [5, 20, 29, 30]. In practice, these assumptions do not hold. Although general-purpose cloud providers guarantee a certain processor speed, memory capacity, and bandwidth for their services, the actual performance is subject to several underlying factors, such as multi-tenancy and varying bandwidth that cause uncertainty. To offer robust services, uncertainty and dynamic performance variations, inherent to heterogeneous and shared cloud infrastructures [41], must be captured.

There is a variety of sources for uncertainty in the cloud that are listed in the table of Fig. 3.1. As it is shown, the size of input and output data, machine heterogeneity, multi-tenancy and virtualization, elasticity, replication, distance from datacenters, migration, failure (in task, middleware, network, and hardware), source of power supply, and environmental variables (e.g., temperature) are the sources that cause uncertainty in one or more system parameters. For instance, size of data causes uncertainty in execution time, communication latency, and memory and storage usages. Among these parameters, the key parameters that impact streaming QoS are, namely *tasks' execution time and arrival time, communication latency, machine performance,* and *memory and storage usages.* The problem is that, often, these uncertain parameters co-occur and cause a compounded uncertainty, which make the whole system unpredictable and fragile. For instance, uncertainty in communication latency and execution time are compounded and deteriorate the streaming QoS [43]. Similarly, multiple tasks pending for execution in a queue have compound execution time uncertainty [15].

Robustness is defined as the degree a system can perform correctly in the presence of uncertainty [37]. Robust system synthesis minimizes the impact of

Sources of Uncertainty

Uncertain Parameters	Data Size/Value	Heterogeneity	Multi Tenancy	Elasticity	Replication	User Distance	Migration	Failures	Power Source	Environment (temperature)
Execution Time	✓	✓	✓		✓		✓	✓	✓	✓
Arrival Rate		✓		✓	✓			✓	✓	✓
Communication Latency	✓				✓	✓		✓		✓
Effective Performance		✓	✓	✓			✓	✓	✓	✓
Memory Footprint	✓				✓		✓	✓		
Storage Usage	✓				✓		✓	✓		

Fig. 3.1 Sources of uncertainty and parameters affected by them in the cloud environment

uncertainties on the system performance. Effective solutions for MSC not only have to be robust against the mentioned uncertain parameters, but also should capture their interfering impacts on each other. Achieving robustness has traditionally been performed by either mitigating the sources of uncertainty or using a probabilistic approach or a worst case approach. The latter approaches treat uncertainty as either random variables or interval variables.

Stream providers' strategy to achieve robustness is the former approach. They mitigate the uncertainty via pre-processing every single multimedia segment in numerous formats (between 90 and 270 versions) [9, 10]. However, pre-processing is not possible for the live multimedia contents. Even for the recorded contents (e.g., VOD), pre-processing of all services is cost-prohibitive, provided the long-tail access pattern to the content [10]. Alternatively, the MSC platform enables lazy (i.e., on-demand) and real-time processing of rarely-accessed and live contents. Note that the lazy processing cannot be outsourced to viewers' thin-clients (e.g., smartphones) that generally have energy and compute limitations [27]. Moreover, software packages needed to process the multimedia contents may be missing on the viewer's device that will raise compatibility issues, hence, is counterproductive.

3.3   Architecture of the Multimedia Streaming Cloud (MSC) Platform

In this part, we provide a bird-eye view of the MSC platform. Recall that, one of the main features of this platform that discriminates it from the general-purpose serverless cloud platforms (e.g., AWS Lambda [40]) is the ability of interactive multimedia streaming that is to dynamically accommodate new services developed by the users (either the stream provider or the viewer).

The MSC platform serves two types of users, namely *stream providers* and *viewers*. Stream providers desire MSC to enable them stream in various forms (e.g., live, recorded, AR/VR, etc.) with a low cost and the minimum administration and development efforts. MSC offers the Object-as-a-Service (OaaS) management and programming abstraction, such that the stream providers can configure live (e.g., security camera) or recorded (e.g., VOD) multimedia sources in form of streaming objects with various real-time constraints (e.g., soft real-time for VOD and hard real-time for live-streaming [26]) and then bind functions to them. The functions can be from the set of publicly available functions or be developed by the stream provider to enable new services on the streaming objects. A viewer of MSC uses an application (e.g., live streaming for disabled people) to issue requests in form of <object,function> to trigger a function call, defined for a particular streaming objects. It is as well possible that the stream provider and viewer be the same. For instance, in a home security system, the owner is both the stream provider and the viewer who triggers a specific function (e.g., face detection) on the camera object.

The computing resources available to MSC are highly heterogeneous, e.g., CPUs, GPUs, FPGAs, and ASICs. In fact, stream processing can take advantage of heterogeneous computing machines offered by clouds to improve both their QoS and cost efficiency. Nowadays, cloud providers (e.g., Twitch [11]) are increasingly making use of such highly heterogeneous cloud datacenters to reduce their energy consumption and minimize their expenditure [24, 36].

Based on the aforementioned expectations, a high-level view of the MSC platform is shown in Fig. 3.2. To achieve its goals, MSC is built upon and extends the currently available open-source frameworks. Forming new objects, monitoring their states, and managing their configurations is carried out via a Single Pane Of Glass (SPOG) framework that provides a unified access to the objects across the continuum. Developing new functions is carried out via a FaaS framework that itself is connected to the SPOG to facilitate binding the functions to the streaming objects. Once the objects are formed, activating them is carried out in a lazy (on-demand) manner—upon calling a function of the object by an application. In this case, the containerized functions are provisioned and managed via a container orchestrator. A container that includes the MSC-engine acts as the object controller that can alter the object's state and allocating resources to manage the requests received by the object. The MSC platform that runs on the edge tier, called MSC-edge, essentially has the same architecture as the one runs on the cloud, except using a lightweight (edge-friendly) container orchestrator (e.g., K3s [21]) and incorporating methods to overcome the lack of elasticity in the edge tier.

Objects are considered first-class citizens in the MSC platform. Any streaming source, either live or recorded, is defined as an object that can persist its state and is bound to a set of functions that can be called on the streaming source. The ability to inherit properties and functions across objects makes the object management organized and convenient. A *streaming request*, issued by a viewer's

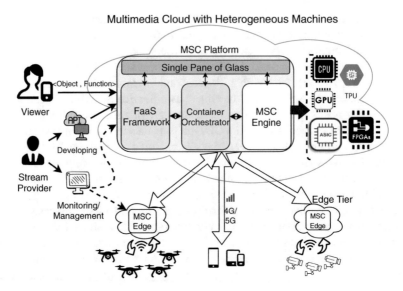

Fig. 3.2 Bird-eye view of the MSC streaming platform operating in the edge-to-cloud continuum

application or another object, is a requester to an streaming object (e.g., captured video) that triggers one or more functions (e.g., face detection) of that object. Even the request to watch the stream is considered as invoking the `playback` function of a particular object. To overcome the lack of elasticity at the edge tier and to support mobility of streamers, MSC can seamlessly migrate objects from one tier (e.g., edge) to another (e.g., cloud).

Figure 3.3 provides a more detailed view to the MSC platform. In this platform, *MSC-Rancher* is the single pane of glass (SPOG) that helps the stream provider to monitor and manage the objects (e.g., to change an object's status and bind/unbind its functions). Upon receiving a function call to an object from a viewer, a *controller* container (a.k.a. pod) that includes MSC-engine to manage the request and the object's state is created. To process the invoked function the *Elasticity Manager* module of the MSC-engine instantiates one or more *worker containers* on potentially heterogeneous machines and hands them over to the application-level scheduler to map the streaming segments to them. Each segment is a requester for a containerized function and is treated as a *task* with an individual deadline, which its presentation time. *Time Estimator* learns and maintains the execution time information of each task on heterogeneous machine types. *Scheduler* uses the estimations to efficiently map tasks to the allocated machines. To minimize the incurred cost of using cloud and even improving QoS, an *Admission Control* component is developed within the MSC-engine whose job is to verify the possibility of reusing (aggregating) function calls of different users on the same object and applying the aggregation without causing starvation for other requests.

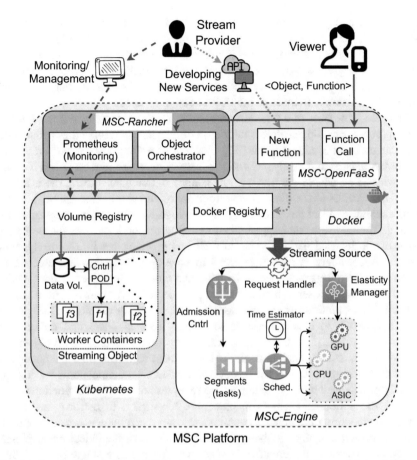

Fig. 3.3 Detailed view of the MSC streaming platform architecture. The workflow of different actions in the platform is shown by different line types and colors

3.3.1 Object-as-a-Service (OaaS) Abstraction in the MSC Platform

Existing FaaS solutions have relieved users from the burden of resource allocation and management. However, FaaS is stateless [14, 19] and does not preserve any state for the data it processes. This implies that, separate from the functions, the user has to be involved in details of managing the state data. For instance, in a FaaS-based application that needs to persist the frame-rate of a security camera, the programmer should use another cloud service, e.g., AWS DynamoDB [38], to persist the state. This makes the development and maintenance of such applications difficult and cumbersome.

To accelerate developing new services, a higher level of abstraction is needed that, in addition to hiding resource allocation details, it hides the details of data management and preserving state of streaming sources from the developers. For this purpose, we borrow the concept of *object* from Object-Oriented Programming that encapsulates both computations (functions) and state in a single entity and offer the notion of *Object-as-a-Service* (OaaS) in the MSC platform. OaaS opens the gate for inheritance of properties and functions across streaming objects, thereby making it easier for streamers to manage multiple streaming sources.

Preserving the state of a function process via OaaS paves the way for migration of the process. Enabling seamless migration of objects can resolve the fundamental elasticity problem of edge systems [22]. Consider the example of a blind person who uses smart glasses and needs real-time process of observed objects enters a coffee shop where few people are playing low-latency online games using the available edge. Upon arrival of the blind person, to make room for the blind application, the game streaming object has to be migrated to cloud without any interruption in the gaming. The opposite can happen when the blind person leaves the place. This is much like a disabled parking spots in a shopping center, but in a more dynamic manner. Accordingly, we leverage OaaS to develop a live migration mechanism for containerized objects between the edge and cloud or across edge tiers, which is useful for mobile users. In addition, we provide stream providers with a unified real-time object monitoring and management tool across various tiers in the system.

Our approach to enable OaaS is to entirely re-think FaaS and define each streaming source (e.g., a recording device or a recorded content) as an object. An individual data volume maintains the object's state and a controller container that includes MSC-engine acts as the object handler and can manipulate its state. A set of lazily provisioned worker containers are to represent the object's functions.

Once the notion of OaaS is in place, we leverage it to perform live object migration via storing the object's running state into the volume and restoring it via a new controller container in the destination tier. To ease the object management, we leverage Rancher and create MSC-Rancher to serve as a single pane of glass through which the stream providers can view and manipulate the status of objects on various tiers.

3.3.2   Enabling Object-as-a-Service (OaaS) Abstraction in the MSC Platform

The object implementation, as shown in Fig. 3.3, include: (a) A *data volume* managed by Kubernetes to persist the state information of the object. The volume only stores metadata, thus, it is not bulky and structured data models (e.g., MySQL) can be used to implement it. (b) A *controller container* that is loaded with the MSC-engine and has sole access to the data volume to change the object's state. (c) One or more *worker containers*—each one representing a function of the object. The set of containers (part b and c) collectively form a *namespace* in Kubernetes.

To form a new object, according to Fig. 3.3, the stream provider interfaces with the unified object manager (called MSC-Rancher and explained in Sect. 3.3.4) to instantiate a new data volume for the object and ask Kubernetes to form a namespace with a controller container within it and mount the volume to it. The controller container manages both the object's state and the segments arriving from the streaming source. Binding of the functions to an object is achieved via persisting the functions' metadata into the volume. Function inheritance achieved based on the type of streaming source (i.e., object type). For instance, fast-forward is a function for recorded (VOD) streaming, while it is not defined for live streaming. Note that basic functions (e.g., playback and transcoding) are inherited to any object, unless the user disables them. MSC-OpenFaaS (see Fig. 3.3) is used to develop a new function for an object and wrap it in form of a Docker image. Next, the function is pushed to the function repository, which is essentially a Docker Image Registry, where users can build, push or deploy their functions. A function can be private or made publicly available in a function marketplace. Once a function is a containerized image in the registry, it can be bound to objects, as explained earlier.

Upon calling an object's function, first, MSC-OpenFaas consults with Object Orchestrator in MSC-Rancher to locate the object. If the object is not active, MSC-Rancher activates it via locating its volume and requesting Kubernetes to mount the volume to the object's controller container. Next, the request is handed over to the Request Handler of MSC-engine and it consults with the object's volume to see if the invoked function is bound to the object. Then, lazy provisioning of the function occurs by asking Kubernetes to pull the corresponding Docker image from the registry and execute the invoked function. We note that the MSC-engine elastically instantiates enough containers for the invoked function, such that its QoS desires are met. By considering a Docker Hub [18] in the architecture to act as an upstream image registry, we can enable pulling images from other cloud systems and deploy MSC in a multi-cloud setting.

3.3.3 Enabling Live Object Migration

The decision for object migration is made by the Elasticity Manager. Assuming such decision has been made, in this part, our aim is to provide the live object migration ability. To migrate an object, its container(s) and data volume have to be migrated. The data volume includes the object state, so its transfer does impose a significant delay.

Container images have a layered architecture where the first layer is the base image (a.k.a root volume) and any installed package on top of that forms a new layer and is stored in a separate image file. This layered approach, known as union mounting, enables fast and space-efficient container packaging. To migrate a container, existing solutions [31] not only transfer the application images, but also the root volume that implies a significant volume migration time, which is counterproductive for low-latency applications. To reduce the object migration time, for each container, we proactively migrate only the layer(s) that do not exist in the destination. We can leverage the MD5 hash of the source layers to find the equivalent layer(s) in the destination. In addition to the layers, the container's execution state, including the memory contents and devices' states, have to be transferred to the destination.

To transfer the containers' layers and the object's data volume, `rsync` [35] can be utilized to transfer the latest changes of the layers to the destination without interrupting the source container. To capture the container's execution state, we use Checkpoint/Restore In Userspace (CRIU) [7] utility that dumps and persists the current state of the container. Then, the state file is transferred using `rsync`. A pre-copy approach should be used to impose a lower downtime to the object in compare to the post-copy. Once the container image and its state are transferred, to avoid any inconsistency, we suspend all the containers in the source and then all the migrated containers are resumed in a new namespace and set to work with the migrated data volume. Finally, the source namespace will be terminated.

3.3.4   Single Pane of Glass to Objects in MSC

MSC operates in a geographically distributed environment. This, in addition to the object migration possibility, raise the need for a single pane of glass for stream providers to compose and monitor objects or to modify their properties and (enable/disable) their functions. Within the MSC platform, Kubernetes clusters are used to allocate resources on edge or cloud tiers. To provide a unified access to users, a management layer on top of these Kubernetes clusters is needed. For that, Rancher [12], an open-source framework for managing and orchestrating Kubernetes clusters, can be extended.

We modify Rancher and create MSC-Rancher to enable it recognizing the object abstraction, via mapping the concept of objects to namespaces in Kubernetes (see Fig. 3.4). To handle the creation and manipulation of objects, MSC-Rancher has to be granted access to the same storage system that Kubernetes has access to. Thus, MSC-Rancher can dynamically create data volumes for new objects and offer them the block storage service (e.g., Ceph). MSC-Rancher will be featured with the ability of real-time monitoring of the location and state of the streaming objects across the continuum. Prometheus feature of the MSC-Rancher is in charge of event monitoring and alerting. We configure Prometheus to access certain parameters of the data volume of the object that is intended to be monitored. Deleting and modifying (binding/unbinding functions of) an object or making it immutable will be achieved by leveraging access to the object's data volume in MSC-Rancher.

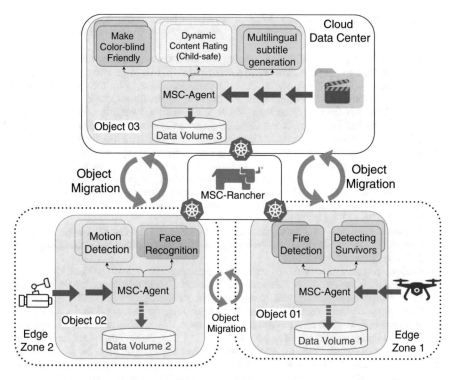

Fig. 3.4 MSC-Rancher: single pane of glass for objects

3.4   Summary

In this chapter, we outlined the MSC platform and elaborated about its components and features, mainly OaaS, without implementing its components. In the next chapters, after surveying possible applications that can benefit from MSC, we elaborate on the ways major components of the MSC platform operate. We also elaborate on a prototype of a MSC platform we developed in our research laboratory that supports most of the expected features mentioned in this and next chapters.

In the next chapter, we will elaborate on the potential applications of the MSC platform for different types of streaming (i.e., live and on-demand) and even different multimedia technologies (e.g., AR/VR, 360-degree, etc.).

References

1. Adnan Ashraf, Fareed Jokhio, Tewodros Deneke, Sébastien Lafond, Ivan Porres, and Johan Lilius.   Stream-based admission control and scheduling for video transcoding in cloud computing. In *Proceedings of the 13th IEEE/ACM International Symposium on Cluster, Cloud and Grid Computing*, CCGrid '13, pages 482–489, May 2013.

2. Kashif Bilal, Aiman Erbad, and Mohamed Hefeeda. Qoe-aware distributed cloud-based live streaming of multisourced multiview videos. *Journal of Network and Computer Applications*, 120:130–144, 2018.
3. Rajkumar Buyya, Satish Narayana Srirama, Giuliano Casale, Rodrigo Calheiros, Yogesh Simmhan, Blesson Varghese, Erol Gelenbe, Bahman Javadi, Luis Miguel Vaquero, Marco A. S. Netto, Adel Nadjaran Toosi, Maria Alejandra Rodriguez, Ignacio M. Llorente, Sabrina De Capitani Di Vimercati, Pierangela Samarati, Dejan Milojicic, Carlos Varela, Rami Bahsoon, Marcos Dias De Assuncao, Omer Rana, Wanlei Zhou, Hai Jin, Wolfgang Gentzsch, Albert Y. Zomaya, and Haiying Shen. A manifesto for future generation cloud computing: Research directions for the next decade. *ACM Computing Survey*, 51(5):105:1–105:38, Nov. 2018.
4. De-Yu Chen and Magda El-Zarki. Improving the quality of 3d immersive interactive cloud based services over unreliable network. In *Proceedings of the 10th International Workshop on Immersive Mixed and Virtual Environment Systems*, MMVE '18, pages 28–33, 2018.
5. Kwei-Bor Chen and Hong-Yi Chang. Complexity of cloud-based transcoding platform for scalable and effective video streaming services. *Multimedia Tools and Applications*, 76(19):19557–19574, Oct. 2017.
6. Andrew Chung, Jun Woo Park, and Gregory R. Ganger. Stratus: Cost-aware container scheduling in the public cloud. In *Proceedings of the ACM Symposium on Cloud Computing*, SoCC '18, pages 121–134, 2018.
7. checkpointing for Linux CRIU. https://criu.org/main_page. Accessed July 20, 2020.
8. M. Darwich, E. Beyazit, M. A. Salehi, and M. Bayoumi. Cost efficient repository management for cloud-based on-demand video streaming. In *Proceedings of 5th IEEE International Conference on Mobile Cloud Computing, Services, and Engineering*, pages 39–44, April 2017.
9. M. Darwich, E. Beyazit, M. A. Salehi, and M. Bayoumi. Cost efficient repository management for cloud-based on-demand video streaming. In *in Proceedings of 5th IEEE International Conference on Mobile Cloud Computing, Services, and Engineering*, pages 39–44, Apr. 2017.
10. Mahmoud Darwich, Mohsen Amini Salehi, Ege Beyazit, and Magdy Bayoumi. Cost-efficient cloud-based video streaming through measuring hotness. *The Computer Journal*, 2018.
11. Live Streaming Service for Gaming. https://www.twitch.tv/. Accessed May 5, 2020.
12. Rancher for Kubernetes Management. https://rancher.com/. Accessed July 22, 2020.
13. How Netflix Tunes Amazon EC2 Instances for Performance. https://aws.amazon.com/solutions/case-studies/netflix/#. Accessed Aug. 5, 2020.
14. Geoffrey Charles Fox, Vatche Ishakian, Vinod Muthusamy, and Aleksander Slominski. Status of serverless computing and function-as-a-service (faas) in industry and research. *ArXiv*, abs/1708.08028, 2017.
15. James Gentry, Chavit Denninnart, and Mohsen Amini Salehi. Robust dynamic resource allocation via probabilistic task pruning in heterogeneous computing systems. In *Proceedings of the 33rd IEEE International Parallel & Distributed Processing Symposium (IPDPS '19)*, May. 2019.
16. J. He, Y. Wen, J. Huang, and D. Wu. On the Cost–QoE Tradeoff for Cloud-Based Video Streaming Under Amazon EC2's Pricing Models. *IEEE Transactions on Circuits and Systems for Video Technology*, 24(4):669–680, Apr. 2014.
17. Qiyun He, Jiangchuan Liu, Chonggang Wang, and Bo Li. Coping with heterogeneous video contributors and viewers in crowdsourced live streaming: A cloud-based approach. *IEEE Transactions on Multimedia*, 18(5):916–928, May 2016.
18. Docker Hub. https://hub.docker.com/. Accessed July 27, 2020.
19. Aman Jain, Ata F. Baarzi, Nader Alfares, George Kesidis, Bhuvan Urgaonkar, and Mahmut Kandemir. Spiitserve: Efficiently splitting complex workloads across faas and iaas. In *Proceedings of the ACM Symposium on Cloud Computing*, SoCC '19, page 487, 2019.
20. Myoungjin Kim, Yun Cui, Seungho Han, and Hanku Lee. Towards efficient design and implementation of a hadoop-based distributed video transcoding system in cloud computing environment. *International Journal of Multimedia and Ubiquitous Engineering*, 8(2):213–224, Mar. 2013.
21. Lightweight Kubernetes. https://k3s.io/. Accessed Aug. 7, 2020.

22. Chunlin Li, Jingpan Bai, Yuan Ge, and Luo Youlong. Heterogeneity-aware elastic provisioning in cloud-assisted edge computing systems. *Future Generation Computer Systems (FGCS)*, 112:1106–1121, 2020.

23. Qiankun Li, Gang Yin, Tao Wang, and Yue Yu. Building a cloud-ready program: A highly scalable implementation based on kubernetes. In *Proceedings of the 2nd International Conference on Advances in Image Processing*, ICAIP '18, pages 159–164, 2018.

24. X. Li, M. A. Salehi, M. Bayoumi, N. Tzeng, and R. Buyya. Cost-efficient and robust on-demand video transcoding using heterogeneous cloud services. *IEEE Transactions on Parallel and Distributed Systems*, 29(3):556–571, Mar. 2018.

25. Xiangbo Li, Mohsen Amini Salehi, Yamini Joshi, Mahmoud Darwich, Landreneau Brad, and Magdi Bayoumi. Performance Analysis and Modelling of Video Stream Transcoding Using Heterogeneous Cloud Services. *IEEE Transactions on Parallel and Distributed Systems (TPDS)*, Sep. 2018.

26. Xiangbo Li, Mohsen Amini Salehi, and Magdy Bayoumi. VLSC: Video Live Streaming Based On Cloud Services. In *Big Data & Cloud Applications Workshop, as part of the 6th IEEE International Conference on Big Data and Cloud Computing Conference*, BDCloud '16, Oct. 2016.

27. Xiangbo Li, Mohsen Amini Salehi, and Magdy Bayoumi. Cloud-based video streaming for energy- and compute-limited thin clients. In *the Stream2015 Workshop at Indiana University*, Oct, 2015.

28. Xiangbo Li, Mohsen Amini Salehi, Magdy Bayoumi, and Rajkumar Buyya. CVSS: A Cost-Efficient and QoS-Aware Video Streaming Using Cloud Services. In *Proceedings of the 16th IEEE/ACM International Conference on Cluster Cloud and Grid Computing*, CCGrid '16, May 2016.

29. Song Lin, Xinfeng Zhang, Qin Yu, Honggang Qi, and Siwei Ma. Parallelizing video transcoding with load balancing on cloud computing. In *Proceedings of the IEEE International Symposium on Circuits and Systems (ISCAS)*, pages 2864–2867, May 2013.

30. A. Marahatta, S. Pirbhulal, F. Zhang, R. M. Parizi, K. R. Choo, and Z. Liu. Classification-based and energy-efficient dynamic task scheduling scheme for virtualized cloud data center. *IEEE Transactions on Cloud Computing*, 2019.

31. S. Nadgowda, S. Suneja, N. Bila, and C. Isci. Voyager: Complete container state migration. In *Proceedings of the 37th IEEE International Conference on Distributed Computing Systems (ICDCS)*, pages 2137–2142, 2017.

32. P. Oikonomou, M. G. Koziri, N. Tziritas, A. N. Dadaliaris, T. Loukopoulos, G. I. Stamoulis, and S. U. Khan. Scheduling video transcoding jobs in the cloud. In *Proceedings of the IEEE International Conference on Internet of Things (iThings) and IEEE Green Computing and Communications (GreenCom) and IEEE Cyber, Physical and Social Computing (CPSCom) and IEEE Smart Data (SmartData)*, pages 442–449, Jul. 2018.

33. OpenFaaS Platform. https://www.openfaas.com/. Accessed July 22, 2020.

34. P. A. L. Rego, M. S. Bonfim, M. D. Ortiz, J. M. Bezerra, D. R. Campelo, and J. N. de Souza. An OpenFlow-Based Elastic Solution for Cloud-CDN Video Streaming Service. In *Proceedings of IEEE Global Communications Conference (GLOBECOM)*, pages 1–7, Dec 2015.

35. rsync Linux Command. https://linux.die.net/man/1/rsync. Accessed July 20, 2020.

36. Z. Ruan and X. Ye. Cost-optimized video dissemination over heterogeneous cloud with slas support. *IEEE Access*, 7:42874–42888, 2019.

37. Mohsen Amini Salehi, Jay Smith, Anthony A. Maciejewski, Howard Jay Siegel, Edwin K. P. Chong, Jonathan Apodaca, Luis D. Briceno, Timothy Renner, Vladimir Shestak, Joshua Ladd, Andrew Sutton, David Janovy, Sudha Govindasamy, Amin Alqudah, Rinku Dewri, and Puneet Prakash. Stochastic-based robust dynamic resource allocation for independent tasks in a heterogeneous computing system. *in Journal of Parallel and Distributed Computing (JPDC)*, 97(C), Nov. 2016.

38. Amazon DynamoDB Service. https://aws.amazon.com/dynamodb/. Accessed June 12, 2020.

39. AWS Interactive Video Streaming (IVS) Service. https://aws.amazon.com/about-aws/whats-new/2020/07/introducing-amazon-ivs/. Accessed July 22, 2020.

40. AWS Lambda Service. https://aws.amazon.com/lambda/. Accessed July 25, 2020.
41. Andrei Tchernykh, Uwe Schwiegelsohn, Vassil Alexandrov, and El-ghazali Talbi. Towards understanding uncertainty in cloud computing resource provisioning. *Procedia Computer Science*, 51(C):1772–1781, Sep. 2015.
42. Xilinx transcoding solution for Twitch. https://www.xilinx.com/publications/powered-by-xilinx/twitch-case-study.pdf. Accessed Aug. 5, 2020.
43. V. Veillon, C. Denninnart, and M. A. Salehi. F-fdn: Federation of fog computing systems for low latency video streaming. In *Proceedings of the 3rd IEEE International Conference on Fog and Edge Computing*, ICFEC '19, pages 1–9, May 2019.
44. M. Zink, R. Sitaraman, and K. Nahrstedt. Scalable 360 video stream delivery: Challenges, solutions, and opportunities. *Proceedings of the IEEE*, 107(4):639–650, April 2019.

Chapter 4
Applications of Multimedia Clouds

4.1 Overview

In the previous chapters, we described the workflow of processes take place to achieve multimedia streaming. We also explained the infrastructural and middleware requirements to build a multimedia cloud. In this chapter, we assume that the multimedia cloud is in place and elaborate on the possible opportunities it can offer in the future of streaming technology. In particular, the platform we explained in Chap. 3 offer high-level abstractions and APIs and hides the details of both resource and data management from stream providers in the cloud. This mitigates burden that stream providers have to currently overcome by their own and make developing new services fast and possible for everyone. In fact, MSC will pave the way of stream providers to become solution-oriented and let them focus on developing advanced streaming services and integrate them to their applications. In that sense, we can say the MSC will democratize the streaming process and will change the future of software development and programming in these domains. That is, software development will become mashing up different services and creating a new service, rather than coding everything from the scratch. Many functionalities/services (e.g., transcoding) will be offered as built-in MSC services for various streaming types.

In this chapter, we first introduce various forms of multimedia streaming and position them with respect to each other. Then, we focus on the widely-used services for each form of streaming that can be potentially offered as builtin services by the MSC platform. Next, we describe emerging smart services that can be developed and offered by the MSC platform.

© Springer Nature Switzerland AG 2021
M. A. Salehi, X. Li, *Multimedia Cloud Computing Systems*,
https://doi.org/10.1007/978-3-030-88451-2_4

4.2   Multimedia Streaming Types

The taxonomy shown in Fig. 4.1 expresses possible ways a multimedia streaming service can be provided to viewers on the Internet. More specifically, video streaming service can be offered in three main fashions: *On Demand* (commonly known as Video On Demand (VOD)) streaming, *live* streaming, and *live-to-VOD* streaming. These types are explained in the rest of this section.

4.2.1   On-Demand Multimedia Streaming

In on-demand streaming, also known as Over-The-Top (OTT) streaming, the multimedia contents (e.g., video files) are already available in a repository and are streamed to viewers upon their requests. By far, VOD is the most common type of multimedia streaming and is offered by major streaming providers, such as YouTube, Netflix, and Amazon Prime Video. Some VOD providers (e.g., Netflix and Hulu) offer professionally-made contents and movies that are subscription-based and viewers are generally required to pay a monthly fee to access their content and services. Some other VOD services (e.g., YouTube) operate based the user-provided contents. Such services are often advertisement-based and free of charge. On-demand streaming has also significant applications in e-learning systems [47], Internet television [42], and in-flight entertainment systems [13]. On-demand multimedia streaming has progressed over time, from *single configuration* format in the past to *adaptive configuration* that is currently achieved, and *personalized* one (a.k.a. interactive) configuration that will be the future of this type of streaming. Details of these configurations are discussed in the next subsections.

On-demand streaming is commonly achieved through a centralized (i.e., server-based) approach in which the multimedia contents are located on a central server repository and streamed to viewers upon receiving of their requests in the server [9, 34] and by the help of a content delivery network (CDN), elaborated in Sect. 2.5 that significantly reduces the steaming latency. Apart from the latency, another challenge in the centralized on-demand streaming approach is the storage requirement to persist multiple versions of each content (e.g., video) that can cover heterogeneous

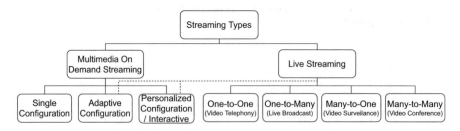

Fig. 4.1 Taxonomy of different types of Internet-based multimedia streaming

display devices. We elaborate on the storage challenge and some solutions for it in Sect. 8.4. We note that, on-demand streaming and particularly VOD can be carried out using Peer-to-Peer (P2P) approach [43] too where the contents are streamed from other peer machines (i.e., other viewers) that are located nearby.

4.2.1.1 Single Configuration On-Demand Streaming

Before 1995, when online multimedia and video streaming was not feasible owing to lack of compression formats, network bandwidth, and hardware limitation. As such, a video could not be viewed until it was completely downloaded on the viewers device. This implies that viewers usually had to wait for a considerable amount of time (from minutes to even hours) before watching the video. Although first tests for streaming multimedia content occurred in 1993 between Xerox Park in Palo Alto and Australia, the technology did not get prevalent sooner than late 1990s and early 2000. The major development that enabled multimedia streaming was the invention of *Progressive download* method that allowed the multimedia (video) content to be played as soon as the player's buffer is filled by the initial segments of the video. This could reduce the user's waiting time to begin watching a video from minutes and hours down to only 3–10 s [2].

Initial progressive download versions were only supporting a single configuration (format) for the streamed content, disregarding the user's display device and/or network bandwidth. It was the user's responsibility to assure its display device support the codec of the streamed content. Moreover, disregarding the network condition could significantly affect the QoE of the users with low network bandwidth. The downloading feature of the progressive download causes three other problems:

1. Since a video is downloaded linearly, if the viewer's network bandwidth is too low, the viewer cannot move forward a video until that part is fully downloaded.
2. if a video file is fully downloaded, but viewer stops watching in the middle, the rest bandwidths are wasted.
3. Copyright is problematic in progressive download because the whole video is downloaded on the viewer's storage device. Progressive Download utilizes HTTP protocol that itself operates based on the TCP protocol, which provides better reliability and error-resilience than UDP, however, it incurs a high network latency [40].

These inherent drawbacks of HTTP-based progressive download raised the need to a dedicated technology for video streaming.

4.2.1.2 Adaptive On-Demand Streaming

To avoid problems of progressive download, a dedicated protocol for real-time streaming (known as RTP) [23] was created. This protocol delivers video contents from a separate streaming server. With traditional HTTP servers handle web requests, streaming servers only handle the streaming requests. The connection is initiated between the player and the streaming server whenever a viewer clicks on a video in an web page. The connection persists until the video is ended or the viewer stops watching it. In compared to stateless HTTP, RTP protocol is considered stateful because of this persistent connection. Therefore, such a dedicated streaming protocols can offer features like random access (e.g., fast forward) within the streamed content. These protocols also allow adaptive streaming, in which multiple encoded streams could be delivered to different players based upon available bandwidth and processing characteristics. The streaming server can monitor the outbound flow, so if the viewer stops watching the video, it stops sending video packet to the viewer.

Although dedicated streaming protocols were attractive in the beginning, its drawback appeared after deployment. A streaming protocol, e.g., RTMP [31] used by Adobe Flash, utilizes different port numbers from HTTP. As such, RTMP packets can be blocked with some firewalls. The persistent connection between the streaming server and viewer players increases the network usage and causes limited scalability for the streaming servers. To address the limitations of streaming protocols, HTTP-based streaming solutions came back to the forefront of streaming technology-adaptive streaming. All adaptive streams are broken into chunks and stream separate videos. There is no persistent connection between the server and the player. Instead of retrieving a single large video file in one request, adaptive streaming technology retrieves a sequence of short video files in an on-demand basis.

Adaptive streaming has the following benefits: First, like streaming server, there is no network wastage, because the video content is delivered on the fly. Therefore, one HTTP server can efficiently serve several streams. Second, HTTP-based streaming is delivered through HTTP protocol, which avoids the firewall issue faced by RTMP. Third, it is less expensive than the dedicated streaming server approach, because there is no dedicated streaming server involved in the process. Fourth, it is scalable and can serve large number of viewers. Fifth, seeking inside the stream is feasible. For instance, when the viewer moves the stream forward, the player just retrieves the required segments as opposed to the entire stream up to the requested point.

There are four main adaptive streaming protocols, namely MPEG Dynamic Adaptive Streaming over HTTP (DASH) [46], Apple HTTP Live Streaming (HLS) [49], and Microsoft Smooth Streaming [3]. MPEG DASH delivers ISO Base Media File Format (ISOBMFF) [5] video segments. It defines a Media Presentation Description (MPD) XML document to provide the locations of each streams and segments, so that players know where to download them. The media segments for DASH is delivered with formats either based on the ISOBMFF [50] or Common Media Application Format (CMAF) standards [14]. Apple's HLS is well-known and implemented on the Apple devices (and nowadays on Android devices too). It utilizes a M3U8 master manifest to include multiple media playlists, each playlist represents one stream version and it contains the location of all the video segments for this stream. HLS video segment is using either MPEG-2 Transport Stream

Table 4.1 Adaptive streaming supported platforms

	Desktop player	Mobile device support	OTT support
MPEG-DASH	dash.js, dash.as, GPAC	Windows, Android Phone	Google TV, Roku, Xbox 360
Apple HTTP Live Streaming (HLS)	iOS, Mac OSX, Flash	iOS/Android3.0+	Apple TV, Boxee, Google TV, Roku
Smooth Streaming	Silverlight	Windows Phone	Google TV, Roku, Xbox 360

(M2TS) [19] or CMAF [14] for H.264 encoded videos, and ISOBMFF for HEVC encoded videos. Smooth Streaming has two separated manifest files, namely SMIL server manifest file and client manifest file. They are all defined in XML format documents. Smooth streaming also delivers video segment with a format (known as ISMV) based on ISOBMFF.

The four adaptive streaming technologies have empowered streaming service providers to deliver the video contents to viewers smoothly even under a low bandwidth Internet connection. However, to support all viewers' platforms, stream providers have to deploy and maintain all these four streaming protocols that subsequently increases complexity and costs. The supported platforms of these four protocols are shown in Table 4.1.

4.2.1.3   Personalized On-Demand (Interactive) Streaming

Although currently adaptive streaming is the most popular type of streaming, we envisage that the next step in the streaming technology will be to where a much larger adaptability and customization on the streaming content will be possible. In fact, current stream providers, such as YouTube, do not offer many streaming options (i.e., services) beyond the standard operations, such as fast forward and pause. There are also some customization services, such as playback speed, that are offered using the facilities of the client machine or browser. However, in personalized streaming a much higher flexibility will be offered to the users to the extend that users (or stream providers) can use the high-level APIs provided by the streaming engine and directly develop new functions that will satisfy their particular desire.

Personalized (a.k.a. interactive) streaming is particularly becoming popular with the prevalence of multimedia streaming not only for video content in the conventional form using public stream providers such as YouTube and Netflix, but it is becoming an integral part of an increasingly wide range of applications, often operating across the edge-to-cloud continuum. This includes the applications in hospitals, traffic control, gaming, disaster management, maintenance, and manufacturing among many others. Interactive streaming allows rapid development of new streaming services and the streaming engine will serve as a platform with high-level management abstractions whose job is to reap the benefits of the edge, fog, and cloud continuum and facilitate real-time execution of interactive streaming services.

A few scenarios where interactive streaming is applicable are as follows: Consider a company (streaming service provider) that develops an application to offer cloud-based (live or on-demand) streaming services to disabled people. To enhance visual recognition of color-blind viewers, they need to develop a near real-time service to increase the contrast of frames' colors. For deaf viewers, they need a service for dynamic multilingual subtitle generation. For blind viewers, they need a service to provide additional audio description [25]. Another child entertainment application needs to develop a service to dynamically extract harmful and illicit content from the videos and make them child-safe. A healthcare application needs to develop AI-based service to monitor certain metrics in premature birth cases and inform the medical crew upon detecting important signs [21]. A situational-awareness application operating based on edge and cloud computing needs a face detection service to track suspects across multiple security cameras. A repair company needs to develop services to live stream from smart glasses to a mechanic for troubleshooting.

4.2.2 Live Multimedia Streaming

In live multimedia streaming, the contents are streamed to the viewer(s), as they are captured by a camera. Live streaming has numerous applications, such as event coverage, live conference and meetings (e.g., Zoom and Webex), situational awareness, and video calls among many others. The live multimedia streaming used in different applications have minor differences that are mainly attributed to the buffer size on the sender and receiver ends [29]. In general, a larger buffer size causes a more stable streaming experience, but imposes a longer latency. This latency can be tolerated in live broadcasting applications, however, latency-sensitive applications (e.g., video telephony, patient care, and online meeting) cannot bear the delay, thus need a shorter buffer size. Based on the buffer size factor, live streaming can be accomplished in four was that are explained below. Disregarding the buffer size, live streaming can be accomplished in adaptive and personalized fashions as described in the previous part.

(a) **One-to-one** (unicast) streaming is when a user streams the contents to another user. This type is primarily used in video chat and video call applications that require two live streams, one from each participant. This streaming type requires short delays to enable smooth conversation between participants. As such, these applications generally operate with a short buffer size and low picture quality to make the delay as small as possible [29]. Skype[1] and video telephony applications [24] like FaceTime[2] are instances of this type of live streaming.

---

[1] https://www.skype.com.

[2] https://support.apple.com/en-us/HT204380.

(b) **One-to-many** (multicast) streaming is when one source streams video to many viewers. A well-known example of this type is live broadcasting which is currently offered by many social network applications, such as Facebook and Instagram. Jo et al. [26] conducted one of the first studies on live streaming. They identified and addressed several challenges in multicast streaming regarding signaling protocols, network stability, and viewer variations. For this type of streaming, often a middle server is considered where transcoding and broadcasting to audience is achieved. Using such as server makes this type of streaming scalable.

(c) **Many-to-one** occurs when several cameras capture scenes and send them to one viewer. The most important application for this type of streaming is multi-camera video surveillance which is used for situational awareness for security purposes or natural disaster management [22]. In this type of streaming, the video contents are collected from multiple cameras and displayed on special multi-screen monitoring devices [18].

(d) **Many-to-many** streaming occurs when a group of users in different geographical locations holds a video conference. In this case, all users stream lively to all others. For this streaming type, Multipoint Control Unit (MCU) [29] method can be used to combine individual participants into a single video stream and broadcast it. Most of video chat applications, e.g., Skype and Google Hangouts, support many-to-many live streaming, in addition to one-to-many streaming.

4.2.3 Live-to-VOD Streaming

In addition to live and VOD streaming, a combination of live and VOD streaming, known as Live-to-VOD [45], is another type of streaming. In this type of streaming, which is mostly used on one-to-many live streaming, the live video stream is recorded and can be readily used in form of VOD streaming.

Using live-to-VOD streaming, viewers who are not online during the live stream can watch the content at a later time. In addition, live-to-VOD can provide VOD-like services to live stream viewers. For instance, live stream viewers can have the rewind ability. Another application of live-to-VOD is to play live contents in different time zones. For example, using live-to-VOD, the same TV program that is live streamed at 8:00 am in the Eastern Time Zone, can be played at 8:00 am in the Pacific Time Zone.

4.2.4 Differences in Processing Live and VOD Streaming

Although the workflow and processes that are applied to live streaming are the same as those for on-demand streaming (VOD), there are some differences between them. Specifically, processing live and VOD streaming have two differences:

Firstly, in live streaming, the multimedia segments are processed as they are generated. This has two implications:

- The generated segments have to be processed (e.g., transcoded) on-the-spot, whereas in VOD, it is possible to pre-process the multimedia contents (i.e., in an offline manner).
- There is no historic processing time information for live multimedia segments [34]. Conversely, in VOD, each segment is processed multiple times and the historic execution time information are available. The historic information are particularly important for the efficient allocation of the streaming tasks on the cloud machines.

Secondly, is the way they are treated for processing. In both live and VOD streaming, to ensure Quality of Experience (QoE), each streaming task is assigned a deadline that must be respected. That is, the task processing must be completed before the assigned deadline that is determined based on the presentation time of the pertinent multimedia segment. If a task cannot meet its assigned deadline for any reason, then, in VOD, the task has to wait until it is processed [33]. Conversely, in live streaming, if a task deadline is violated, it must be dropped (i.e., discarded) to keep up with the live streaming [34]. In other words, there is no reason to process an expired live segment.

The third difference between VOD and live streaming is again related to the way deadlines are assigned to the streaming tasks. In fact, in multimedia streaming, if a task misses its deadline, all the tasks behind it, i.e., those process later segments in the stream, should update their streaming deadlines (presentation times) accordingly. This is known as the dynamic deadline. However, this is not the case in live streaming where the tasks have hard and unchangeable deadlines.

4.3   Basic Services Offered by MSC

4.3.1   Multimedia Content Transcoding

Multimedia contents are originally encoded with one specific spatial resolution, bit rate, frame rate, and compression standard (codec). To play the multimedia on various devices, streaming service providers usually have to adjust the original videos in terms of the viewer's device and network bandwidth. The process of this adjustment is called transcoding [1, 52] and is one of the frequent operations carried out on the multimedia contents.

Transcoding is a compute-intensive operation [32], hence, in VOD, it is generally performed in an off-line manner, known as pre-transcoding [35]. Conversely, in live streaming, it is not naturally possible to perform pre-transcoding. As such and because of the latency imposed by the transcoding operation, live contents are often transcoded to one or a few formats. This is the reason that live streams are not as high-quality as VOD.

Because of the high-frequency usage, we consider transcoding as a basic service that any MSC is expected to provide. In the following parts, we describe various transcoding operations.

4.3.1.1 Bit Rate Transcoding

Video bit rate is the number of bits used to encode a unit time of video. Bit rate directly impacts on video quality, as higher bit rate produces better quality, while higher bit rate consumes larger network bandwidth and storage.

In order to stream videos to viewers with different network conditions (i.e., adaptive video streaming), streaming service providers convert the video contents to multiple bit rates [54]. Given the popularity of adaptive streaming, bit rate can be considered as the most basic streaming service.

4.3.1.2 Spatial Resolution Transcoding

Resolution represents the dimensional size of a video, which indicates the number of pixels on each video frame. As such, higher resolution contains more pixels and details that also results into a larger size. Video resolution must match with the screen size. Playing a low resolution video on a large screen causes blurry quality due to the upsampling, whereas playing a high resolution content on a small screen wastes the bandwidth, because the viewer usually does notice the difference due to the limited pixels on the screen. To adapt to the diverse screen sizes of the users' devices, the original video contents have to be transcoded to multiple spatial resolutions [4].

4.3.1.3 Frame Rate Transcoding

Playing multimedia contents (video) is nothing but changing still frames at a certain rate, so that the human visual system feel the object is moving. Specifically, frame rate is defined as the number of frames shown in each second. Videos and movies are usually recorded at high frame rate to produce smooth transitions, however, devices may not support such high frame rates. As such, in some cases, the frame rate has to be reduced by removing some of the frames. On the other hand, increasing the frame rate is more complicated than reducing it, since non-existent frames have to be injected into the video. In general, to cover a larger set of user devices, videos are pre-transcoded to different frame rates [15].

4.3.1.4   Video Compression Standard (Codec) Transcoding

Video Compression standard is the key to compress a raw video, the encoding process mainly goes through four steps: prediction, transform, quantization, and entropy coding, while decoding is a just reverted encoding process. With different codecs manufactured on different devices (e.g., DVD player with MPEG-2 [20], BluRay player with H.264 [55], 4K TV with HEVC [48]), an encoded video may have to be converted to the supported codec on that device. Changing codec is the most compute-intensive type of transcoding [32] because it has to decode the bitstream with the old codec first and then encode it again with the new codec. For that reason, codec transcoding is commonly carried out in an off-line manner and only for VOD streaming.

4.3.2   Video Packaging

Transmitting an encoded/transcoded video segment from the server to viewer's display device involves multiple layers of network protocols, namely physical layer, data link layer, network layer, transport layer, session layer, presentation layer, and application layer [27]. The protocols of these layers dictate video packaging details, such as stream file header syntax, payload data, authorization, and error handling. Since video streaming protocols operate under the application layer, they potentially can use different protocols in the underlying layers to transmit data packets.

4.3.3   Analytical Services of Multimedia Streaming

4.3.3.1   Impact of QoE on Viewers' Behavior

Prior studies indicate that the quality of video streaming impacts on viewers' reception to the video and the revenue of the stream provider [28]. According to the studies, high startup delay and interruptions remarkably increases the likelihood of terminating multimedia streaming. Florin et al. [11] discuss the impact of video quality on viewers' interest. They demonstrate that the percentage of time spent on buffering (i.e., buffering ratio) has the largest impact on the user regardless of the content types. Moreover, the average bit-rate of live streaming has shown to be effective on the viewers' interest.

Accordingly, in MSC services are required to collect these type of information that can help streaming providers to analyze their viewers' satisfaction and try to maximize their engagement via minimizing the buffer time and increasing the average bit-rate. Some of the prior work in this area includes a study by Dutta et al. [12] who propose an approach to improve Quality-of-Experience (QoE) aware on-demand transcoding via Mobile Edge Computing (MEC). Their scheme involves an autonomic creation of a transcoding service as a Virtual Network Function (VNF) and ensures dynamic rate switching of the streamed video to maintain the desired quality. Their approach reduced latency and provided a better quality of experience. In another study, Wang et al. [53] propose an adaptive wireless video transcoding framework for user diversity that is based on the emerging edge computing paradigm by deploying edge transcoding servers close to viewers. In their approach, the core network only needs to send the source video stream to the edge transcoding servers rather than one stream for each viewer. their proposed method reduced the transcoding operations over the network. Also, the authors developed efficient bandwidth adjustment algorithms that allocates the spectrum resources to individual mobile users.

4.3.3.2   Access Pattern to Multimedia Streams

Analysis of access pattern to multimedia contents in a repository follows a long-tail distribution [8]. That is, few popular videos, known as *hot* contents that construct around 5% of the repository, are accessed very often while a large portion of non-popular contents are accessed infrequently. The studies also reveal that viewers are typically interested in recently posted contents. Moreover, the popularity of new contents fluctuates remarkably whereas the popularity of old contents are more stable and does not fluctuate significantly [7].

Multimedia access rate indicates the number of times a content is accessed by a viewer, however, it does not implicate if the accessed content is played completely or not. Some studies (e.g., [37]) shows that the beginning segments of a stream are played more often than the rest of it. Miranda et al. [37] show that in a video stream, the views are distributed following a long tail distribution. More specifically, the distribution of views of the segments (GOPs) in a video stream can be calculated by the Power-law [39] model.

The access rate of segments in all video streams in a repository does not necessarily follow a long-tail pattern. In some cases, some segments in the middle or end of the stream are accessed more frequently than other segments. For instance, in streaming a soccer match, the segments with attractive content (e.g., when a goal is scored) have a substantially higher access rate than other segments. Similarly, in an educational video, the important part of teaching, can be more frequently watched than others. The access pattern of these multimedia streams is known as non-long-tail access pattern [10].

4.3.3.3   Recommendation Systems for Multimedia Streaming

Provided the access pattern of multimedia contents of a given viewer, MSC is able to provide services to stream providers to predict the video categories the viewer prefers and recommend them to the viewers or consider them in the viewer's search. The recommendation strategy can be applied to the viewers located in the same geographical area with similar interests too. To improve the accuracy of prediction and recommendation, recommendation algorithms based on machine learning [38] and deep learning [30] approaches have been developed. The most successful example is Netflix and YouTube machine-learning-based recommendation systems as explained in [16].

4.4   Advanced Services Offered by MSC

4.4.1   Smart (AI-Based) Multimedia Streaming Services

With the significant progress of machine learning methods, many new services can be developed to make the streaming much more flexible than before. In fact, the emergence of these methods and variety of use-cases in different contexts is one of the main motivations of developing special-purpose clouds and MSC where the stream providers (or even viewers) can flexibly develop new functions depending on their particular demands.

A few motivational examples of the services that can be offered using MSC can be a stream provider that produces specialized services for handicapped people. To enhance visual recognition of color-blind viewers, the stream provider needs to develop a real-time service to increase the contrast of frames' colors. For deaf viewers, they need a service for dynamic multilingual subtitle generation. For blind viewers, they need a service to provide additional audio description [25]. Another child entertainment application needs to develop a service to dynamically extract harmful and illicit content from the videos and make them child-safe. A healthcare application needs to develop a machine learning based service to monitor certain metrics in premature birth cases and inform the medical crew upon detecting important signs [21]. A situational-awareness application needs a face detection service to track suspects across multiple security cameras. A repair company develop services to live stream from Google Glass to a mechanic for troubleshooting. A live-stream provider can develop a function for dynamic multilingual subtitle generation. An e-learning application can develop a function to dynamically summarize educational videos.

4.4.2   Augmented Reality (AR) and Virtual Reality (VR) Streaming

Virtual reality (VR) is a technology that gives the user/viewer an illusion of being somewhere else. VR works based on headsets (e.g., Oculus Rift) that enable the user to interact with the visualized environment. For instance, using this technology, the user can lift a virtual object or drive a car. Alternatively, Augmented Reality (AR), which also operate based on smart glasses (e.g., Microsoft HoloLens), projects virtual objects to the real-world scenes that the user looks at. In summary, we can say that VR replaces the reality whereas AR adds to the reality [17]. Both VR and AR are among the flourishing markets in the computing and major players such as Facebook and YouTube already can stream them to the users. However, AR/VR streaming services (and particularly VR) require 4K+ resolution and 60 frame-rate configuration that implies a huge data volume in addition to the complex rendering algorithms that has to be executed on the viewer's device, which makes such streaming services both compute- and bandwidth-hungry. High-end processing demanded at the user-side to execute rendering algorithms can be procured by edge computing systems, so that VR streaming becomes feasible on thin clients (e.g., smartphones).

For a realistic AR streaming experience, objects imposed to the real scenes should be delivered to the user device with both high quality (in terms of pho-torealism) and low latency. Currently, a download-and-play approach is used for AR streaming, where the whole scene is deemed a monolithic entity for delivery. However, this approach results in a high start-up latency and thus a poor QoE. To facilitate AR streaming, MSC can incorporate methods to apply the adaptive streaming principle from the video to the AR context [41]. In this method, the AR objects are pre-processed and made available at different Levels-Of-Detail (LODs) that can be streamed independently from each other. The LOD adaptation method dynamically decides the object and its level of LOD that should be fetched from the server. The method prioritizes contents that are more likely to be viewed by the user and chooses the LOD that maximizes the object's perceived visual quality based on the available bandwidth such that a timely delivery of the AR objects is ensured.

4.4.3   Holographic Multimedia Streaming

Holographic-type Communication (HTC) is a new immersive technology based on combination of AR and VR that is anticipated to become prevalent streaming in the 5G networks. It can display full 3D objects captured by RGB depth (a.k.a. RGB-D) sensor cameras, so that the viewers can stream objects in 6-Degree-of-Freedom (6DoF) using VR devices. It is predicted that the HTC technology will help in emerging next generation applications that can support all human senses (vision, smell, hearing, taste, touch, and balance) [44]. Such applications will need network bandwidth in the scale of Gbps and even Tbps to enable the immersive technology for real-time user interactions. Streaming the holographic contents can be facilitated by the edge computing at the user-end and federated fog delivery networks (F-FDNs) supported by MSC that are explained in Sect. 7.4.

4.4.4   360° Multimedia Streaming

Similar to Virtual Reality (VR), 360° videos provide the viewer with a 360° environment. However, VR and 360-videos are not the same thing and there are some certain differences between them. While VR provides an immersive experience by taking the viewer into a digital world using a particular headset (e.g., Samsung Gear VR Glass and Oculus Rift), 360-video is a live action and films the reality as it is seen [6]. Although 360-videos are captured using specific cameras that can cover multiple angles of the scene, they can be viewed on any 360-compatible device, such as smartphone applications and computers. Unlike VR where the viewer determines the next scene and can interact with the surrounding environment (e.g., shooting to a target or lifting an object), in 360-videos the viewer is passive and progression of the video is solely determined by the broadcaster. 360-videos are yet to be prevalent, but they are expected to dominate the streaming market in the near future when there are more affordable cameras and compatible display devices.

Capturing a 360-video is carried out via a set of cameras that are fixed on a circle or a sphere uniformly. The captured images of the cameras have at least 3840×1920 (4K) resolution. They are collected and stitched together, much like a panoramic image, to ultimately form a 360-degree video. As storing and presenting 360-degree videos in the spherical domain is difficult, they are projected onto a two-dimensional (2D) space that can be represented by the EquiRectangular (ERP) format [51]. Then, the ERP images can be processed further to be represented in form of a spherical video.

Streaming of the 360-videos and performing various functions of them can be supported by MSC. In particular, MSC can include built-in services for QoE-aware and uninterrupted 360-video streaming. For instance, it is proven that viewers are only attracted to a part of the entire 360-degree video at a time, known as Field of View (FoV) [36]. Thus, to make 360-video streaming feasible MSC can process and transmit only the FoV part of the 360-degree video. Accordingly, tile-based adaptive streaming is a suitable approach for streaming 360-degree videos [56]. In this approach, after projecting the sphere onto a 2D plane, the 360-video picture with ERP format is split into 24 tiles with 4 rows and 6 columns that includes a block of FoV. Upon turning the viewer's head to another direction and changing the FoV, the tiles with high quality that cover the FoV are shifted accordingly. Yuan et al. have shown that DASH is a reliable protocol that can adapt streaming bit-rate to the available network bandwidth. It can accommodate tiling and achieve real-time 360-degree video streaming.

4.5 Summary

In this section, we focused on the potential applications for the MSC platform. We introduced basic streaming services that MSC should offer in the builtin manner and more advanced services that can be programmed for by the users of the MSC platform.

From the next chapter, we elaborate on how different components of the MSC platform can be implemented. Specifically, in the next chapter, we discuss the virtualization system that is appropriate for multimedia processing and the inconsistently heterogeneous computing infrastructure needed for a domain-specific cloud system. Then, we explain how such computing infrastructure can be efficiently handled by the MSC platform.

References

1. Ishfaq Ahmad, Xiaohui Wei, Yu Sun, and Ya-Qin Zhang. Video transcoding: an overview of various techniques and research issues. *IEEE Transactions on Multimedia*, 7(5):793–804, Oct. 2005.
2. Selim Balcisoy, Marta Karczewicz, and Tolga Capin. Progressive downloading of timed multimedia content, June 9 2004. US Patent App. 10/865,670.
3. Ali Begen, Tankut Akgul, and Mark Baugher. Watching video over the web: Part 1: Streaming protocols. *IEEE Internet Computing*, 15(2):54–63, 2011.
4. Niklas Bjork and Charilaos Christopoulos. Transcoder architectures for video coding. *IEEE Transactions on Consumer Electronics*, 44(1):88–98, Feb. 1998.
5. Nassima Bouzakaria, Cyril Concolato, and Jean Le Feuvre. Overhead and performance of low latency live streaming using mpeg-dash. In *Proceedings of the 5th International Conference on Information, Intelligence, Systems and Applications*, pages 92–97, 2014.
6. Aaron Burch. INFOGRAPHIC – VIRTUAL REALITY VS 360 VIDEOS. https:// touchstoneresearch.com/infographic-virtual-reality-vs-360-videos/, 2016. [Online; accessed 19-May-2021].
7. Meeyoung Cha, Haewoon Kwak, Pablo Rodriguez, Yong-Yeol Ahn, and Sue Moon. I tube, you tube, everybody tubes: analyzing the world's largest user generated content video system. In *Proceedings of the 7th ACM SIGCOMM conference on Internet measurement*, pages 1–14. ACM, 2007.
8. Xu Cheng, Jiangchuan Liu, and Cameron Dale. Understanding the characteristics of internet short video sharing: A youtube-based measurement study. *IEEE Transactions on Multimedia*, 15(5):1184–1194, Aug. 2013.
9. Mahmoud Darwich, Ege Beyazit, Mohsen Amini Salehi, and Magdy Bayoumi. Cost efficient repository management for cloud-based on-demand video streaming. In *Proceedings of the 5th IEEE International Conference on Mobile Cloud Computing, Services, and Engineering*, pages 39–44, Apr. 2017.
10. Mahmoud Darwich, Mohsen Amini Salehi, Ege Beyazit, and Magdy Bayoumi. Cost efficient cloud-based video streaming based on quantifying video stream hotness. *The Computer Journal*, pages 1085–1092, June 2018.
11. Florin Dobrian, Vyas Sekar, Asad Awan, Ion Stoica, Dilip Joseph, Aditya Ganjam, Jibin Zhan, and Hui Zhang. Understanding the impact of video quality on user engagement. In *Proceedings of the ACM SIGCOMM Computer Communication Review*, volume 41, pages 362–373. ACM, 2011.

12. Sunny Dutta, Tarik Taleb, Pantelis A Frangoudis, and Adlen Ksentini.   On-the-fly qoe-aware transcoding in the mobile edge. In *Proceedings of the EEE Conference on Global Communications Conference (GLOBECOM).*, pages 1–6, 2016.

13. Gokhan Erdemir, Osman Selvi, Veysi Ertekin, and Gökhan Eşgi. Project PISCES: Developing an in-flight entertainment system for smart devices. 2017.

14. Common Media Application Format.   https://mpeg.chiariglione.org/standards/mpeg-a/common-media-application-format/text-isoiec-cd-23000-19-common-media-application. Jun. 2016.

15. Sumeer Goel, Yasser Ismail, and Magdy Bayoumi. High-speed motion estimation architecture for real-time video transmission. *The Computer Journal*, 55(1):35–46, Apr. 2012.

16. Carlos A Gomez-Uribe and Neil Hunt. The netflix recommender system: Algorithms, business value, and innovation.   *ACM Transactions on Management Information Systems (TMIS)*, 6(4):13, 2016.

17. Will Greenwald.   Augmented Reality (AR) vs. Virtual Reality (VR): What's the Difference? https://www.pcmag.com/news/augmented-reality-ar-vs-virtual-reality-vr-whats-the-difference, 2021. [Online; accessed 19-May-2021].

18. Giovanni Gualdi, Andrea Prati, and Rita Cucchiara.   Video streaming for mobile video surveillance. *IEEE Transactions on Multimedia*, 10(6):1142–1154, 2008.

19. C Hanna, D Gillies, E Cochon, A Dorner, J Alred, and M Hinkle. Demultiplexer ic for mpeg2 transport streams. *IEEE Transactions on Consumer Electronics*, 41(3):699–706, 1995.

20. Barry G Haskell, Atul Puri, and Arun N Netravali. *Digital video: an introduction to MPEG-2.* Springer Science and Business Media, Dec. 1996.

21. Enhancing Healthcare and Eliminating Human Error in NICUs. https://www.wowza.com/wp-content/uploads/child-health-imprints-case-study.pdf. Accessed Jul. 5, 2020.

22. Matin Hosseini, Mohsen Amini Salehi, and Raju Gottumukkala.   Enabling interactive video stream prioritization for public safety monitoring through effective batch scheduling.   In *Proceedings of the 19th IEEE International Conference on High Performance Computing and Communications*, HPCC '17, Dec. 2017.

23. Van Jacobson, Ron Frederick, Steve Casner, and H Schulzrinne. Rtp: A transport protocol for real-time applications. 2003.

24. Shraboni Jana, Eilwoo Baik, Amit Pande, and Prasant Mohapatra.   Improving mobile video telephony.   In *Proceedings of the 11th Annual IEEE International Conference on Sensing, Communication, and Networking*, SECON '14, pages 495–503, 2014.

25. Qin Jin and Junwei Liang.   Video description generation using audio and visual cues.   In *Proceedings of the ACM International Conference on Multimedia Retrieval*, pages 239–242, 2016.

26. Jinyong Jo and JongWon Kim.   Synchronized one-to-many media streaming with adaptive playout control.   In *proceeeding of the International Society for Optics and Photonics on Multimedia Systems and Applications V*, volume 4861, pages 71–83, 2002.

27. Christine E Jones, Krishna M Sivalingam, Prathima Agrawal, and Jyh Cheng Chen. A survey of energy efficient network protocols for wireless networks. *Wireless networks*, 7(4):343–358, 2001.

28. S Shunmuga Krishnan and Ramesh K Sitaraman.   Video stream quality impacts viewer behavior: inferring causality using quasi-experimental designs. *IEEE/ACM Transactions on Networking*, 21(6):2001–2014, 2013.

29. Eetu Latja. *Parallel Acceleration of H.265 Video Processing*. PhD thesis, Aalto University, 2017.

30. Yann LeCun, Yoshua Bengio, and Geoffrey Hinton. Deep learning. *Nature*, 521(7553):436, 2015.

31. Brian Lesser. *Programming flash communication server*. O'Reilly Media, Inc., 2005.

32. Xiangbo Li, Mohsen Amini Salehi, Yamini Joshi, Mahmoud Darwich, Brad Landreneau, and Magdi Bayoumi.   Performance analysis and modelling of video stream transcoding using heterogeneous cloud services. *Accepted in IEEE Transactions on Parallel and Distributed Systems (TPDS)*, Sep. 2018.

33. Xiangbo Li, Mohsen Amini Salehi, and Magdy Bayoumi. High Perform On-Demand Video Transcoding Using Cloud Services. In *Proceedings of the 16th ACM/IEEE International Conference on Cluster Cloud and Grid Computing*, CCGrid '16, pages 600–603, May 2016.

34. Xiangbo Li, Mohsen Amini Salehi, and Magdy Bayoumi. VLSC: Video Live Streaming Using Cloud Services. In *Proceedings of the 6th IEEE International Conference on Big Data and Cloud Computing Conference*, BDCloud '16, pages 595–600, Oct. 2016.

35. Xiangbo Li, Mohsen Amini Salehi, Magdy Bayoumi, Nian-Feng Tzeng, and Rajkumar Buyya. Cost-efficient and robust on-demand video transcoding using heterogeneous cloud services. *IEEE Transactions on Parallel and Distributed Systems (TPDS)*, 29(3):556–571, 2018.

36. Chengming Liu, Nuowen Kan, Junni Zou, Qin Yang, and Hongkai Xiong. Server-side rate adaptation for multi-user 360-degree video streaming. In *Proceedings of the 25th IEEE International Conference on Image Processing (ICIP)*, pages 3264–3268, 2018.

37. Lucas CO Miranda, Rodrygo LT Santos, and Alberto HF Laender. Characterizing video access patterns in mainstream media portals. In *Proceedings of the 22nd International Conference on World Wide Web*, pages 1085–1092. ACM, 2013.

38. Nasser M Nasrabadi. Pattern recognition and machine learning. *Journal of electronic imaging*, 16(4):049901, 2007.

39. Mark EJ Newman. Power laws, pareto distributions and zipf's law. *Contemporary physics*, 46(5):323–351, 2005.

40. Venkata N Padmanabhan and Jeffrey C Mogul. Improving http latency. *Computer Networks and ISDN Systems*, 28(1–2):25–35, 1995.

41. Stefano Petrangeli, Gwendal Simon, Haoliang Wang, and Vishy Swaminathan. Dynamic adaptive streaming for augmented reality applications. In *Proceedings of the IEEE International Symposium on Multimedia (ISM)*, pages 56–567, 2019.

42. F. F. Al Quayed and S. S. Zaghloul. Analysis and evaluation of internet protocol television (IPTV). In *Proceedings of the Third International Conference on e-Technologies and Networks for Development (ICeND2014)*, pages 162–164, April 2014.

43. Naeem Ramzan, Hyunggon Park, and Ebroul Izquierdo. Video streaming over p2p networks: Challenges and opportunities. *Signal Processing: Image Communication*, 27(5):401–411, 2012.

44. Ioannis Selinis, Ning Wang, Bin Da, Delei Yu, and Rahim Tafazolli. On the Internet-scale Streaming of Holographic-type Content with Assured User Quality of Experiences. In *Proceedings of the IFIP Networking Conference*, pages 136–144, 2020.

45. Martin Smole. Live-to-VoD Streaming. https://bitmovin.com/bitmovins-live-vod-service/, Feb. 2017.

46. Thomas Stockhammer. Dynamic adaptive streaming over http: standards and design principles. In *Proceedings of the 2nd annual ACM conference on Multimedia systems*, MMSYS '11, pages 133–144, Feb. 2011.

47. George Suciu, Muneeb Anwar, and Roxana Mihalcioiu. Virtualized video and cloud computing for efficient elearning. In *Proceedings of The International Scientific Conference eLearning and Software for Education*, volume 2, page 205, 2017.

48. Gary J Sullivan, J-R Ohm, Woo-Jin Han, and Thomas Wiegand. Overview of the high efficiency video coding (HEVC) standard. *Circuits and Systems for Video Technology, IEEE Transactions on*, 22(12):1649–1668, Sep. 2012.

49. Truong Cong Thang, Hung T Le, Anh T Pham, and Yong Man Ro. An evaluation of bitrate adaptation methods for http live streaming. *IEEE Journal on Selected Areas in Communications*, 32(4):693–705, 2014.

50. Christian Timmerer and Christopher Müller. Http streaming of mpeg media. *Streaming Day*, 2010.

51. Sik-Ho Tsang and Yui-Lam Chan. 360-Degree Intra Coding Mode for Equirectangular Projection Format Videos. In *Proceedings of the IEEE International Symposium on Circuits and Systems (ISCAS)*, pages 1–5, 2020.

52. Anthony Vetro, Charilaos Christopoulos, and Huifang Sun. Video transcoding architectures and techniques: an overview. *IEEE Magazine on Signal Processing*, 20(2):18–29, Mar. 2003.

53. Desheng Wang, Yanrong Peng, Xiaoqiang Ma, Wenting Ding, Hongbo Jiang, Fei Chen, and Jiangchuan Liu. Adaptive wireless video streaming based on edge computing: Opportunities and approaches. *IEEE Transactions on services Computing*, 12(5):685–697, 2018.
54. Oliver Werner. Requantization for transcoding of MPEG-2 intraframes. *IEEE Transactions on Image Processing*, 8:179–191, Feb. 1999.
55. Thomas Wiegand, Gary J Sullivan, Gisle Bjontegaard, and Ajay Luthra. Overview of the h. 264/avc video coding standard. *IEEE Transactions on circuits and systems for video technology*, 13(7):560–576, 2003.
56. Hui Yuan, Shiyun Zhao, Junhui Hou, Xuekai Wei, and Sam Kwong. Spatial and temporal consistency-aware dynamic adaptive streaming for 360-degree videos. *IEEE Journal of Selected Topics in Signal Processing*, 14(1):177–193, 2019.

Chapter 5
Computing Infrastructure for Multimedia Streaming Clouds (MSC)

5.1 Overview

Computing services are the first and foremost requirement in offering interactive multimedia streaming services. Accordingly, knowing the details of computing resources needed for efficient multimedia streaming is vital for cost- and QoS-efficient offering of such services. When we talk about the computing services, at least the following three dimensions of the services have to be considered:

1. The appropriate execution (a.k.a. virtualization) platform. Nowadays, cloud compute services are offered via a variety of execution platforms, such as bare-metal, virtual machines (VMs), containers, and virtualized containers. Each one of these platforms has their own pros and cons and knowing them is necessary to optimally configure MSC.
2. The appropriate type of cloud machines that well suite execution of multimedia streams. Apart from the type of computing platform (e.g., VM-based and container-based) for multimedia streaming, the type of machines provisioned to process streaming tasks are also influential in the latency and incurred cost of streaming. For instance, clouds offer various VM types with diverse configurations (e.g., GPU based, CPU based, IO based, and Memory based), or various reservation types (e.g., on-demand, spot, and advance reservation). Choosing machine types with high affinity to process multimedia tasks can not only make MSC more cost-efficient, but also can improve the real-time quality of the streaming services. We investigate the impact of heterogeneous computing systems offered by cloud providers in satisfying the efficiency goals.
3. How to optimally make use of the allocated heterogeneous computing machines. Therefore, we also investigate the role of scheduling tasks of invoked functions on the allocated machines and policies for resource provisioning.

To better understand the role of computing in MSC, we should know that different steps of the streaming process are commonly implemented in form of

© Springer Nature Switzerland AG 2021
M. A. Salehi, X. Li, *Multimedia Cloud Computing Systems*,
https://doi.org/10.1007/978-3-030-88451-2_5

independent micro-services [1] and deployed in a loosely coupled manner on a certain type of virtualization platform (e.g., containers) that are allocated on independent servers within the cloud. Services like web server, request ingestion, encoding, transcoding, and packaging are examples of such micro-services that are deployed in datacenters for streaming. For the sake of reliability and fault tolerance, each of these micro-services is deployed on multiple servers and together they form a large distributed system. A load balancer is deployed for the servers of each micro-service. It assigns streaming tasks to an appropriate server with the goal of minimizing latency and to cover possible faults in the servers.

Considering the importance of computing in MSC, in this chapter, we dive deep on different aspects of the computing and particularly explore how efficiently processing of the multimedia streaming tasks within the large distributed system with respect to the viewers' expected QoS can cause cost- and energy-efficiency.

5.2   Virtualization Platforms for MSC

Virtualization platforms emulate and isolate compute, storage, and network resources within a host. Current virtualization platforms are categorized based on the level of abstraction they provide. In particular, VMs provide a hardware layer abstraction, known as *hardware virtualization*, whereas containers enable abstraction from the operating system (OS) layer, known as *OS virtualization*.

Hardware virtualization in form of virtual machines (VMs) is an indispensable part of cloud computing technology that offers isolation, manageability, consolidation, and reliability [2] to cloud-based applications. However, performance overhead, resulted from several abstraction layers in the hypervisor [3–6], has historically been a side-effect of the virtualization technology. More recently, a lightweight form of virtualization, known as containerization, that provides abstraction at the application layer has gained popularity in the cloud and has caused a paradigm shift in offering computing services. Serverless computing [7, 8] that is offered by various cloud providers under different names (e.g., AWS Lambda [9], Azure Service Fabric[10]) operates based on the container technology.

Nowadays, major cloud providers offer a range of *execution platforms* (namely, bare-metal, VMs, containers, and containers on top of VMs) to carry out multimedia processing. Technically, all of these platforms can be used by MSC, however, the challenge is to choose the execution platform that imposes the lowest overhead. The overhead increases execution time of the tasks running inside the platform. However, its magnitude can remarkably vary, depending on the way it is configured on the underlying hardware resources and the task type. Specifically, CPU provisioning for the virtualized platforms can be configured either through CPU-quota or CPU-set (a.k.a *CPU pinning*) [11]. In the former, at each scheduling event, the middleware of the host machine decides about allocating the proper CPU core(s) to each VM/container (a.k.a. *vanilla mode*). In the latter, certain CPU cores are statically bound to each VM/container by the solution architect. Note that the side-effect of pinning (i.e., not using the host scheduling) can appear in a lower CPU utilization, hence, it should be used carefully for certain application types and processes.

Hardware Virtualization (VM)
Hardware virtualization operates based on a hypervisor that enables one or more isolated guest operating systems (VMs) on a physical host [12, 13]. KVM [5] is a popular open-source hypervisor extensively used by cloud providers. For instance, AWS developed a KVM-based hypervisor called *Nitro* [14] and uses it for its C5 VM types. Many datacenter management platforms have been developed around the KVM hypervisor. For instance, Hyper Converged Infrastructure (HCI) platforms [15] (e.g., Nutanix [16], Maxta [17], and Cloudistics [18]) that enable integrated software defined datacenters have adopted KVM as their underlying hypervisor.

OS Virtualization (Container)
Container is a lightweight and portable virtualization solution in which the host OS kernel is shared across multiple isolated user-space environments. Besides the use of containers in clouds, the technology has changed the landscape of application deployment and managing critical layers of the IT infrastructure. For instance, containers are being utilized in storage appliances (e.g., EMC Unity [19]) to reduce the fail-over time and improve their availability. In addition to the negligible overhead, containers are more storage-efficient, have shorter cloning and application deployment time, faster scale out, and offer Continuous Integration/Continuous Delivery (CI/CD) [20]. Nonetheless, conflicts between processes sharing the kernel and lack of cross middleware portability are known drawbacks of the containerization [21].

In contrast to VMs, containers are transparent from the host OS perspective. That is, the processes created by a container are visible to the host OS as native processes, however, the container itself is not a process. All processes created via a container have access to the same set of resources and libraries. A container is an abstraction created by the coupling of *namespace* and *cgroups* modules of the host OS. A namespace that is assigned to a container creates an abstraction for the processes of the container and offers them an isolated user space, such as network configurations, storage space, and software packages.

Control Groups (a.k.a cgroups) is a kernel module that enforces and monitors resource usage limitations for a given group of processes [22, 23]. Cgroups module of the host OS is in charge of enforcing resource constraints designated for a container instance. As an example, for a container instance with two CPU cores, cgroups oversees its usage not to go beyond the two cores across the entire host. It is noteworthy that the way cgroups enforces constraints is a decisive factor from the performance overhead perspective.

Docker [24] is the most widely adopted container technology in the cloud era, hence, we consider it as the container platform in this study. However, we believe that our findings can be extrapolated to other containerization techniques that operates based on cgroups (e.g., Singularity). Figure 5.1 illustrates the architecture of the Docker container. Docker Engine (DockerD) receives container management

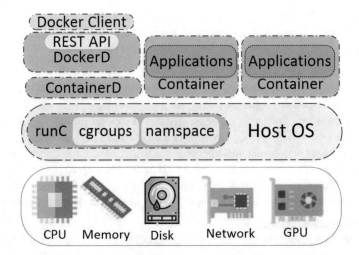

Fig. 5.1 Main modules of Docker. Containers are coupling of namespace and cgroups modules of the host OS kernel. Docker daemon interacts with Container daemon (ContainerD) and runC kernel module to manage containers

requests via its APIs. The engine is in charge of creating container instances and enforcing their specifications via containerD service. ContainerD utilizes runC module of the OS kernel to create namespace and cgroups for each container instance.

The micro-services used for multimedia streaming are commonly implemented via container technologies [25] and in a serverless computing paradigm [26]. Docker containers scale up and down much faster than VMs and have faster startup (boot up) times that gives them an advantage to VMs in handling fluctuating video streaming demands. In addition, Docker containers are used in video packaging, handling arriving streaming requests (known as request ingestion), and inserting advertisements within/between video streams.

5.2.1   Case-Study: Appropriate Virtualization Platform for Multimedia Processing Using FFmpeg

To study the appropriate virtualization platform for MSC, we consider a case-study where FFmpeg is used to process the multimedia contents. FFmpeg offers a wide variety of video transcoding functions, such as those to change video resolution, bit-rate, frame rate, and codec. Changing the codec is known to be the most CPU-intensive transcoding operation [27, 28] with small memory footprint (around 50 MB in our observations). Hence, we employ it in this case-study to represent a CPU-intensive workload. This also makes the overhead of the execution platform more visible and makes it easier to harvest. FFmpeg is a multi-threaded application and can utilize up to 16 CPU cores to transcode a video. Hence, we do not allocate more than 16 cores to each execution platform.

To understand the best-performing (i.e., the least overhead) virtualization platform for cloud-based multimedia processing, three virtualization platforms, namely Virtual Machines (VMs), containers (CN), and containers within VMs (VMCN) are considered. As alluded, each of the three platforms can be deployed with and without CPU pinning, that makes the total considered cases six. These cases are compared against the bare-metal platform, which is the baseline setting with no virtualization overhead. We note that it is not convenient and common to implement pinning on the bare-metal, hence, this setting is used only in the vanilla mode. Figure 5.2 provides a schematic view of the four execution platforms and Table 5.1 elaborates on the specifications of each platform used in the case-study. The abbreviations mentioned in the first column of the table are used henceforth to represent each execution platform. Note that each execution platform can be instantiated using any instance type of Table 5.2.

As increasing the number of cores allocated to a certain virtualization platform implies more housekeeping and controls on the assigned cores to the platform, our hypothesis is that the imposed overhead of various platforms correlates with their sizes (number of assigned cores). In other words, our hypothesis is that scale up is a decisive factor on the of the imposed overhead of various virtualization platforms. Accordingly, we conduct the analysis with respect to different number of cores

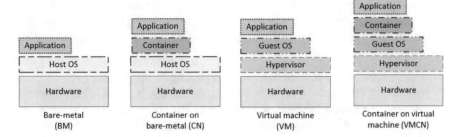

Fig. 5.2 The four execution platforms used for performance evaluation of different application types

Table 5.1 Characteristics of different execution platforms used in the evaluations. First column shows the abbreviation of the execution platform used henceforth in the case-study

Abbr.	Platform	Specifications
BM	Bare-Metal	Ubuntu 18.04.3, Kernel 5.4.5
VM	Virtual Machine	Qemu 2.11.1, Libvirt 4
		Ubuntu 18.04.3, Kernel 5.4.5
CN	Container on	Docker 19.03.6,
	Bare-Metal	Ubuntu 18.04 image
VMCN	Container on VM	As above

Table 5.2 List of instance types used for evaluation. These instance types represent the scale up of the allocated number of cores in the case-study

Instance type	No. of cores	Memory (GB)
Large	2	8
×Large	4	16
2×Large	8	32
4×Large	16	64

assigned to each platform (i.e., scale up of the resources). Table 5.2 describes the configuration of instance types used for the evaluation.

The host server for this case-study is a DELL PowerEdge R830 with 4×Intel Xeon E5-4628Lv4 processors with 112 homogeneous cores, 384 GB memory (24 × 16 GB DRAM), and RAID1 (2 × 900 GB HDD) storage. Each processor is 1.80 GHz with 35 MB cache and 14 processing cores (28 threads). The performance metric measured in the case-study is the *execution time* of each application type. Also, to quantify the overhead of a certain virtualized platform, *overhead ratio* is used and defined as the average execution time offered by a given virtualized platform to the average execution time of bare-metal. We examine a source video segment[1] that has a large codec transcoding time. The reason that we examine one video segment is to concentrate on the overhead resulted from the execution platform and remove any uncertainty in the analysis, caused by the video characteristics. The source video segment is 30 MB in High Definition (HD) format. The codec is changed from AVC (H.264) to HEVC (H.265). The evaluation was conducted 20 times and the mean and confidence interval of the results were collected.

Results of the evaluation are shown in Fig. 5.3 where the vertical axis shows the average execution time for each case and the horizontal axis shows different instance types (scale up). We note that the confidence interval in most of the cases are negligible. Specific observations and analysis of Fig. 5.3 are enumerated in the following list.

1. VMCN imposes the highest overhead and pinning it cannot reduce the overhead remarkably. Alternatively, CN platforms (particularly, pinned CN) are shown to impose the minimal overhead with respect to BM. Importantly, we observe that as the number of cores increases, the overhead of vanilla CN and both VMCN platforms decrease.
2. The imposed overhead of VM platforms (vanilla or pinned) across all instance types is remarkable to the extent that causing the execution times to remains at least twice as much as BM. Unexpectedly, pinning does not mitigate the imposed overhead for VMs when FFmpeg application is deployed.
3. By adding the containerization layer on top of VM (i.e., the case of VMCN), even a larger performance overhead is imposed. The maximum and minimum imposed overhead ratios are 4 and 1, respectively. However, as the number

---

[1] The video file is free-licensed and is publicly available in the following address: https://peach.blender.org/download/.

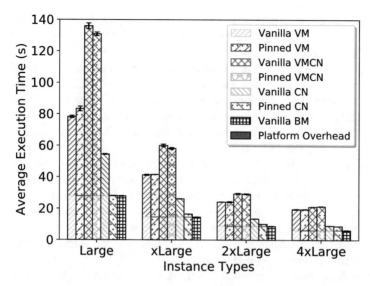

Fig. 5.3 Comparing execution time of FFmpeg on different execution platforms under varying number of CPU cores. Horizontal axis indicates the number of CPU cores in form of different instance types

of CPU cores allocated to the VMCN increases, the overhead is mitigated drastically, such that for 4×Large, the overhead imposed by VMCN is almost the same as VM. Furthermore, overhead ratio of VM and VMCN (vanilla and pinned) remains almost the same across all instance types.
4. Unlike VM and VMCN, pinning CN significantly reduces the overhead, particularly when containers are allocated with fewer processing cores (e.g., Large). This suggests that pinned CN is a suitable virtualization platform for CPU-bound applications, such as FFmpeg.

As a short takeaway of this case-study, we can conclude that pinned containers impose the least overhead for video processing tasks among other virtualization platforms. However, we note that due to the importance of latency, particularly in live streaming, some current stream providers use bare-metal as their execution platform. We will discuss this further in a case-study explained in Sect. 5.6.

5.3   Heterogeneous Computing for Multimedia Streaming Clouds (MSC)

Apart from diverse execution platforms that were discussed in the previous section, Cloud service providers offer heterogeneous machines (VMs) with diverse architectures and prices to satisfy various types and levels of computational requirements of their clients. Heterogeneity of these VMs is based on both underlying hardware characteristics and their hourly cost. Such heterogeneity enables cloud users to build a cluster of heterogeneous VMs to process high performance computations in the cloud. Heterogeneous systems are categorized as *consistent* and *inconsistent* [29] environments. The former refers to environments in which some machines (VMs) are faster than others whereas the latter explains an environment in which tasks have diverse execution times on heterogeneous machines. For instance, machine A may be faster than machine B for task 1 but slower than other machines for task 2 [30]. We also say that machine A has a higher affinity with task 1. In fact, cloud providers offer several categories of VMs that are inconsistently heterogeneous. Nevertheless, there is a consistent heterogeneity within VMs in each one of those categories.

For instance, Amazon EC2 offers `General-Purpose`, `CPU-Optimized`, and `GPU` machine types that have different architectural characteristics (i.e., inconsistent heterogeneity) and remarkably diverse costs. Within each VM type, several instance types are offered (i.e., consistent heterogeneity within each type). In such a heterogeneous environment, different function calls (tasks) can potentially have various execution times on these machines.

The *task-machine affinity* of a task type i on a machine (or VM) type j is defined as how tasks of type i matches (i.e., can take advantage of) the architectural characteristics of machine type j. Higher affinity implies faster execution time of tasks type i on machine type j [31, 32]. For instance, changing codec is proven to be CPU-intensive, whereas, real-time analysis of the view information for videos is memory-intensive. Importantly, two tasks can have nearly the same execution times on two heterogeneous machines, however, their incurred costs can be significantly different.

Dimensions of the heterogeneity in the Cloud necessitates developing optimal methods for *mapping* video (multimedia) tasks to VMs and for *elasticity management* within MSC to reduce the cost while providing decent QoS to viewers. Such methods should rely on accurate performance information of tasks and their incurred costs on heterogeneous machines. Hence, a deep analysis of the task-machine affinity of transcoding tasks with heterogeneous Cloud machines is essential.

Expected Time to Compute (ETC) [33, 34] and *Estimated Computation Speed* (ECS) [29, 35] matrices are commonly used to model and explain the task-machine affinity. However, the both ETC and ECS are defined based on only the execution time as their performance metric and neglect the cost difference across heterogeneous VMs. The question arises is how we can have a model that captures both the execution time and cost differences of heterogeneous machines? answering this question can be useful for resource provisioning methods to allocate appropriate type of machines for incoming tasks.

In this part, we provide a case study on the potentials of heterogeneous cloud resources for transcoding operation, as a very popular type of processing needed for multimedia streaming. Assuming VMs as the virtualization platform, the challenges are as follows: (1) How can we recognize the task-machine affinity of different transcoding tasks with heterogeneous cloud VMs? (2) How to model the trade-off between performance and cost of heterogeneous VMs for different transcoding tasks?

To answer the first question, we need to find appropriate factors in video transcoding tasks that can determine the task-machine affinity of transcoding tasks with heterogeneous VMs. In particular, we investigate two factors, namely video transcoding operation and the video content type. For that purpose, we analyze the task-machine affinity of transcoding tasks on heterogeneous cloud VMs when the tasks are partitioned based on the type of their transcoding operation and when they are partitioned based on the video content types. We note that, it is difficult to categorize video tasks based on their content type, because the content type is not known prior to the task execution. Hence, in the next step, we find factors that indicate the video content type that can be used for categorizing the videos.

To answer the second question, we present a model to quantify the suitability of heterogeneous VMs for a given transcoding task. The model encompasses both the execution time of the task on a VM type and the incurred cost of using it.

In summary, in this part, we elaborate on the following topics:

- Analyzing the performance of different video transcoding operations on heterogeneous cloud VMs.
- Analyzing the performance of video content types on the heterogeneous cloud VMs.
- Explaining influential factors on the execution time of the video transcoding operation.
- Explaining a model to capture (and quantify) the cost and performance trade-off of heterogeneous VMs for video transcoding tasks.

5.3.1 Heterogeneous Resource Provisioning in MSC

In the case of Amazon EC2 cloud, six categories of VM types are offered that are described below:

- **General Purpose VMs:** This VM type has a fair amount of CPU, memory, and networks for many applications, such as web servers and small- or mid-size database servers. General-purpose VMs are the least expensive one and have lower computing power in comparison with other VM types. Generally, to process a large set of tasks, either many or few of these VMs should be allocated for a long time [36].
- **CPU Optimized VMs:** This VM type offers a higher processing power in comparison with other VM types, which makes them ideal for compute-intensive tasks. They are currently mostly applied for high-traffic web application servers, batch processing, video encoding, and high performance computing applications (e.g., genome analysis and high-energy physics) [37].
- **Memory Optimized VMs:** Memory-Optimized VM type is designed for processing tasks with large memory demand. This VM type has the lowest cost per GB of memory (RAM) compared to other types. Applications such as high

performance databases, distributed cache, and memory analytics [38] usually demand Memory-Optimized VMs.

- **GPU Optimized VMs:** The GPU-Optimized VMs are applied for compute-intensive tasks (i.e., tasks that involve huge mathematical operations). Many large-scale simulations, such as computational chemistry, rendering, and financial analysis are conducted on GPU-Optimized VMs [39].
- **Storage Optimized and Dense Storage VMs:** These VM types are utilized in cases where low storage cost and high data density is necessary. This VM type is designed for large (big) data requirements such as Hadoop clusters and data warehousing applications [40].

Our analysis in this part is based on the VM types offered by the Amazon Cloud. The reason we chose Amazon is that it is the mainstream cloud provider and many video SSPs utilize its services [41]. However, we would like to note that the analysis is general and can be applied to any heterogeneous computing (HC) environment.

5.3.2   Case-Study: Performance Analysis of Video Transcoding Operations on Heterogeneous Cloud VMs

To keep the generality and to avoid limiting the analysis to the VM types offered by Amazon EC2, we select one VM type from different VM categories in Amazon EC2 that represents the characteristics of that category (see Sect. 5.3.1).

In particular, for the General-Purpose, CPU-Optimized, Memory-Optimized, and GPU VM types we choose `m4.large`, `c4.xlarge`, `r3.xlarge`, and `g2.2xlarge`, respectively. We did not consider any of the Storage-Optimized and Dense-Storage VM types in our evaluations, as we observed that IO and storage are not influential factors for video transcoding tasks. The characteristics and the cost of the chosen VM types are illustrated in Table 5.3. In this table, vCPU represents virtual CPU. Amazon uses what it calls "EC2 Compute Units" or ECUs, as a measure of virtual CPU power. It defines one ECU as the equivalent of a 2007 Intel Xeon or AMD Opteron CPU running at 1 GHz to 1.2 GHz clock rate. More details about the characteristics of the VM types can be found at Amazon EC2 website.[2]

Table 5.3 Cost of heterogeneous VMs in Amazon EC2 cloud

VM type	General (m4.large)	CPU Opt. (c4.xlarge)	Mem. Opt. (r3.xlarge)	GPU (g2.xlarge)
vCPU	2	4	4	8
Memory (GB)	8	7.5	30.5	15
Hourly cost ($)	0.15	0.20	0.33	0.65

---

[2] https://aws.amazon.com/ec2/instance-types/.

We note that the characteristics and types of the VMs are based on what is offered by Amazon Cloud at the time of conducting this evaluation and they are subject to change, as Amazon makes changes in its VM offerings frequently.

To analyze the transcoding time, we utilized a set of benchmark videos. The benchmarking videos are publicly available for reproducibility purposes.[3] Videos in the benchmark are diverse both in terms of the content types and length. The benchmark includes a combination of slow, fast, and mixed motion video content types. The length of the videos in the benchmark varies in the range of [10, 600] seconds. The size and frame number of the benchmark videos ranges from 5MB to 313MB, and 240 to 10,464, respectively.

We used `FFmpeg` to transcode the videos. State-of-the-art FFmpeg transcoder is a cascaded transcoder with sequential transcoding algorithm, that means the incoming source video stream is fully decoded before re-encoding into the target video stream with the desired codec, bitrate, and frame rate [42, 43]. For each one of the benchmarking videos, four different transcoding operations, namely codec conversion, resolution reduction, bit rate adjustment, and frame rate reduction were carried out on heterogeneous VMs.

Each transcoding operation has been repeated for 30 times on each video to remove any randomness (e.g., due to VM malfunctioning or other temporal issues).[4] The mean transcoding time on each VM for a given GOP is considered for comparison and analysis.

5.3.2.1 Analyzing the Execution Time of Different Video Transcoding Operations

The first question we answer is to identify if a certain transcoding operation has a stronger task-machine affinity with a particular cloud VM type.

To answer this question, we compared the transcoding time (execution time) of various transcoding operations using different VM types. We measured the transcoding time of the first nine GOPs in all videos in the benchmark on different VM types and reported and the mean of their transcoding times. The reason we choose nine GOPs is that the shortest video exists in the benchmark has nine GOPs. We should note that, because GOPs are transcoded independently and there are diverse types of video contents in the repository, the nine GOPs are representative of other GOPs in the benchmark.

Figure 5.4 shows the transcoding time of different transcoding operations on heterogeneous VMs. We can observe that the execution times of different transcoding operations are not the same, however, regardless of the VM type, they follow the same pattern. Figure 5.4a–d demonstrates that although the execution time of each transcoding operation varies on different VM instances, in general,

---

[3] The videos can be downloaded from: https://goo.gl/TE5iJ5.

[4] The workload traces are available at: https://goo.gl/B6T5aj.

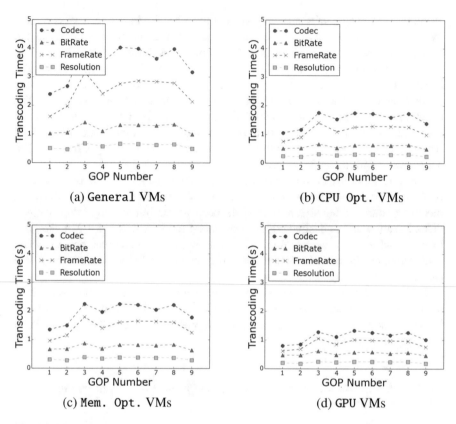

Fig. 5.4 Mean transcoding time (in seconds) on GOPs of benchmark videos on distinct VM types. (**a**) Mean transcoding time of different transcoding operations on General VM. (**b–d**) show mean transcoding time of different transcoding operations using CPU Opt., Mem. Opt., and GPU, respectively

transcoding time has the same pattern across General, CPU Opt., Mem. Opt. and GPU VM types.

The results confirm that, regardless of the VM type utilized, converting video codec always takes more time than other transcoding operations. This is because changing codec implies decoding the original format of the video and then, encoding it to a new codec. These conversions make the transcoding time longer. We also observe that changing resolution has the least transcoding time regardless of the VM type. The reason is that the transcoding is achieved by utilizing filtering and subsampling [44, 45] which works directly in the compressed domain and avoids the computationally expensive steps of converting to the pixel domain. Therefore, it takes less time than other transcoding operations.

5.3.2.2   Analyzing the Task-Machine Affinity of Video Transcoding Operations with Heterogeneous VMs

As mentioned in Sect. 5.3.1, cloud providers offer VMs that are heterogeneous both in terms of performance and cost. An important question for video stream providers to reduce their cost and improve their Quality of Service (QoS) is: what is the task-machine affinity of video transcoding operations with heterogeneous cloud VMs?

As we noticed in Sect. 5.3.2.1, although execution times of various video transcoding operations are different, codec transcoding has the highest execution time and changing spatial resolution generally has the lowest execution time. Considering this pattern, to study the task-machine affinity of video transcoding on heterogeneous VMs, we only consider one transcoding operation (e.g., codec transcoding) on heterogeneous VMs. Hence, we measure the codec transcoding time of benchmark videos on heterogeneous VM types.

Figure 5.5 expresses the analysis for one video[5] in the benchmark. In this figure, we can observe that, in general, GPU VM provides a better execution time in comparison with other VM types. This is because transcoding operations include substantial mathematical operations and GPU VM types are well suited for such kind of operations. General VM provides the lowest performance as it includes less powerful processing units (see Table 5.3).

More importantly, in Fig. 5.5, we observe that the transcoding times of different GOPs significantly varying on the four VM types. For some GOPs, the GPU VM remarkably outperforms other VMs (e.g., GOP 6, 7, and 8) whereas for some other GOPs (e.g., GOP 9, 12, and 13) the difference in transcoding times is negligible.

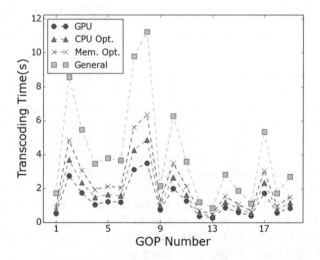

Fig. 5.5 Execution time of codec transcoding for a video in the benchmark on different VM types

---

[5] This is `big_buck_bunny_720p_h264_02tolibx264` video in the benchmark.

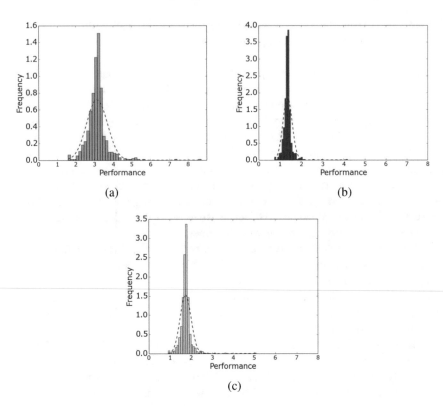

Fig. 5.6 Performance ratio of transcoding on different VM types with respect to GPU VM. Horizontal axis shows the performance ratio and the vertical axis shows the frequency of the performance ratio for all GOPs of videos in the benchmark. (**a**) Performance ratio of General to GPU. (**b**) Performance ratio of CPU-Opt. to GPU (**c**) Performance ratio of Mem-Opt. to GPU

To better understand the performance variations in transcoding different GOPs, we compared the performance of these four VM types for all videos in the benchmark in detail. Although GPU takes the least time to perform a transcoding operation, we are interested to know the significance of the outperformance of the GPU across different GOPs. Thus, we normalized the transcoding time of GOP i on a given VM type, by dividing it by the transcoding time of GOP i on GPU. The result of this analysis is shown in Fig. 5.6. In all sub-figures of Fig. 5.6, the horizontal axis shows the performance ratio and the vertical access shows the frequency of that ratio across all GOPs in a video. That is, the number of times each performance ratio has occurred for all GOPs. We fit a Bell curve on the histograms of these sub-figures and the results conform with the Normal distribution. Mean and Standard Deviation of the fitted Normal distribution, are as follows:

1. In Fig. 5.6a, performance ratio of General VM lies within the range 2.781 ± 1.524.

Table 5.4 Performance ratio of different VM types with respect to GPU VM, for all GOPs of the videos in the benchmark. Each entry shows the percentage of GOPs with performance ratio <1.0

	Codec	Frame rate	Bit rate	Resolution
General	0%	2.4%	2.7%	2.4%
CPU Opt.	2.2%	**24.8%**	**28.0%**	3.9%
Mem. Opt.	0.6%	2.8%	4.2%	2.5%

Bold values show a significant performance ratio of different VM types WRT GPU

Table 5.5 Performance ratio of different VM types with respect to GPU VM, for all GOPs of the videos in the benchmark. Each entry shows the percentage of GOPs with performance ratio ≤1.2

	Codec	Frame rate	Bit rate	Resolution
General	0%	2.72%	2.87%	2.72%
CPU Opt.	12.28%	**33.33%**	**63.93%**	22.28%
Mem. Opt.	1.36%	23.78%	23.63%	3.49%

Bold values show a significant performance ratio of different VM types WRT GPU

Table 5.6 Percentage of GOPs with performance <1.2 and maximum GPU time 2.1 s

	Codec	Frame rate	Bit rate	Resolution
General	14.70%	10.46%	4.70%	2.73%
CPU Opt.	26.82%	**41.07%**	**65.31%**	22.58%
Mem. Opt.	16.07%	31.52%	25.60%	3.49%

Bold values show a significant performance ratio of different VM types WRT GPU

2. In Fig. 5.6b, performance ratio of CPU Opt. VM lies within the range 1.263 ± 0.508.
3. In Fig. 5.6c, performance ratio of Mem. Opt. VM lies within the range 1.608 ± 0.652.

We also measured the percentage of GOPs transcoded on VMs other than GPU with performance ratio < 1.0. That is, the percentage of GOPs that their transcoding time is less than the transcoding time on the GPU. The results are shown in Table 5.4. We see that the percentage of GOPs that have transcoding time strictly lower than the GPU for different transcoding operations. In addition, to see the percentage of transcoding tasks that have close execution time to the GPU, in Table 5.5, the percentage of tasks that have performance ratio lower than 1.2 are reported. Finally, in Table 5.6 we report the percentage of GOPs who performance ratio is less than 1.2 and the processing time on GPU is short (less than 2.1 seconds).

Summary of Our Observations
1. We observe that in cases that transcoding time of other VM types are lower than GPU, the transcoding time differences are low (less than 0.24 s). We note that 0.24 s is relatively low and negligible when compared with the delay caused by network.
2. In all cases that other VM types outperform the GPU VM, the transcoding time on the GPU was low (less than 2.1 s). That is, when the GPU takes a low time to transcode a GOP, other VM types may outperform it.

3. From the two previous observations, we conclude that, in a cloud environment with heterogeneous VMs, making use of expensive VM types for tasks with short execution time is not beneficiary. However, understanding the exact execution time threshold requires benchmarking in that particular context and study the performance cost ratio of using different VM types.
4. According to Fig. 5.6, none of the transcoding types need extensive memory space (i.e., transcoding is not a memory intensive operation). Therefore, video stream providers would not benefit from instantiating memory-optimized VM types for video transcoding.

5.3.2.3   Analyzing the Impact of Video Content Type on Transcoding Time

As we observed in the previous section, the transcoding time of a GOP can vary significantly on different VM types. For instance, in Fig. 5.5, transcoding time difference between GPU and CPU Opt. VM types for GOP 8 is $\simeq$7 s while the difference for GOP 13 is less than a half second. What is this performance difference attributed to? Answering this question enables us to allocate the appropriate VM types depending on the GOP type, hence, reducing the transcoding time and its incurred cost.

Our investigation revealed that the reason for the transcoding time variations is the content type of the GOPs. To further investigate the impact of video content type on the transcoding performance, we performed codec transcoding on each video content type on different VM types. Results of the investigation are reported in Fig. 5.7.

Figure 5.7a shows that the transcoding times of the slow motion videos are distinct from each other across different VM types. In particular, GPU and General VM types, respectively, provide the best and worst performance for this type of video content.

In contrast, Fig. 5.7b shows that the outperformance of GPU VM is not statistically and practically significant when transcoding fast motion videos. Although GPU still provides a slightly faster transcoding time than other VM types, the difference is negligible. For some GOPs (e.g., 4, 5, 13, 16, and 31) the transcoding time on GPU is almost the same as other VM types.

To confirm this finding, we performed the transcoding operation on a mixed motion video and the result is depicted in Fig. 5.7c. As we can see in this subfigure, GPU outperforms others VMs significantly for some GOPs (e.g., GOP 30–37) while provides almost same transcoding time for other GOPs. We noticed that the difference in transcoding time is remarkable for GOPs of the video that contains slow motion content and it is negligible for fast motion GOPs.

The reason for the performance variations on different video content types is that, in fast motion videos, due to the high frequency of changing scenes, the number of frames in a GOP and, therefore, the GOP size is small. In contrast, slow motion GOPs include more frames and they are larger in size. When we transcode a large number of small size GOPs (i.e., the case for fast motion videos) there is little

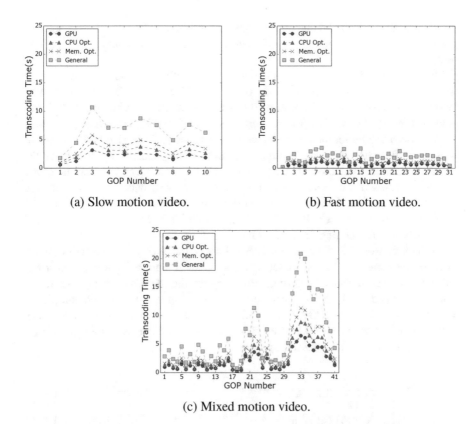

(a) Slow motion video. (b) Fast motion video.

(c) Mixed motion video.

Fig. 5.7 Transcoding time (in seconds) of video streams on different cloud VMs for various video content types. (**a–c**) Demonstrate the transcoding time obtained from different VM types when applied on slow motion, fast motion and mixed motion video content types, respectively

computation to be performed for each GOP and the performance of the VM is dominated by the overhead of switching between different GOPs. On the contrary, when in transcoding slow motion videos we deal with few numbers of GOPs that are large in size (i.e., they are compute intensive). Transcoding such videos can take advantage of compute-heavy (e.g., GPU) VMs.

In the next section, the impact of GOP size and the number of frames in a GOP on video transcoding is investigated.

5.3.2.4 Analyzing the Impact of GOP Size and Number of Frames on Transcoding Time

In Sect. 5.3.2.3, it was concluded that the transcoding time of GOPs varies significantly on different VMs depending on the video content types. However, automatic categorization of GOPs based on their video content type is a difficult task. We need an intuitive factor to categorize GOPs on different VM types. In this section, the other factors that influence GOP transcoding time on different VM types are investigated.

In Sect. 5.3.2.3, it was discussed that a GOP with slow motion content type benefits more from a computationally powerful VM. Such a GOP has a large size and includes many frames. Therefore, it is needed to analyze the impact of GOP *size* and *number of frames* on the transcoding time of each GOP on different VM types.

We use a regression analysis to study the impact of GOP size and number of frames on the GOP transcoding time. We consider the transcoding time of GOPs in all benchmark videos of the benchmark that is a mixture of slow, fast, and mixed motion video contents. Due to the large amount of data, the second-degree regression is used for the analysis. The horizontal axis shows The GOP size (in MB) and number of frames for all GOPs in Figs. 5.8 and 5.9, respectively. The vertical axes show the transcoding times of GOPs (in seconds).

In both figures, it is observed that, regardless of the VM type, transcoding times increase by increasing both the GOP size and the GOP number of frames. As it can be seen, the coefficient of determination (R^2) for the regression analyses. As we can see in this table, both GOP size and number of frames show a high confidence of relationship to transcoding time, while the number of frames in a GOP shows a higher R^2 value for all VM types. Therefore, the number of frames provides a stronger regression with transcoding time.

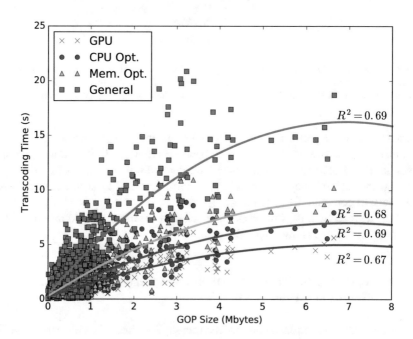

Fig. 5.8 Second degree regression to study the influence of GOP size on the transcoding time

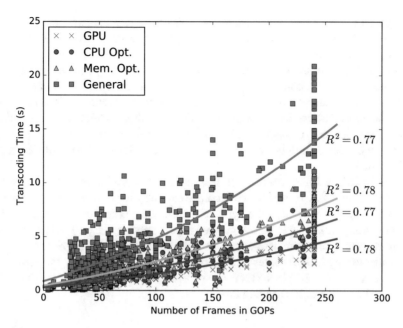

Fig. 5.9 Second degree regression to study the influence of number of frames in a GOP on the transcoding time

In Fig. 5.9, it is also observed that when the number of frames in a GOP is small, the performance of GPU is very close to other VM types whereas for a larger number of frames, the performance gap between GPU and others VM types rises. This implies that GOPs with few numbers of frames are better to be assigned to cost-efficient VM types whereas GOPs with a large number of frames can benefit from computationally powerful VM types.

5.3.2.5   Summary and Discussion

It is necessary to come up with a trade-off between performance and cost of using heterogeneous cloud machines for multimedia processing. As a case-study, to understand the affinity of different transcoding tasks and heterogeneous VM types, we provided a detailed study and analysis of different transcoding operations on heterogeneous VMs. In summary, the main findings of this analysis are as follows:

1. The execution times of different transcoding operations follow a pattern: video codec and adjusting frame rate transcoding require more computation time than bit rate and spatial resolution transcoding.
2. Although GPU VM type mostly provides a faster execution time than other VM types, in some cases the execution time difference is negligible. In particular, it is observed that when transcoding tasks are categorized based on transcoding

type, up to 63% of bit rate transcoding tasks can be executed on VM types other than GPU with nearly the same transcoding time (see Table 5.5) while incurring a significantly lower cost.

3. It is noticed that the execution time of the transcoding operation on heterogeneous VMs has a correlation with the video content type. GOPs that contain slow motion video content are larger in size and include more frames in compare to GOPs of fast motion videos. Thus, GOPs with slow motion video content can benefit from computationally powerful VMs whereas fast motion ones can be executed on less powerful and more cost-efficient VMs with a similar performance.

4. Cloud VMs exhibit inconsistent heterogeneity behavior in executing video transcoding tasks. However, the inconsistent behavior is more related to video content type rather than the type of transcoding operation. As such, video transcoding tasks (GOPs) are suggested to be categorized based on their content type to gain more from heterogeneous VMs offered by cloud providers.

5. As identifying GOPs' content types prior to execution is difficult, the number of frames (or frame size) in the GOP can be used as an intuitive factor that indicates the content type of transcoding tasks.

5.4 Performance-Cost Trade-Off of Multimedia Processing on Heterogeneous Cloud VMs

As discussed in the previous section, machines offered by cloud providers are heterogeneous both in terms of performance and cost [46]. Hence, allocating VMs that are cost- and performance-efficient for processing (e.g., transcoding) tasks is an open challenge for cloud solution architects and MSC, as well.

As we discussed in Sect. 5.3.2.2, computationally-powerful VMs do not always provide the best performance for multimedia processing (e.g., transcoding) tasks. This is particularly important when we consider the significant cost difference between the VM types. We also discussed that the processing time has a correlation with the GOP size and number frames in GOPs. Specifically, when the GOP size or the number of frames is small, the performance difference of heterogeneous VMs is negligible. Alternatively, the performance difference of using heterogeneous VMs to process large size GOPs is significant. Thus, it may be worthwhile to allocate a powerful and costly VM to transcode such GOPs.

To cope with the heterogeneous VM allocation challenge, we require a construct to identify the appropriateness of various VM types for different GOPs. Such a construct can be helpful in allocation and mapping (i.e., scheduling) of GOPs to the appropriate VMs for transcoding. In this section, we present a construct termed GOP *Suitability Matrix* that maintains the suitability value of each VM type for each GOP type. Also, as discussed the GOP types can be determined based on the number (range) of frames or the GOP size range. Such a matrix can be used by video stream providers to allocate VMs that offer the best performance and cost trade-off for multimedia processing.

5.4.1 Modeling Performance Versus Cost Trade-Off of Transcoding Tasks on Heterogeneous VMs

Recall from Table 5.3 that GPU VM, in general, provides the best performance while having the highest cost. Also, General VM type provides the lowest transcoding performance and is the least expensive one when compared to other VM types.

Performance gap, denoted Δ_i, is defined as the performance difference VM type i and GPU. For a given GOP, a large value of Δ_i indicates that VM type i remarkably performs worse than GPU, hence, GPU should be assigned a higher suitability value than VM i.

Determination of the trade-off between performance and cost of utilizing heterogeneous VMs, in the first place, depends on the business policy of the streaming service provider (here, we call it *user*). That is, a user should determine how important is the performance, denoted p, and the incurred cost, denoted c, for the system. As these parameters complement each other (i.e., $p + c = 1$), the user only needs to provide one of these parameters. For instance, a user can provide $p = 0.6$ (that implies $c = 0.4$) to indicate a higher performance preference.

Performance threshold gap, denoted Δ_{th}, is defined as the threshold of the performance gap between GPU and other VM types. The value of Δ_{th} is determined based on the user preference of p and c. As user cost and performance preferences are not crisp values, a model based on fuzzy membership functions [47] can be considered for them. As shown in Fig. 5.10, we define two membership functions for the cost and performance preferences. According to this figure, the membership value of one preference (e.g., performance) decreases when the other preference (e.g., cost) increases.

Value of the user's performance (or cost) preference is considered as the membership value of the fuzzy membership function (vertical axis in Fig. 5.10) and is used to obtain the performance threshold gap (horizontal axis in Fig. 5.10). More specifically, by using the performance preference (p), the value of Δ_{th} can be obtained based on Eq. (5.1).[6]

$$\Delta_{th} = \frac{\ln \frac{1-p}{p}}{\alpha} + \beta \tag{5.1}$$

where α is the inflection point in the membership function and β is the slope at α. In Fig. 5.10, the values of α and β are experimentally found to be 1 and 5, respectively.

---

[6] Similarly, the value of Δ_{th} can be obtained from the cost preference value: $\Delta_{th} = \frac{\ln \frac{c}{1-c}}{\alpha} - \beta$.

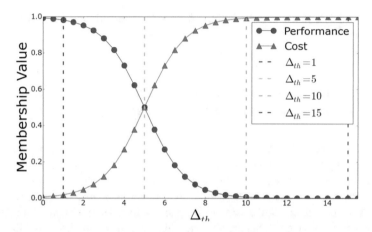

Fig. 5.10 Membership functions for performance and cost preferences. The user-provided values for the cost or performance are considered as the membership value (vertical axis). Then, the corresponding value on the horizontal axis is considered as Δ_{th}

Based on the value of Δ_{th}, the trade-off between performance and cost for transcoding a given GOP can be determined. For that purpose, the *weight* of the VM type i, denoted W_i, to transcode a given GOP is determined based on Eq. (5.2) that encompasses both the performance and cost factors. The first part, in Eq. (5.2), considers the performance factor and calculates the difference of performance gap from Δ_{th}. Performance gaps greater than the threshold (Δ_{th}) cause a low (negative) weight value which implies higher Suitability for performance-oriented VM types. In this part, the denominator determines the sum of performance gaps for all N VM types. The second part, in Eq. (5.2), considers the cost factor. This part functions based on the cost of transcoding a given GOP on VM type i, denoted φ_i. The cost of transcoding a GOP on VM i is obtained from the transcoding time of the GOP on VM i and the hourly cost of VM type i in the cloud. This part of the equation favors VM types that incur a lower cost for transcoding a given GOP.

$$W_i = \frac{\Delta_{th} - \Delta_i}{\sum\limits_{n=1}^{N} \Delta_n} \cdot \left(1 - \frac{\varphi_i}{\sum\limits_{n=1}^{N} \varphi_n}\right) \tag{5.2}$$

To normalize the value of W_i and determine the final suitability values, denoted S_i, between [0, 1] we use Eq. (5.3) as follows:

$$S_i = \frac{W_i - \max\limits_{i}(W_i)}{\max\limits_{i}(W_i) - \min\limits_{i}(W_i)} \tag{5.3}$$

where max_i and min_i are the largest and smallest values among W_is, respectively. In transcoding a video stream, each GOP has different Suitability values on different VM types. These suitability values construct a *Suitability Matrix* for each video stream.

5.4.2 Case Study of the Cost Performance Trade-Off Model

To have a better understanding of the Suitability Matrix construct, four suitability matrices with different performance and cost preference values provided by the user are compared.

Table 5.7a shows the Suitability Matrix for a given video when the user has a performance-oriented preference—$p = 0.98$. As it can be seen, in this case, the Suitability value of GPU and CPU Opt. VMs is higher than the other VM types. We observe that the Suitability values for (General) VM are mostly 0.

When user's performance preference drops to 0.5 (and cost raises to 0.5), as demonstrated in Table 5.7b, the Suitability value of GPU decreases while the General VM gets higher Suitability values. By further decreasing the user performance preference and increasing the cost preference, the Suitability value of the GPU drops to almost 0 while the Suitability values of cost-efficient VMs (General) are increased (see Table 5.7c and 5.7d). It is noteworthy that CPU Opt. VM type mostly maintains a high Suitability value regardless of Δ_{th} value. This is because the CPU Opt. VMs has a high performance and its cost is relatively low.

Performance Evaluation of the Trade-Off Model

For evaluation, CloudSim [48], which is a discrete event simulator, was used for modeling and evaluating the performance of the scheduling methods and VM provisioning policies. The modeling was conducted based on the characteristics and cost of the VM types in Amazon EC2. the startup delay, deadline miss rate of video streams, and the incurred cost of using cloud VMs to process different number of streaming tasks (from 100 or 1000) arriving during the same time period were used for measurement. For the sake of accuracy, each experiment has been conducted 30 times and the mean and 95% confidence interval of the results are reported. For this experiment, the performance ratio $p=40\%$ (and cost ratio $c=60\%$) was considered.

To demonstrate the efficacy of the trade-off model, the performance and the incurred cost were compared when the scheduling method uses the suitability matrix against a naïve suitability matrix that has been proposed in [49]. The naïve method operates simply based on a trade-off between the performance (T_i) and the cost (C_i) for a given GOP on VM type i, as shown in Eq. (5.4), while it does not consider the performance variation that the user can decide as it is in the described approach.

$$S_i = k \cdot T_i + (1 - k) \cdot C_i \tag{5.4}$$

Table 5.7 Suitability matrices for different values of performance and cost preferences. Tables (a) to (d), show that as the performance preference p decrease (and cost-preference c increases), the value of Δ_{th} grows. Accordingly, the maximum Suitability value changes from GPU (performance-oriented VM) in Table 5.7a to General type (cost-oriented VM) in Table 5.7d

(a) Suitability Matrix, when $p = 98\%$, $c = 2\%$, and $\Delta_{th} = 1$

VM type	General	CPU Opt.	Mem. Opt.	GPU
GOP_1	**0.00**	1.00	0.78	**0.98**
GOP_2	**0.00**	1.00	0.68	**0.26**
GOP_3	**0.00**	1.00	0.67	**0.30**
GOP_4	**0.00**	1.00	0.61	**0.01**
GOP_5	**0.00**	1.00	0.71	**0.60**
GOP_6	**0.00**	1.00	0.80	**0.89**
GOP_7	**0.00**	0.91	0.74	**1.00**
GOP_8	**0.00**	0.88	0.72	**1.00**
GOP_9	**0.00**	0.87	0.72	**1.00**
GOP_{10}	**0.00**	0.86	0.71	**1.00**
...			...	...

(b) Suitability Matrix, when $p = 50\%$, $c = 50\%$, and $\Delta_{th} = 5$

VM type	General	CPU Opt.	Mem. Opt.	GPU
GOP_1	0.00	1.00	0.63	0.03
GOP_2	0.69	1.00	0.78	0.00
GOP_3	0.67	1.00	0.78	0.00
GOP_4	0.75	1.00	0.78	0.00
GOP_5	0.57	1.00	0.74	0.00
GOP_6	0.26	1.00	0.71	0.00
GOP_7	0.00	1.00	0.72	0.54
GOP_8	0.00	1.00	0.75	0.70
GOP_9	0.00	1.00	0.77	0.77
GOP_{10}	0.00	1.00	0.77	0.77
...			...	...

(c) Suitability Matrix, when $p = 1\%$, $c = 99\%$, and $\Delta_{th} = 10$

VM type	General	CPU Opt.	Mem. Opt.	GPU
GOP_1	0.48	1.00	0.73	0.00
GOP_2	0.79	1.00	0.80	0.00
GOP_3	0.79	1.00	0.80	0.00
GOP_4	0.83	1.00	0.80	0.00
GOP_5	0.74	1.00	0.78	0.00
GOP_6	0.59	1.00	0.77	0.00
GOP_7	0.06	1.00	0.65	0.00
GOP_8	0.00	1.00	0.68	0.20
GOP_9	0.00	1.00	0.71	0.35
GOP_{10}	0.00	1.00	0.70	0.32
...			...	...

(d) Suitability Matrix, when $p = 0.01\%$, $c = 99.99\%$, and $\Delta_{th} = 15$

VM type	General	CPU Opt.	Mem. Opt.	GPU
GOP_1	**0.63**	1.00	0.76	**0.00**
GOP_2	**0.82**	1.00	0.81	**0.00**
GOP_3	**0.83**	1.00	0.81	**0.00**
GOP_4	**0.85**	1.00	0.81	**0.00**
GOP_5	**0.79**	1.00	0.80	**0.00**
GOP_6	**0.69**	1.00	0.79	**0.00**
GOP_7	**0.37**	1.00	0.72	**0.00**
GOP_8	**0.19**	1.00	0.69	**0.00**
GOP_9	**0.04**	1.00	0.66	**0.00**
GOP_{10}	**0.08**	1.00	0.67	**0.00**
...			...	...

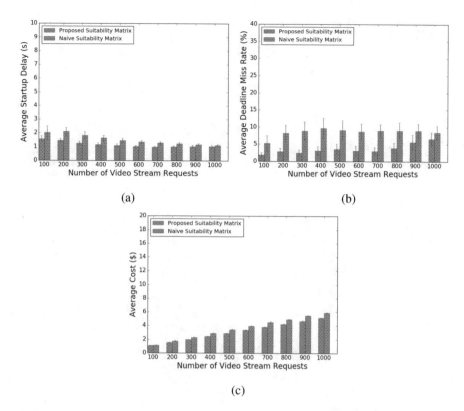

(a)

(b)

(c)

Fig. 5.11 Performance and cost comparison when our proposed suitability matrix is used against the a naïve suitability matrix. Horizontal axes in all subfigures show the number of streaming tasks. (**a**) Comparison of startup delay. (**b**) Comparison of deadline miss rate. (**c**) Comparison of cost

As seen in Fig. 5.11, the resource allocation system that uses our proposed suitability matrix leads to a lower startup delay and a lower deadline miss rate at even a lower cost. The reason is that the method can more accurately assign GOP types based on user's preference. To further investigate the impact of the streaming provider's preference on the performance (and cost) when our suitability matrix is deployed, in the second experiment, the performance and the incurred cost with two performance ratios, namely $p = 40\%$ and $p = 99\%$ were compared. Figure 5.12 expresses that for the higher value of performance ratio, both the startup delay and deadline miss rate are improved. The improvement is more remarkable when there are more tasks in the system. In addition, it can be seen that the incurred cost significantly increases for a higher performance ratio. The experiment testifies that the performance and incurred cost resulted from deploying the suitability matrix conforms with the discretion of the streaming service provider.

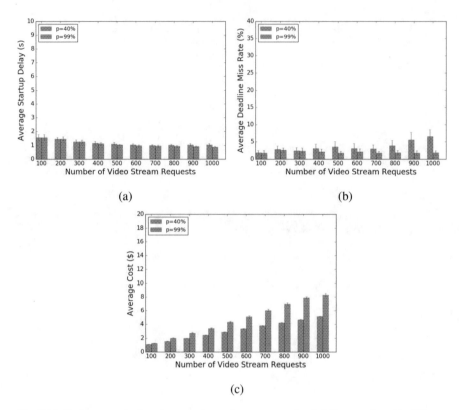

Fig. 5.12 Performance and cost comparison of our proposed suitability matrix with different performance rates, $p = 40\%$ versus $p = 99\%$. Horizontal axes in all subfigures show the number of streaming tasks. (**a**) Comparison of startup delay. (**b**) Comparison of deadline miss rate. (**c**) Comparison of incurred cost

5.5 Scheduling of Multimedia Segments on Heterogeneous Machines in MSC

In the previous part, we showed that heterogeneous cloud machines can be helpful in improving the performance and cost of multimedia cloud systems. In this section, our focus is on *how* to optimally make use of the heterogeneous capability of cloud systems to process multimedia tasks. In particular, the challenge is how to construct a heterogeneous cluster of VMs to minimize the incurred cost of streaming providers while the QoS demands of viewers are respected? More importantly, the heterogeneous VM cluster should be self-configurable. That is, based on the arriving multimedia (e.g., transcoding) tasks, the *number* and the *type* of VMs within the cluster should be dynamically altered to maximize the affinity with VMs and reduce the incurred cost.

For that purpose, in this part, we explain the QoS-aware scheduling component of MSC that maps the tasks to a heterogeneous VM cluster with respect to the viewers' QoS demands. We also explain the resource (e.g., VM) provisioner (a.k.a. elasticity manager) component of the MSC that forms a self-configurable heterogeneous VM cluster to minimize the incurred cost of the streaming providers while maintaining a robust QoS for the viewers.

5.5.1 QoS-Aware Multimedia Task Scheduler

Details of the multimedia task scheduler are shown in Fig. 5.13. According to the figure, segments (GOPs) of the requested video streams are batched in a queue upon arrival to be mapped to VMs by the scheduler. To avoid any execution delay, the required data for the GOPs are fetched in the local queue of the VMs, before the processing started. Previous studies [50] show that the local queue size should be short. Accordingly, the local queue size is considered to be 2 in all VMs. We assume that the GOP tasks in the local queue are scheduled in the *first come first serve* (FCFS) fashion. Once a free slot appears in a VM local queue, the scheduling method is notified to map a GOP task from those in the batch queue to the free slot. The GOP scheduler assumed to be non-preemptive and non-multi-tasking.

The scheduler goal is to satisfy the QoS demands of viewers by minimizing the average deadline miss rate and the average startup delay of the multimedia streams. The scheduling method maps the GOP tasks to a heterogeneous cluster of VMs where GOPs have different execution times on different VM types. In such a system, optimal mapping of GOP tasks to heterogeneous VMs is an NP-complete problem.

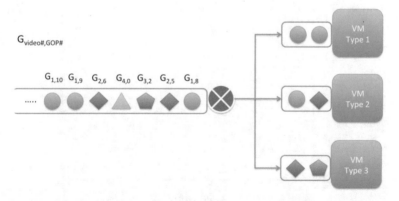

Fig. 5.13 QoS-aware multimedia scheduler that functions based on the utility value of the GOPs. Each item in the queue represents a segment (GOP) of a multimedia stream and is represented as $G_{i,j}$

Utility-Based GOP Task Prioritization

One approach to minimize the average startup delay of multimedia streams is to consider a separate dedicated queue for the startup GOPs of the streams [27]. Such a queue can only prioritize a constant number of GOPs at the beginning of the streams, with the rest of the GOPs treated as normal priority. In practice, however, the priority of GOPs should be decreased gradually as the video stream moves forward.

To implement the gradual prioritization of GOPs in a video stream, we define a *utility function* that operates on a video stream and assigns *utility values* to each GOP. Equation (5.5) shows the utility function the admission control policy uses for assigning utility values. In Eq. (5.5), c is a constant and i is the order number of GOP in the multimedia stream. We experimentally realized that $c = 0.1$ provides the prioritization we need for the GOP tasks.

$$U = (\frac{1}{e})^{c \cdot i} \tag{5.5}$$

The utility values assigned to a given video stream are depicted in Fig. 5.14. In this figure, the horizontal axis is the GOP number and the vertical axis is the utility value. As we can see, the utility function assigns higher utility values (i.e., higher priority) to earlier GOPs in the stream. The utility value drops for the latter GOPs in the stream. It is worthy to mention that the proposed Eq. (5.5) serves the purpose of utility priority for this architecture, however, there are still some rooms for improvement or better function to represent the utility priority. The exploration can be an extended future direction work.

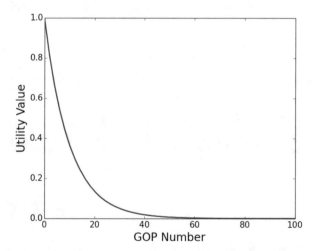

Fig. 5.14 Utility values of different GOP tasks to indicate their processing priority within a multimedia stream

Estimating Task Completion Time on Heterogeneous VMs

For each GOP j from multimedia stream i, denoted G_{ij}, the arrival time and the deadline (denoted δ_{ij}) are available. The GOP deadline is relative to the beginning of the multimedia stream. Therefore, to obtain the absolute deadline for G_{ij} (denoted Δ_{ij}) the relative deadline must be added to the presentation start time of the video stream (denoted ψ_i). That is, $\Delta_{ij} = \delta_{ij} + \psi_i$.

Recall that the estimated execution time for G_{ij} on VM type m is available via the ETC matrix. To capture randomness in the estimated execution time of GOPs, let τ_{ij}^m be the worst-case transcoding time estimation. That is, in the scheduling, we consider τ_{ij}^m as the sum of mean historic execution times of G_{ij} plus its standard deviation on VM_m. The scheduling method also needs to estimate the tasks' *completion times* to be able to efficiently map them to VMs. To estimate the completion time of an arriving GOP task G_n on VM_m, we add up the estimated remaining execution time of the currently executing GOP in VM_m with the estimated execution time of all tasks ahead of G_n in the local queue of VM_m. Finally, we add the estimated execution time of G_n (i.e., τ_n^m). Recall that each GOP task has a different execution time on different VM types that can be obtained from the ETC matrix. Let t_r denote the remaining estimated execution time of the currently executing task on VM_m, and let t_c be the current time. Then, we can estimate the *task completion time* of G_n on VM_m (denoted φ_n^m) as follows:

$$\varphi_n^m = t_c + t_r + \sum_{p=1}^{N} \tau_p^m + \tau_n^m \qquad (5.6)$$

where τ_p^m denotes the worst case estimated execution time of any task waiting ahead of G_n in local queue of VM_m and N is the number of waiting tasks in local queue of VM_m.

Mapping Heuristics

Mapping heuristics that operate on a batch queue generally function in two phases. In Phase 1, it identifies the machine with minimum expected completion time (i.e., VM) for each task in the batch queue and generates task-machine pairs. Then, in Phase 2, the heuristic recognizes the pair that maximizes a performance objective over all task-machine pairs identified in Phase 1. Based on this mechanism, MinCompletion-MinCompletion (MM) [50], MinCompletion-SoonestDeadline (MSD) [50], and MinCompletion-MaxUrgency (MMU) [50] are defined as follows:

MinCompletion-MinCompletion (MM) In the first phase, the heuristic finds the machine (i.e., VM) that provides the minimum expected completion time for the GOP task. In the second phase, the heuristic selects the pair that has the minimum completion time from all the task-machine pairs generated in the first phase. Then, the heuristics maps the task to that machine, removes it from batch queue and repeats the process until all tasks are assigned or there is no free slot left on local machine queues.

MinCompletion-SoonestDeadline (MSD) The heuristic selects the minimum expected completion time VM for each task in the first phase. In the second phase, MSD assigns the task that has the soonest deadline from the list of task-machine pairs found in the first phase.

MinCompletion-MaxUrgency (MMU) In the first phase of MMU, the heuristic identifies the shortest expected completion time machine for each task. In the second phase, MMU selects the assignment whose task urgency is the greatest (i.e., has the shortest slack) from the task-matching pairs.

Although these mapping heuristics are extensively employed in heterogeneous computing systems, none of them consider the task precedence based on the utility value.

Utility-Based Mapping Heuristics

Recall that each GOP is assigned a utility value that shows its precedence. Therefore, in the *first phase* of the utility-based scheduling method, as shown in Fig. 5.15, the GOPs with the highest utility values are selected and put into a virtual queue. The rest of the scheduling method is applied on the virtual queue rather than the whole batch queue. Given the large number of GOPs in the batch queue, making use of the virtual queue reduces the scheduling overhead. In the *second phase*, similar to the heuristics introduced earlier, the task-VM pairs are formed based on the VM that provides the minimum expected completion time for each GOP in the priority queue. Then, in the *third phase*, the mapping decision is made by combining a performance objective (e.g., SoonestDeadline) and the utility values of the GOP tasks. For combining, we prioritize the GOP with the highest utility value from the pairings of a VM, if and only if it does not violate the deadline of the task selected based on the performance objective.

To clarify further, we explain the third phase using an example. Let GOP tasks G_a and G_b denote pairs for VM_m. Also, let SoonestDeadline be the performance objective. Assume that G_a has a sooner deadline, whereas G_b has a higher utility value. In this case, G_b can be assigned to VM_m, if and only if it does not violate

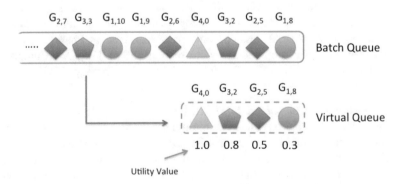

Fig. 5.15 Virtual Queue to hold GOPs with the highest utility values from different video streams. GOPs in Virtual Queue are ready for mapping to VMs

the deadline of G_a. To assure that assigning G_b does not cause a violation of the deadline of G_a, we assume that G_b has already been assigned to VM_m and run the mapping heuristic again to see if G_a can still meet its deadline or not.

Based on the way the third phase of our proposed mapping heuristic functions, we can have three variations, namely Utility-based MinCompletion-MinCompletion (MMUT), Utility-based MinCompletion-SoonestDeadline (MSDUT), and Utility-based MinCompletion-MaximumUrgency (MMUUT).

5.5.2 Self-Configurable Heterogeneous VM Provisioner

The goal of the VM Provisioner component is to maintain a robust QoS while minimizing the incurred cost to the stream provider. To that end, the component includes VM provisioning policies that make decisions for *allocating* and *deallocating* VMs from cloud.

To achieve the QoS robustness, the stream provider needs to define the acceptable QoS boundaries. Therefore, the stream provider considers an upper bound threshold for the deadline miss rate of GOPs that can be tolerated, denoted β. Similarly, it considers a lower bound threshold for the deadline miss rate, denoted α, that enables the provisioning policies to reduce the incurred cost of the stream provider through deallocating VM(s). The strategy of the VM provisioning to maintain QoS robustness is to manage the VM allocation/deallocation so that the deadline miss rate at any given time t, denoted γ_t, remains between α and β. That is, at any given time t, we should have $\alpha \leq \gamma_t \leq \beta$.

The VM Provisioner component follows the *scale up early and scale down slowly* principle. That is, VM(s) are allocated from the cloud as soon as a provisioning decision is made. However, as the stream provider has already paid for the current charging cycle of the allocated VMs, the deallocation decisions are not practiced until the end of the current charging cycle. In general, any cloud-based VM provisioning policy needs to deal with two main questions:

1. *When* to provision VMs?
2. *How many* VMs to provision?

The self-configurable VM provisioning, however, introduces a third question to the VM provisioning policies:

3. *What type* of VM(s) to provision?

In the next subsections, we first provide a method to determine the suitability of VM types for GOP tasks, then we introduce two provisioning policies, namely periodic and remedial, that work together to answer the three aforementioned questions.

Identifying Suitability of VM Types for GOP Tasks

Recall that each GOP task has different execution times on different VM types. In general, GPU provides a shorter execution time compared with other VM types. However, for some GOPs, the execution time on GPU is close to other VM types while its cost is significantly higher. Therefore, we need a measure to determine the suitability of a VM type for a GOP based on the two factors.

For a given GOP task, we define *suitability*, denoted S_i, as a measure to quantify the appropriateness of a VM type i for executing the GOP task both in terms of performance and cost. We calculate the suitability measure for a task based on Eq. (5.7). The measure establishes a trade-off between the performance (T_i) and the cost (C_i) for a given GOP on VM type i.

$$S_i = k \cdot T_i + (1 - k) \cdot C_i \qquad (5.7)$$

The value of T_i is defined based on Eq. (5.8).

$$T_i = \frac{t_i - t_{min}}{t_{max} - t_{min}} \qquad (5.8)$$

where t_i is the GOP execution time on VM type i (obtained from the ETC matrix). Also, t_{max} and t_{min} are the maximum and minimum GOP execution times across all VM types, respectively. In Eq. (5.7), the value of C_i is determined according to Eq. (5.9).

$$C_i = \frac{c_i - c_{min}}{c_{max} - c_{min}} \qquad (5.9)$$

where c_i is the cost of transcoding the same GOP on VM type i. Also, c_{max} and c_{min} are the maximum and minimum GOP transcoding costs across all VMs, respectively.

Based on Eq. (5.7), for a given GOP task, we define the *GOP type* based on the type of VM that provides the highest suitability measure. Later, the VM provisioning policies will utilize the concept of GOP type in their provisioning decisions.

Periodic VM Provisioning Policy

This VM provisioning policy occurs periodically (we term it *provisioning event*) to make VM allocation or deallocation decisions. The policy includes two methods, namely *Allocation* and *Deallocation*.

Allocation Method: Algorithm 1 provides a pseudo-code for the VM allocation method. The method is triggered *when* the deadline miss rate (γ_t) goes beyond the upper bound threshold β (line 2 in the Algorithm).

To determine *what type* of VM(s) to be allocated, we need to understand the demand for different VM types. Such demand can be understood from the concept of GOP type, introduced in Sect. 6.3.1. In fact, the number of GOP tasks from different types can guide us to the types of VMs that are required. More specifically, we

---

Algorithm 1 Pseudo-code for the VM allocation method

Input:
    β: upper bound threshold
    r: streaming request arrival rate
Output:
    n: list of number of VMs of each type to be allocated.

1: $\gamma_t \leftarrow$ current deadline miss rate
2: **if** $\gamma_t \geq \beta$ **then**
3:     **for** each VM type i **do**
4:         $\sigma_i \leftarrow$ deadline miss rate for each GOP type i
5:         $\phi_i \leftarrow$ ratio of each GOP type i in the batch queue
6:         Calculate the demand (ω_i) for each VM type
7:         $\rho_i \leftarrow$ minimum utilization in VMs of type i
8:         **if** $\omega_i \geq \omega_{th}$ and $\rho_i \geq \rho_{th}$ **then**
9:             $n_i \leftarrow \lfloor \frac{r \cdot \omega_i}{\beta} \rfloor$
10:           Allocate n_i VM type i
11:         **end if**
12:     **end for**
13: **end if**

---

can identify the type of required VMs based on two factors: (a) the proportion of deadline miss rate for each GOP type, denoted σ_i, and (b) the proportion of GOPs of each type waiting for execution in the batch queue, denoted ϕ_i. In fact, factor (a) indicates the current QoS violation status of the system, whereas factor (b) indicates the QoS violation status of the system in the near future.

Based on these factors, we define the *demand* for each VM type i, denoted ω_i, according to Eq. (5.10). The constant factor $0 \leq k \leq 1$, in this equation, determines the weight assigned to the current deadline miss rate status and to the future status of the system. For implementation, we experimentally realized that $k = 0.3$ produces the best results (see line 6).

$$\omega_i = k \cdot \sigma_i + (1 - k) \cdot \phi_i \tag{5.10}$$

If the demand for VM type i is greater than the allocation threshold (ω_{th} in line 8), and also the utilization of corresponding VM type (ρ_i) is greater than the utilization threshold (ρ_{th}), then the policy decides to allocate from VM type i.

Once we determine the type of VMs that needs to be allocated, the last question to be answered is *how many* VMs of each type to be allocated (lines 8–11 in the Algorithm). The number of allocations of each VM type depends on how far is the deadline miss rate of GOP type i is from β. For that purpose, we use the ratio of ω_i / β to determine the number of VM(s) of type i that has to be allocated (line 9). The number of VM(s) allocated also depends on the arrival rate of GOP tasks to the system. Therefore, the GOP arrival rate, denoted r, is also considered in line 9 of Algorithm 1.

Deallocation Method: The VM deallocation method functions are based on the lower bound threshold (α). That is, it is triggered *when* the deadline miss rate (γ_t) is less than α. Once the deallocation method is executed, it terminates at most one VM. The reason is that, if the VM deallocation decision is practiced aggressively, it can cause loss of processing power and results in QoS violation in the system. Therefore, the only question in this part is *which* VM should be deallocated.

In the first glance, it seems that the deallocation method can simply choose the VM with the lowest utilization for deallocation. However, this is not the case when we are dealing with a heterogeneous VM cluster. The utilizations of the VMs are subject to the degree of heterogeneity in the VM cluster. For instance, when the VM cluster is in a mostly homogeneous configuration, the task scheduler has no tendency to a particular VM type. This causes all VMs in the cluster to have a similar and high utilization. Hence, if the deallocation method functions just based on the utilization, it cannot terminate VM(s) in a homogeneous cluster, even if the deadline miss rate is low.

The challenge is how to identify the degree of heterogeneity in a VM cluster. To cope with this challenge, we need to quantify the VM cluster heterogeneity. Then, we can apply the appropriate deallocation method accordingly.

We define *degree of heterogeneity*, denoted η, as a quantity that explains the VM diversity (i.e., heterogeneity) that exists within the current configuration of the VM cluster. We utilize the Shannon Wiener equitability [51] function to quantify the degree of heterogeneity within our VM cluster. The function works based on the Shannon Wiener Diversity Index that is represented in Eq. (5.11).

$$H = -\sum_{i=1}^{N} p_i \cdot \ln p_i \qquad (5.11)$$

where, N is the number of VM types, p_i is the ratio of VM type i of the total number of VMs. Then, the degree of heterogeneity is defined as follows:

$$\eta = H/H_{max} \qquad (5.12)$$

Higher values of η indicates a higher degree of heterogeneity in a cluster and vice versa. Once we know the degree of heterogeneity in a VM cluster, we can build the deallocation method accordingly. Algorithm 2 provides the pseudo-code proposed for the VM deallocation method.

The deallocation method is carried out in four main steps. In the first step, the VM(s) with the lowest utilization are chosen (lines 3–4 in Algorithm 2). In the second step, ties are broken by selecting the least powerful VM (line 5). If more than one VM remains, in the third step (line 6), ties are broken based on the VM with the minimum remaining time to its charging cycle.

For a VM cluster that tends to a heterogeneous configuration (i.e., $\eta \geq \eta_{th}$), the policy deallocates the selected VM (termed VM_j in the algorithm) if its utilization is less than the VM utilization threshold (i.e., $\rho_j < \rho_{th}$). In contrast, in a VM cluster

---

Algorithm 2 Pseudo-code for the VM deallocation method

Input:
   α: lower bound threshold

1: $\gamma_t \leftarrow$ current deadline miss rate
2: **if** $\gamma_t \leq \alpha$ **then**
3:    calculate the utilization of each VM in the cluster
4:    find VM(s) with the lowest utilization
5:    resolve ties by choosing the least powerful VM(s)
6:    $VM_j \leftarrow$ resolve ties by selecting VM with minimum remaining time to its charging cycle
7:    $\eta \leftarrow$ calculate the degree of heterogeneity
8:    **if** $\eta \geq \eta_{th}$ and $\rho_j \geq \rho_{th}$ **then**
9:       No deallocation
10:   **else**
11:      Deallocate VM_j
12:   **end if**
13: **end if**

---

that tends to a homogeneous configuration, even if the utilization is high, the policy can deallocate VM_j based on the deadline miss rate (lines 8–12).

It is worth noting that the deallocation method is also executed at the end of the charging cycle of the current VMs to deallocate the VMs that are underutilized.

Remedial VM Provisioning Policy

The periodic VM provision policy cannot cover request arrivals to the batch queue that occur in the interval of two provisioning events.

To cope with the shortage of the periodic policy, we propose a lightweight remedial provisioning policy that can improve the overall performance of the VM Provisioner component. By injecting this policy into the intervals of the periodic provisioning policy, we can perform the periodic policy less frequently.

In fact, the remedial provisioning policy provides a quick prediction of the system based on the state of the virtual queue. Recall that the Virtual Queue includes the distinction of streaming requests waiting for transcoding in the batch queue. Hence, the length of the Virtual Queue implies the intensity of streaming requests waiting for processing. Such long batch queue increases the chance of a QoS violation in the near future. Thus, our lightweight remedial policy only checks the size of the Virtual Queue (denoted Q_s). Then, it uses Eq. (5.13) to decide for the number of VMs that should be allocated.

$$n = \lfloor \frac{Q_s}{\theta \cdot \beta} \rfloor \tag{5.13}$$

where n is the *number* of VM(s) that should be allocated; Q_s is the size of the Virtual Queue. θ is a constant factor that determines the aggressiveness of the VM allocation in the policy. That is, lower values of θ leads to allocating more VMs and vice versa. In the implementation, we considered $\theta = 10$. In the remedial policy, we allocate a VM type that, in general, provides a high performance per cost ratio (in the experiments, we used c4.xlarge).

Experiment results indicate that the remedial provisioning policy does not incur any extra cost to the stream service provider. Nonetheless, it increases the robustness of the QoS by reducing the average deadline miss rate and average startup delay.

5.6   Case-Study: Making Use of Heterogeneous Computing in Live-Streaming Industry

Heterogeneous computing has been widely used in live-streaming industry as well as other types of multimedia streaming. Along with cost and efficiency, latency is also essential in the specific case of live streaming, which can be a critical factor when allocating computing resources/machines.

Common software encoders (e.g., x264,[7] x265[8]) nowadays have been optimized to encode high quality video contents. It also has the flexibility to be installed on any type computing resources (e.g., bare-metal, cloud VMs). However, such encoding efficiency is at the cost of computing complexity. In other words, it causes relatively higher latency. For example, the latest AV1 software encoder[9] can produce the same quality as x264 at a 48.66% lower bandwidth and the same quality as x265 at 16.22% lower bandwidth [52], but it requires twice of encoding time even in comparison with x265 [53].

As for encoding speed, hardware encoders, such as Intel quick sync video [54], usually encode video contents much faster at the cost of lower quality and flexibility. To achieve both speed and quality, Xilinx's FPGA encoder [55] is definitely the winner, but it comes with a higher computing cost.

To balance the cost, efficiency and speed of video encoding, live streaming industry usually utilizing heterogeneous computing resources. For example, for popular and large viewers events (e.g., super bowl, concerts etc.), FPGA can be used to encoding the streams with high video quality and low streaming latency. Alternatively, for normal live streaming, Intel quick sync or x264 can be used, which generally depends on stream popularity, as shown in Fig. 5.16. However, due to technical hardships, the mentioned heterogeneity is mainly at a high-level. That is, each multimedia stream is scheduled to different computing resources and the whole transcoding procedure takes place in one resource and then is distributed to the viewers. Although to achieve lower level heterogeneity (i.e., scheduling segments of each stream to different computing resources) is also feasible, it generally introduces more complexity into the architecture design, which needs be carefully balanced off.

---

[7] https://www.videolan.org/developers/x264.html.

[8] https://www.videolan.org/developers/x265.html.

[9] https://aomedia.googlesource.com/aom/.

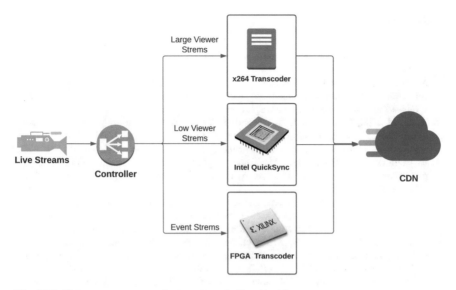

Fig. 5.16 Heterogeneous computing resources in live streaming

It is noteworthy to mention that cloud also provides heterogeneous computing resources that can be utilized for video processing, it also guarantee the service availability and error resilience. However, such benefits come at the cost of networking complication, which may cause higher latency and leaves stream providers with no control, more details will be discussed at Sect. 8.2. That is why large live streaming platforms usually use a hybrid architecture of local and cloud resources. In particular, they perform computing intensive (heavy-duty) video processing tasks (e.g., transcode, package, etc.) on bare-metal and specialized hardware within their premises. Other more general services, such as management (e.g., scheduling) and database services, are performed on public cloud providers (e.g., AWS).

5.7   Summary

This chapter described the computing aspect (also called execution engine) of the MSC platform. We covered the virtualization technology for the worker machines in MSC and provided the performance evaluation and scheduling of the heterogeneous machines for multimedia streaming. In the next chapter, we explain the Admission Control module of the MSC platform and elaborate how reusing can improve the response time, resource cost, and energy consumption within a domain-specific cloud.

References

1. S. Newman, *Building microservices: designing fine-grained systems.*   O'Reilly Media, Inc., 2015.
2. M. Parashar, M. AbdelBaky, I. Rodero, and A. Devarakonda, "Cloud paradigms and practices for computational and data-enabled science and engineering," *Computing in Science & Engineering*, vol. 15, no. 4, pp. 10–18, Jul 2013.
3. Z. Li, M. Kihl, Q. Lu, and J. A. Andersson, "Performance overhead comparison between hypervisor and container based virtualization," in *Proceedings of the 31st IEEE International Conference on Advanced Information Networking and Applications*, ser. AINA '17, Mar. 2017.
4. R. Morabito, J. Kjällman, and M. Komu, "Hypervisors vs. lightweight virtualization: a performance comparison," in *Proceedings of the IEEE International Conference on Cloud Engineering*, Mar. 2015.
5. W. Felter, A. Ferreira, R. Rajamony, and J. Rubio, "An updated performance comparison of virtual machines and linux containers," in *Proceedings of the IEEE international symposium on performance analysis of systems and software*, ser. ISPASS '15, Mar. 2015, pp. 171–172.
6. R. K. Barik, R. K. Lenka, R. K. Rahul, and D. Ghose, "Performance analysis of virtual machines and containers in cloud computing," in *Proceedings of the IEEE International Conference on Computing, Communication and Automation*, ser. ICCCA '16, Apr. 2016.
7. L. Wang, M. Li, Y. Zhang, T. Ristenpart, and M. Swift, "Peeking behind the curtains of serverless platforms," in *Proceedings of the 2018 USENIX Annual Technical Conference*, ser. USENIX ATC '18, July 2018, pp. 133–146.
8. W. Lloyd, S. Ramesh, S. Chinthalapati, L. Ly, and S. Pallickara, "Serverless computing: An investigation of factors influencing microservice performance," in *Proceedings of the 2018 IEEE International Conference on Cloud Engineering*, ser. (IC2E'18), Apr. 2018, pp. 159–169.
9. A. W. Services. Amazon web services. [Online]. Available: https://aws.amazon.com/lambda/
10. M. A. Services. Azure service fabric. [Online]. Available: https://azure.microsoft.com/en-us/services/service-fabric/
11. A. Podzimek, L. Bulej, L. Y. Chen, W. Binder, and P. Tuma, "Analyzing the impact of cpu pinning and partial cpu loads on performance and energy efficiency," in *Proceedings of the 15th IEEE/ACM International Symposium on Cluster, Cloud and Grid Computing*, May 2015, pp. 1–10.
12. M. Amini Salehi, B. Javadi, and R. Buyya, "Resource provisioning based on leases preemption in InterGrid," in *Proceeding of the 34th Australasian Computer Science Conference*, ser. ACSC '11, 2011, pp. 25–34.
13. M. A. Salehi and R. Buyya, "Contention-aware resource management system in a virtualized grid federation," in *PhD Symposium of the 18th international conference on High performance computing*, ser. HiPC '11, Dec. 2011.
14. Amazon, "Aws nitro system." [Online]. Available: https://aws.amazon.com/ec2/nitro/
15. HCI, "Hci: Hyper converge infrastructure." [Online]. Available: https://en.wikipedia.org/wiki/Hyper-converged_infrastructure
16. N. technologies, "Nutanix: Hyper converge infrastructure." [Online]. Available: https://www.nutanix.com/
17. Maxta, "Maxta: Hyper converge infrastructure." [Online]. Available: https://www.maxta.com/
18. Cloudistics, "Cloudistics: Hyper converge infrastructure." [Online]. Available: https://www.cloudistics.com/
19. D. Technologies, "Dell emc unity xt all-flash unified storage." [Online]. Available: https://www.delltechnologies.com/en-us/storage/unity.htm
20. A. F. Nogueira, J. C. Ribeiro, M. Zenha-Rela, and A. Craske, "Improving la redoute's ci/cd pipeline and devops processes by applying machine learning techniques," in *Proceedings of the 11th International Conference on the Quality of Information and Communications Technology*, ser. QUATIC '18, Sep. 2018, pp. 282–286.

21. C. Dupont, R. Giaffreda, and L. Capra, "Edge computing in IoT context: Horizontal and vertical linux container migration," in *Proceedings of the Global Internet of Things Summit*, ser. GIoTS '17, Jun. 2017, pp. 1–4.

22. Kernel-ORG, "Cgroup in kernel.org." [Online]. Available: https://www.kernel.org/doc/Documentation/cgroup-v1/cgroups.txt

23. J. Bacik, "IO and cgroups, the current and future work." Boston, MA: USENIX Association, Feb 2019.

24. C. Yu and F. Huan, "Live migration of docker containers through logging and replay," in *Proceedings of the 3rd International Conference on Mechatronics and Industrial Informatics*, ser. ICMII '15, Oct. 2015.

25. J. Thönes, "Microservices," *IEEE software*, vol. 32, no. 1, pp. 116–116, 2015.

26. L. Ao, L. Izhikevich, G. M. Voelker, and G. Porter, "Sprocket: A serverless video processing framework," in *Proceedings of the ACM Symposium on Cloud Computing*, ser. SoCC '18, 2018, pp. 263–274.

27. X. Li, M. A. Salehi, M. Bayoumi, N.-F. Tzeng, and R. Buyya, "Cost-efficient and robust on-demand video stream transcoding using heterogeneous cloud services," *IEEE Transactions on Parallel and Distributed Systems (TPDS)*, vol. 29, no. 3, pp. 556–571, Mar. 2018.

28. X. Li, M. A. Salehi, Y. Joshi, M. K. Darwich, B. Landreneau, and M. Bayoumi, "Performance analysis and modeling of video transcoding using heterogeneous cloud services," *IEEE Transactions on Parallel and Distributed Systems*, vol. 30, no. 4, p. 910–922, Apr. 2019.

29. A. M. Al-Qawasmeh, A. A. Maciejewski, R. G. Roberts, and H. J. Siegel, "Characterizing task-machine affinity in heterogeneous computing environments," in *Proceedings of 25th IEEE International Symposium on Parallel and Distributed Processing Workshops and Phd Forum*, ser. IPDPSW '11, pp. 34–44, May 2011.

30. M. A. Salehi, J. Smith, A. A. Maciejewski, H. J. Siegel, E. K. P. Chong, J. Apodaca, L. D. Briceno, T. Renner, V. Shestak, J. Ladd, A. Sutton, D. Janovy, S. Govindasamy, A. Alqudah, R. Dewri, and P. Prakash, "Stochastic-based robust dynamic resource allocation in heterogeneous computing system," *Journal of Parallel and Distributed Computing (JPDC)*, vol. 97, pp. 96–111, June 2016.

31. A. M. Al-Qawasmeh, A. A. Maciejewski, R. G. Roberts, and H. J. Siegel, "Characterizing task-machine affinity in heterogeneous computing environments," in *Parallel and Distributed Processing Workshops and Phd Forum (IPDPSW), 2011 IEEE International Symposium on*. IEEE, 2011, pp. 34–44.

32. M. Maheswaran, S. Ali, H. J. Siegel, D. Hensgen, and R. F. Freund, "Dynamic mapping of a class of independent tasks onto heterogeneous computing systems," *Journal of parallel and distributed computing*, vol. 59, no. 2, pp. 107–131, 1999.

33. B. Khemka, A. A. Maciejewski, and H. J. Siegel, "A performance comparison of resource allocation policies in distributed computing environments with random failures," in *Proceedings of the International Conference on Parallel and Distributed Processing Techniques and Applications*, ser. PDPTA '12, pp. 1, June 2012.

34. S. Ali, H. J. Siegel, M. Maheswaran, D. Hensgen, and S. Ali, "Representing task and machine heterogeneities for heterogeneous computing systems," *Journal of Applied Science and Engineering*, vol. 3, no. 3, pp. 195–207, Sep. 2000.

35. A. M. Al-Qawasmeh, A. A. Maciejewski, and H. J. Siegel, "Characterizing heterogeneous computing environments using singular value decomposition," in *Proceedings of the IEEE International Symposium on Parallel & Distributed Processing, Workshops and Phd Forum*, ser. IPDPSW '10, pp. 1–9, Apr. 2010.

36. G. Lee and R. H. Katz, "Heterogeneity-aware resource allocation and scheduling in the cloud," in *Proceedings of the 3rd USENIX Conference on Hot Topics in Cloud Computing*, ser. HotCloud '11, pp. 4, Oct. 2011.

37. K. R. Jackson, L. Ramakrishnan, K. Muriki, S. Canon, S. Cholia, J. Shalf, H. J. Wasserman, and N. J. Wright, "Performance analysis of high performance computing applications on the amazon web services cloud," in *Proceedings of the 2nd IEEE International Conference on Cloud Computing Technology and Science*, ser. CloudCom '10, pp. 159–168, Nov. 2010.

38. G. B. Berriman, G. Juve, E. Deelman, M. Regelson, and P. Plavchan, "The application of cloud computing to astronomy: A study of cost and performance," in *Proceedings of the 6th IEEE International Conference on-Science Workshops*, pp. 1–7, Oct. 2010.
39. R. R. Expósito, G. L. Taboada, S. Ramos, J. Touriño, and R. Doallo, "General-purpose computation on GPUs for high performance cloud computing," *Concurrency and Computation: Practice and Experience*, vol. 25, no. 12, pp. 1628–1642, May 2012.
40. K. P. Puttaswamy, C. Kruegel, and B. Y. Zhao, "Silverline: toward data confidentiality in storage-intensive cloud applications," in *Proceedings of the 2nd ACM Symposium on Cloud Computing*, pp. 10, Oct. 2011.
41. V. K. Adhikari, Y. Guo, F. Hao, M. Varvello, V. Hilt, M. Steiner, and Z.-L. Zhang, "Unreeling netflix: Understanding and improving multi-cdn movie delivery," in *Proceedings the 31st Annual IEEE International Conference on Computer Communications*, ser. INFOCOM '12, pp. 1620–1628, Mar. 2012.
42. I. Ahmad, X. Wei, Y. Sun, and Y.-Q. Zhang, "Video transcoding: an overview of various techniques and research issues," *IEEE Transactions on Multimedia*, vol. 7, no. 5, pp. 793–804, Oct. 2005.
43. A. Vetro, C. Christopoulos, and H. Sun, "Video transcoding architectures and techniques: an overview," *IEEE Magazine on Signal Processing*, vol. 20, no. 2, pp. 18–29, Mar. 2003.
44. T. Shanableh and M. Ghanbari, "Heterogeneous video transcoding to lower spatio-temporal resolutions and different encoding formats," *IEEE Transactions on Multimedia*, vol. 2, no. 2, pp. 101–110, June 2000.
45. P. Yin, M. Wu, and B. Liu, "Video transcoding by reducing spatial resolution," in *Proceedings of International Conference on Image Processing*, ser. ICIP '00, vol. 1, pp. 972–975, Sep. 2000.
46. T. Dillon, C. Wu, and E. Chang, "Cloud computing: issues and challenges," in *Proceedings of the 24th IEEE international conference on advanced information networking and applications*, ser. AINA '10, pp. 27–33, Apr. 2010.
47. M. L. Puri and D. A. Ralescu, "Differentials of fuzzy functions," *Journal of Mathematical Analysis and Applications*, vol. 91, no. 2, pp. 552–558, Feb. 1983.
48. R. N. Calheiros, R. Ranjan, A. Beloglazov, C. A. De Rose, and R. Buyya, "Cloudsim: a toolkit for modeling and simulation of cloud computing environments and evaluation of resource provisioning algorithms," *Software: Practice and Experience*, vol. 41, pp. 23–50, Aug. 2011.
49. X. Li, M. A. Salehi, M. Bayoumi, N. F. Tzeng, and R. Buyya, "Cost-efficient and robust on-demand video transcoding using heterogeneous cloud services," *IEEE Transactions on Parallel and Distributed Systems (TPDS)*, vol. 29, no. 3, pp. 556–571, March 2018.
50. M. A. Salehi, J. Smith, A. A. Maciejewski, H. J. Siegel, E. K. Chong, J. Apodaca, L. D. Briceño, T. Renner, V. Shestak, J. Ladd *et al.*, "Stochastic-based robust dynamic resource allocation for independent tasks in a heterogeneous computing system," *Journal of Parallel and Distributed Computing (JPDC)*, vol. 97, pp. 96–111, Nov. 2016.
51. I. F. Spellerberg and P. J. Fedor, "A tribute to Claude Shannon (1916–2001) and a plea for more rigorous use of species richness, species diversity and the 'Shannon–Wiener' index," *Global ecology and biogeography*, vol. 12, no. 3, pp. 177–179, May 2003.
52. "Promising Initial Results with AV1 Testing," https://streaminglearningcenter.com/blogs/promising-initial-results-with-av1-testing.html, accessed on June. 07, 2021.
53. "AV1 Now Only 2X Slower than X265," https://streaminglearningcenter.com/blogs/av1-now-only-2x-slower-than-x265.html, accessed on June. 07, 2021.
54. "Intel Quick Sync Encoder," https://www.intel.com/content/www/us/en/architecture-and-technology/quick-sync-video/quick-sync-video-general.html, accessed on June. 07, 2021.
55. "How VP9 Delivers Value for Twitch's Esports Live Streaming," https://blog.twitch.tv/en/2018/12/19/how-v-p9-delivers-value-for-twitch-s-esports-live-streaming-35db26f6322f/, accessed on June. 07, 2021.

Chapter 6
Service Reuse in Multimedia Clouds

6.1 Overview

MSC is a serverless computing (a.k.a. Function-as-a-Service (FaaS)) platform that can carry out on-demand and cost-efficient processing of multimedia content. Usually, a service that is offered to end-users is split into several micro-services [19] where each micro-service can be hosted by the serverless computing platform.

Behind the scene, the serverless MSC platform seamlessly handles the resource allocation and execution of the micro-services on the MSC resources. A common practice is to let multiple users send their micro-service requests (a.k.a. *task requests*) to the provider's scheduling queue. Each task in MSC has an individual deadline that failing to meet it compromises the Quality of Service (QoS) expected by the viewer requesting that micro-service. The scheduler allocates the tasks to an elastic pool of computing resources, often provisioned in form of containers, such that their QoS expectations are fulfilled.

As multimedia streaming requests have spatiotemporal characteristic [26], there is a great opportunity to reuse the computation carried out for one micro-service. Multiple viewers can stream the same multimedia content and invoke the same function on them, possibly with various configurations and arguments. At the back-end, these function calls can create similar or identical tasks in MSC. In particular, during peak times (i.e., when the system is oversubscribed) the likelihood of having mergeable tasks increases.

The serverless MSC platform is prone to the oversubscription for the following reasons: (a) Even though the underlying cloud system supplies virtually unlimited resources, there is generally a budget constraint that prevents platforms to lavishly acquire resources [5]; (b) The MSC platform can be employed on a system with limited resources, such as fog/edge systems. These systems naturally fall short on the elasticity and scalability aspects [17]; (c) The request arrival pattern is often uncertain and includes peak periods [4]; and (d) To maximize their profit, cloud providers tend to increase the number of tasks served on the minimum number of machines.

© Springer Nature Switzerland AG 2021
M. A. Salehi, X. Li, *Multimedia Cloud Computing Systems*,
https://doi.org/10.1007/978-3-030-88451-2_6

A large body of research has been dedicated to mitigating the oversubscription problem in the computing system. The approaches undertaken in these research works follow two main lines of thinking: *First*, resource allocation based approaches (e.g., [1, 12, 18]) that try to minimize the impact of oversubscription through efficient mapping (scheduling) of the tasks to the resources. *Second*, approaches based on the computational reuse (e.g., [6, 28]) that avoid or mitigate the oversubscription through efficient caching of the computational results. The latter is particularly effective when there is a redundancy in arriving tasks.

Although both of the aforementioned approaches are effective, they are limited in certain ways. The allocation-based approaches mitigate the impact of oversubscription, but cannot entirely resolve it, according to the definition of the oversubscription. In addition, many of the approaches are based on complex scheduling algorithms that impose extra overhead to the already overwhelmed system [11]. The reusing approaches that operate based on caching are also limited, because they can only reuse the computations for tasks that are identical to the ones already completed and cached [27]. In other words, if two tasks share part of their computation, caching cannot reuse result of the shared part [3].

In this chapter, we introduce mechanism and methods to achieve reusing and alleviate the oversubscription via aggregating similar function calls (tasks) in the scheduling queue of the MSC platform. As shown in Fig. 6.1, the mechanism can aggregate (i.e., merge) not only identical tasks, but also those that partially share their computation. We note that the mechanism complements existing allocation- and caching-based approaches and is not a replacement for them. In fact, the merging mechanism makes the scheduling queue less busy and potentially lighten up the scheduling process. Caching-based approaches are also complemented by capturing the in-progress tasks and those that are partially similar.

To reuse part of a function call, a question that needs to be addressed is how to identify *mergeable* functions? An arriving task (i.e., function call) can potentially have multiple mergeable pairs with varying levels of similarity. In addition, the solution to detect similar functions should not impose an extensive overhead to the system. The other concern in merging functions is to form large compound tasks that potentially causes missing the deadline of either the merged tasks or other pending tasks waiting behind the merged task. As such, merging function calls raises the following two problems: (a) *What are different types of mergeable functions and how to detect them?* (b) *How to perform merging without endangering other tasks in the system?*

In this context, the mechanism we introduce can detect identical and similar tasks and reuse the whole or part of the computation by merging them. Intelligently achieving task merging can benefit both the viewers, by enabling more functions to complete on time, and the stream providers, by improving the resource utilization and reducing their incurred cost of using services.

We explain the development of an Admission Control module (see Fig. 6.1) for the MSC platform that detects different levels of similarity between tasks and performs merging by considering the tasks' deadlines. In particular, we explain efficient methods to identify mergeable tasks. Also, we explain methods for proper

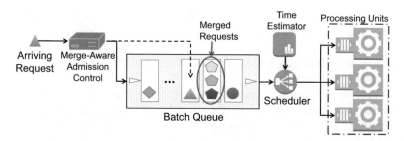

Fig. 6.1 Overview of the function aggregation procedure. A new function call arrives to Admission Control can be merged to an existing task in the Batch Queue. The shapes represents different functions (task types) in the system and shape color represents different configurations of the function

positioning of merged tasks in the scheduling queue. Next, we determine the appropriateness and potential side-effects of merging tasks with respect to the oversubscription level of the system. Lastly, we analyze the performance of merging on the viewer's QoS and the cost of utilizing the processing units.

Although we develop this mechanism in the context of multimedia streaming on a serverless cloud platform, the idea of function aggregation is valid for other domains. However, we note that identifying mergeable functions is domain-specific and requires task profiling in a certain context. The rest of the chapter is organized as follows: We discuss descriptive and predictive methods to measure the benefit of merging two or more tasks in Sects. 6.2 and 6.3, respectively. In Sect. 6.4, we present overview of the reusing system and then, in Sect. 6.5, we propose an efficient method to identify mergeable tasks; In Sect. 6.6, we present merge appropriateness determination and merge position finder; In Sect. 6.7, we discuss ways to quantify oversubscription levels and ways to use quantified oversubscription level to enhance tasks merging decision. And finally, we provide a summary of this chapter in Sect. 6.8.

6.2   Is Function Aggregation (Merging) Beneficial? A Case-Study on Video Transcoding

To avoid the side-effect of task merging and deadline violation, informed merging decisions should be made. Specifically, we need to know how much saving can be accomplished by merging two or more tasks and then, the merging is carried out, only if the it is worthwhile. However, to date, a little attention has been paid in the literature to profile the execution-time of the merging functions and understand their behavior.

The challenge in profiling the task merging is that the number of possible combinations (i.e., merging cases) is interactable and it is not feasible to examine and understand the behavior of all possible cases. Therefore, a method that can

predict the execution-time of the merged task is required. Furthermore, task merging
is naturally application-specific and there is not much gain in generic task-merging.
Accordingly, in this part, we provide a case-study on merge-saving of video
processing tasks. We choose various video transcoding operations as different task
types that can be merged.

We first strategically benchmark a variety of merging cases to understand the
influential factors on merging effectiveness. We perform a descriptive analysis
to understand the merging behavior for different number of merged tasks with
various parameters. Then, in the next section, we develop a method to estimate
the execution-time saving resulted from merging any two or more given tasks.
The proposed method operates based on a machine learning model that is trained
using our observations in the benchmarking part. The model operates based on
Gradient Boosting Decision Tree (GBDT) [10], to predict the execution-time saving
of unforeseen merging cases.

6.2.1 Introducing Video Benchmark Dataset

We used 3159 video segments to construct the benchmark dataset. The video
segments are gathered from a set of 100 open-license videos in YouTube [25].
To build a representative dataset, we assured that the chosen videos cover diverse
content types with distinct motion patterns (i.e., fast or slow pace) and various
object categories.

To systematically analyze the evaluation results and eliminate the impact of
different video formats that affect the execution-time, we split all the videos to 2-s
video segments with the standardized format detailed in Table 6.1. It is noteworthy
that segmenting videos is a common practice in stream providers and the 2-s is
to comply with the MPEG transport streaming [2, 9] standard. We choose H.264
as the unified codec, because it is still the most common and widely compatible
format for video streaming. It is worth noting that we selected libx264 [24] as the
encoders to change all the proposed video formats. The benchmark dataset contains
3159 video segments that are publicly available[1] for reproducibility purposes, with
detailed description of the each video.[2]

Table 6.1 Standardized specifications for videos in the collected video benchmark dataset

	Codec	Frame-rate	Resolution	Container
Standardized format	H.264 (High)	30 fps	1280×720	MPEG transport stream (TS)

---

[1] https://bit.ly/3gKNijT.

[2] https://bit.ly/2YMIwwb.

6.2.2 Case-Study: Benchmarking Execution-Time of Video Transcoding Tasks

Based on the video segments of the collected dataset, we perform a set of benchmark services that consists of four primary video transcoding functions (task types), namely changing bit-rate, frame-rate, resolution, and codec. Early evaluation of the collected execution-time revealed a remarkable variation in the execution-time of some task types. Specifically, we noticed that codec execution-time is far beyond the other three task types. Accordingly, we categorize the tasks types into two groups: *First* group is called Video Information Conversion (*VIC*) that includes changing bit-rate, frame-rate, or resolution task types. Tasks of this group have a low variation in their execution-times, when processing different video segments on the same machine type. *Second* group is Video Compression Conversion that only includes the codec task type (hence, we call it the Codec group). In contrast to the first group, the codec execution-time (and subsequently its merge-saving) for different video segments varies remarkably even on the same machine type.

To limit the degree of freedom in execution-time, we configured each transcoding function to change only one specification of the videos in the benchmark dataset. The characteristics (parameters) of the evaluated transcoding functions are listed in Table 6.2. According to the table, there are 4 function (task) types and collectively 18 transcoding tasks, including 5 different parameters in tasks changing bit-rate, 5 parameter for tasks changing frame-rate, 5 parameters in tasks that change resolution, and 3 parameters in tasks changing codec.

To evaluate a variety of task merging cases, we compare the time difference between executing the 18 video transcoding tasks individually against executing them in various merged forms. Our preliminary evaluations [7, 8] showed that there is little gain in merging more than five tasks. In addition, we observed that it is unlikely to find more than five (similar, but not identical) mergeable tasks at any given moment in the system. As such, in the benchmarking, the maximum number of merged tasks (a.k.a. degree of merging) is limited to five. Even with this limitation, exhaustively examining all possible permutations of merging 18 tasks (in batches

Table 6.2 The list of parameters employed to form various transcoding tasks. Each transcoding task changes only one specification of the videos in the standardized benchmark dataset. Accordingly, there are collectively 18 transcoding tasks: 5 for bit-rate changing, 5 for frame-rate changing, 5 for resolution changing, and 3 for codec changing

Video information conversion (VIC)			
Bit-rate	Frame-rate	Resolution	Codec
384K	10 fps	352 × 288	MPEG-4
512K	15 fps	680 × 320	H.265/HEVC
768K	20 fps	720 × 480	VP9
1024K	30 fps	1280 × 800	–
1536K	40 fps	1920 × 1080	–

of 2, 3, 4, 5 tasks) collectively leads to $C(18, 2) + C(18, 3) + C(18, 4) + C(18, 5)$ cases, where $C(x, y)$ refers to y-combinations from a set of x tasks. That entails 12,597 experiments per video segment. As performing this many experiments is time prohibitive, we reduce the number of possible test cases to some highly representative merging cases for each video segment. Details of the conducted benchmarking is as follows:

1. We measured the execution-time of the 18 tasks on each one of the 3159 video segments in the dataset individually. This means that, in this step, we collected 56,862 execution-times for individual tasks.
2. We measured the execution-time of merged tasks with the same operation and 2–5 various parameters. That is, each merged transcoding task is composed of one operation (e.g., changing resolution) with two to five different parameters (e.g., based on the possible values of resolution, mentioned in Table 6.2). Then, to measure the magnitude of saving resulted by the task merging (henceforth, referred to as *merge-saving*), the resulting execution-times are compared against execution-time of individual tasks, generated in Step (a).
3. In our initial evaluations, we observed more consistent behavior in merge-saving of the VIC group, as opposed those mergings included codec. As such, our evaluations were focused on the merging cases with various operations within the VIC group. Each operation can have various parameters. For instance, consider video A with bit-rate b_1, frame-rate f_1, and resolution r_1. We merge multiple transcoding tasks on A to change: its resolution to r_2, its bit-rate to b_2 and its frame-rate to f_2 and f_3. Then to measure the magnitude of merge-saving, the resulting execution-times are compared against execution-time of individual transcoding time from (a).
4. We benchmark and analyze execution-time of merged tasks with codec operation and operations from the VIC group. The process is similar to (c). However, each merged task is composed of one codec changing operation with one or more VIC class operations.

6.2.3 Analyzing the Impact of Merging Video Tasks

Evaluating the Impact on the Makespan Time

To understand the task merging performance behavior, we evaluate the total transcoding time (a.k.a. makespan) of the tasks in the VIC group under two scenarios: transcoding with and without merging. We consider merging of two to five parameters for bit-rate, frame-rate, and resolution separately—shown as $2P$ to $5P$ in the horizontal axes of Fig. 6.2. The difference between transcoding time when executing each task individually versus when the tasks are merged represents the merge-saving.

We observe that, in all cases, there is an increasing trend in the merge-saving when the degree of merging is increased. Interestingly, we observe that the ratio

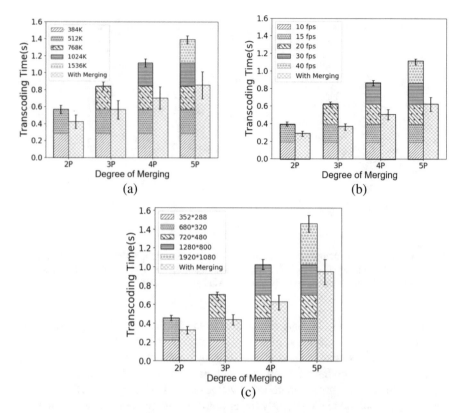

Fig. 6.2 Comparison of the total transcoding time (i.e. makespan) (in seconds) to execute multiple tasks with two to five parameters (2P–5P in the horizontal axes) within the VIC group in two scenarios: executing individual tasks sequentially (without task merging) versus executing them as a merged task. Sub-figures (**a**), (**b**), and (**c**) represent transcoding time of bit-rate changing operation, frame-rate changing operation, and resolution changing operation, respectively

of merge-saving generally increases for the higher degrees of merging. The only exception is in Fig. 6.2c (changing resolution) that by increasing the degree of merging from 4P to 5P, the merge-saving ratio is not increased. In general, we can conclude that all task merging with operations within the VIC group consistently and substantially save the execution-time.

Evaluating the Impact on Execution-Time Saving

Changing the view to focus on execution-time saving percentage, Fig. 6.3 shows that, on average, when two tasks in the VIC group are merged (2P), the execution-time is saved by 26%. The saving increases to 37% when three tasks merged together. From there, the saving taper off to around 40% for four and five tasks merging (4P and 5P). We do not observe significant extra merge-savings after 5P. In addition, forming a large merged task complicates the scheduling and increase the potential side-effects (in the form of delaying) the completion of the large task itself

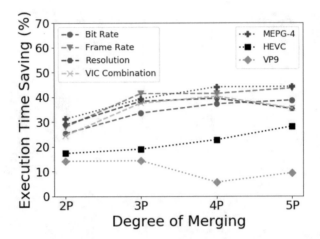

Fig. 6.3 The result of merge-saving across varying numbers of the videos transcoding tasks. Figure show the makespan saving when tasks merged within the VIC group and the makespan saving when codec transcoding tasks merged with VIC group, respectively

or other pending tasks [7]. This observation holds for the merged tasks compose of multiple different operations within the VIC group (denoted as *VIC Combination*).

For merged tasks that include codec changing operations, the results are far from consistent. Merge-saving of tasks that include MPEG-4 codec changing behave similarly to the VIC group operations. Merge-savings of tasks with HEVC codec changing operation are consistently lower than any aforementioned cases for every degree of merging. The minimum saving is observed when the merged task includes VP9 codec changing operation. In this case, the saving is even reduced when the degree of merging increased from 3P to 4P.

The results suggest that the significant gain in merging takes place in the first three tasks merging. We can conclude that, to strike a balance between efficiency gain and potential side-effects of task merging, the system should target to form groups of about three tasks, rather than forming the biggest possible group of task merging. It is also worth mentioning that codec changing operations have a significantly (up to eight times) longer execution-time than VIC group operations. Merging a codec changing task to VIC group tasks does not necessarily offer a significant merge-saving, yet can jeopardizes the users' QoS. That is, merging a short task from the VIC group to a large task from the codec group can significantly delay the completion time of the short task and degrades its QoS (e.g., in terms of missing the task's deadline).

6.3   Predicting the Execution-Time Saving of Aggregating Functions

6.3.1   A Model to Predict Execution-Time Saving

In the benchmarking case-study, we noticed that the number of cases that tasks can be merged in a system is interactable (see Sect. 6.2.2). That is, it is not feasible to pre-generate the knowledge of the merge-saving of all task types with all possible parameter values and for all video files. However, such a knowledge is crucial to decide about performing a task merging case [7]. As such, in this part, we are to leverage our findings in the benchmarking section and develop a machine learning model that can predict the merge-saving of any given set of mergeable tasks based on the task types and characteristics of the video segments.

In total, 81,327 data points, obtained from the benchmarking, were used to train the proposed model. For training and validating the model, we extracted metadata of the benchmark videos and transcoding configurations. A short sample of these metadata is shown in Table 6.3. As we can see in the table, for each video, we collected its essential static features, including duration, segment size, frame-rate (FR), width, and height (for the sake of better presentation, only few columns are shown in the table). Then, we concatenate the static features to the specification of merged task's transcoding configuration. The transcoding configuration includes the number of bit-rate changing (B), spatial resolution/frame-rate changing (S), resolution changing (R), and the type of codec changing included in the merged task. The output of the machine learning model is the merge-saving, i.e., the percentage of improvement in execution-time upon merging several tasks versus not merging them.

Since the three codec transcoding parameters behave significantly different, the codec operation parameters are marked separately in Table 6.3, as MPEG4, VP9, and HEVC columns. In contrast, for the ones in the VIC group, we observed that their configurations (i.e., parameter values) have little influence on the merge-saving, in compare with their degree of merging. As such, for elements of the VIC group, we consider the number of operations (sub-tasks) in the merged task as opposed to the value of their parameters. Accordingly, the integer values in the B, S, and R columns represents the number of those operations included in the merged task. The main benefit of marking the table in this manner is to create a robust model that can infer the merge-saving even for unforeseen parameters. Arguably, if we bind the elements of VIC group to their parameter values in the training, then the model cannot efficiently predict the merge-saving of a merge request whose parameter values are out of the scope of the training dataset.

Table 6.3 A sample of the training dataset. Left side columns show static features of videos, such as duration, size, frame-rate (FR), and dimensions. B, S, and R columns represent bit-rates, frame-rate, and resolution changing operation sub-tasks in the particular merged task. Codec changing operation parameters are marked separately with one possible parameter per column (as MPEG-4, VP9, and HEVC.) The Saving column indicates the merge-saving caused by a particular task merging

Duration (s)	Size (KB)	FR	Width	Height	B	S	R	MPEG-4	VP9	HEVC	Saving
2.0	876	30	1280	720	1	0	0	1	0	0	33.60%
2.0	1085	30	1280	720	1	2	1	0	0	0	39.17%
2.0	1231	30	1280	720	1	1	1	0	1	0	20.22%
1.2	969	30	1280	720	0	0	1	0	1	0	27.89%
2.0	864	30	1280	720	1	3	1	0	0	0	23.33%
2.0	1091	30	1280	720	1	1	1	0	0	1	21.95%
0.9	347	30	1280	720	1	0	1	0	0	0	31.32%
…	…	…	…	…	…	…	…	…	…	…	…

6.3.2 Gradient Boosting Decision Tree (GBDT) to Predict the Execution-Time Saving

Decision tree [23] is a known form of prediction model that functions based on a tree-based structure. Starting from the head node, the model performs a test on a feature at each one of its internal nodes. Ultimately, the traversal leads to a leaf node that includes the prediction [20]. In particular, decision trees are proven to be appropriate for predicting numerical of unknown data [14]. Because merge-saving prediction can be considered as a kind of numerical prediction problem, we choose decision trees to predict the saving. However, solutions based on a single decision tree are generally prone to the over-fitting problem [14]. That means, the model is excessively attached to the training dataset such that, at the inference time, its prediction cannot cover slight variations in the input.

Accordingly, to devise a prediction model that is robust against over-fitting, we utilize a optimal method of decision trees, known as Gradient Boosted Decision Trees (GBDT) [10]. This is an iterative construct based on boosted ensemble of weak-learner decision trees. In fact, GBDT combine the multiple boosted weak-learners into a high accuracy and robust model. The boosting technique uses a process in which subsequent predictors learn from errors of the previous predictors. The objective of each iteration is to reduce the prediction error, which is calculate by a loss function [10], to the minimum possible.

The pseudo-code, shown in Fig. 6.4, elaborates on how the merge-saving prediction model is trained based on GBDT. In Step 2 of the pseudo-code, a subset of the benchmark dataset is generated and is used as the training dataset, denoted as t. We considered 80% of the benchmarked dataset in t. In Step 4, the main loop of the training model aims at creating one weak model based (decision tree) per iteration. Within the loop, the initial decision tree, denoted as $B_0(x)$, is created with random number and trained based on t in Step 4.1. Note that x represents

1. Let T be the merge-saving benchmark dataset
2. Create training dataset t, where $t \subset T$
3. Let M be the number of decision trees (and iterations)
4. For $m \leftarrow 1$ to M do

4.1. Train decision tree $B_0(x)$ from t
4.2. Compute the prediction error (r_{mi}) of the $B_{m-1}(x)$
4.3. $B_m(x) \leftarrow$ Update $B_0(x)$ based on r_{mi}
4.4. Save $B_m(x)$

   5. Build the ultimate merge-saving prediction model $(B_M(x))$
             from all saved $B_m(x)$

Fig. 6.4 Pseudo-code to build the prediction model of the execution-time saving of a merged task

the input features of the merged task, as expressed in Table 6.3. In this step, there are various hyper-parameters that affect form of the decision tree being created. Notable hyper-parameters (among many others [14]) that impact the accuracy of the prediction model are the learning rate (denoted as L), maximum depth of the individual regression estimators (denoted as D), the minimum number of samples required to split an internal node (denoted as S), and the minimum number of samples needed to be at a leaf node (denoted as J). In Sect. 6.3.3, we elaborate on the appropriate values of these hyper-parameters such that the prediction accuracy of the merge-saving prediction model is maximized.

Let r_{mi} denote the prediction error of record $i \in t$. Recall that the core idea of GBDT is to learn from and improve upon the mistakes of the previous iteration. Accordingly, in Step 4.2, we calculate r_{mi} of the model created in the previous iteration (i.e., $B_{m-1}(x)$). The value of r_{mi} is calculated based on Eq. (6.1). In this equation, y_i is the ground truth (i.e., actual saving in Table 6.3) for the prediction made by $B_{m-1}(x_i)$. Also, $L(y_i, B_{m-1}(x_i))$ denotes the loss function and it is calculated as explained in [10].

$$r_{mi} = -\left[\frac{\partial L(y_i, B_{m-1}(x_i))}{\partial B_{m-1}(x_i)} \right] \tag{6.1}$$

In Step 4.3, the decision tree is updated (called $B_m(x)$) based on the value of r_{mi}. At the end of each iteration (Step 4.4) the updated decision tree is saved. In Step 5, the ensemble of created decision trees form the merge-saving prediction model. Details of forming the ensemble can be found in [10].

6.3.3   Performance Evaluation of the Execution-Time Saving Predictor

To maximize the prediction accuracy and efficiency, it is critical to determine the optimal combination of parameter values used in the GBDT model. As such, in this section, first, we examine various parameters that influence the accuracy of the prediction model. The best performance is achieved by deliberately selecting the fittest combination of these parameters. The predicted time-saving is primarily used for scheduling purposes where prediction errors can perturb the scheduler. As such, we consider Root Mean Square Error (RMSE) as the primary performance evaluation metric.

Once we optimally configure the proposed GBDT model, in the second part, we measure and analyze its prediction accuracy with respect to other methods that can alternatively employed to predict the merge-saving.

Tuning the Learning Rate of the Predictor Method

Gradient boosting predictors become robust when the model is sufficiently learned. However, over-fitting can occur, if they learn too fast with too little variation in the input. The learning rate (L) of the predictor indicates how fast it can learns at each iteration. This parameter is generally considered along with the number of trees (denoted as M) that is used to train the model. Parameter M is also known as the iterations parameter, because each iteration generates one tree.

In this part, the objective is to tune the predictor with the appropriate learning rate. For that purpose, we examine the RMSE metric when the learning rate L changes in the range of [0.5, 0.005]. Each learning rate is examined when number of trees varies in the range of [350, 6000].

Figure 6.5 demonstrates the relationship between RMSE and M for different values of L. We observe that when the number of trees is low (i.e., short training), higher learning rates lead to a faster converge of the model. Therefore, the model achieves high accuracy in a lower number of iterations. However, the high learning rate can be susceptible to noise on the gradient that impacts the accuracy when leaned with a relative high number of tree.

We observe the maximum prediction accuracy for low learning rates and high number of trees. Increasing M and decreasing L make the model less susceptible to the noise, however, it make the model more complex and time consuming. Accordingly, to strike a balance between accuracy and the model complexity, we configure $M = 350$ and $L = 0.1$.

Tuning the Value of Regression Estimator Maximum Depth

Maximum Depth (D) is a parameter that controls the number of decision trees allowed in the model. The optimal value of D varies from one model to another, depending on the interaction of features within the training dataset and other training parameters. This parameter can be ignored when there are only few features. However, in our model, the optimal depth value should be limited based on the interplay of the input parameters.

Figure 6.5 shows the correlation between the maximum depth of the tree in the range of [3, 12] in the horizontal axis and its corresponding error rate (RMSE). We notice that, as the value of D increases, the prediction accuracy continues to increase until D reaches 12 where we have an inflection point and we observe over-fitting. Therefore, we set $D = 11$ as the appropriate value for the task merging prediction method.

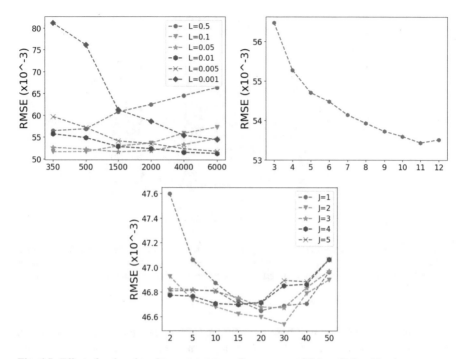

Fig. 6.5 Effect of various learning parameters on the accuracy of the prediction. Y-axis represents the error rate. X-axis of (**a**), (**b**), and (**c**) represent the number of trees in the GBDT algorithm, maximum depth of the decision tree, and the minimum number of samples to split a node (parameter S). Each line of (**a**) and (**c**) represent learning rate L and J values respectively

Tuning the Value of Minimum Samples to Create Internal- and Leaf-Node

In this part, we evaluate the parameters that control the minimum sample to create a new internal node and the minimum sample to create a new leaf node (S and J parameters, respectively) and measure their impact on the accuracy of the prediction model.

The value of J parameter correlates with the value of S parameter. Accordingly, in Fig. 6.5, we explore the prediction accuracy (by means of the RMSE value in the vertical axis) obtained when the values of S varies in the range of [2, 50]. The experiment is conducted for different values of J (in the range of [1, 5]).

We observe that regardless of the J value, by increasing the value of S a reverse bell curve shape is emerged. The lowest error rate, however, varies depending on the value of J parameter. The rebound of error rate indicates overfitting and should be avoided. From this experiment, we configure $J = 2$ and $S = 30$ that offer the lowest error rate.

Evaluating Improvement in the Prediction Accuracy

In this part, we evaluate accuracy of the proposed prediction model (when configured as: $\{M = 350, L = 0.1, D = 11, S = 30, J = 2\}$) against two alternative

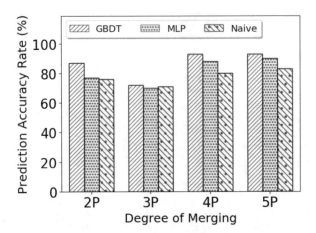

Fig. 6.6 Comparing the prediction accuracy of proposed execution-time saving prediction model (GBDT) against MLP and Naïve approaches. The horizontal axis represents the number of tasks merged to create a merged task and vertical axis represents the percentage of cases accurately predicted

prediction methods. The first baseline approach, called *Naïve* predictor, carries out the prediction based on a lookup table of mean execution-time saving for each operation. Another baseline approach is based on machine learning and uses a multi-layer perceptron (MLP) [22] for prediction.

The prediction accuracy is reported as the percentage of correct predictions, denoted as C and is defined based on Eq. (6.2). In this equation, A represents the total number of test cases, P is the predicted execution-time saving ratio, E is the observed execution-time saving ratio, and τ is the acceptable error rate, which is set to 0.12 in Fig. 6.6.

$$C = 100\% \times \frac{1}{A} \sum_{i=1}^{A} \begin{cases} 0, & |P_i - E_i| > \tau \\ 1, & |P_i - E_i| \leq \tau \end{cases} \tag{6.2}$$

We observed that the GBDT model significantly outperforms the prediction accuracy of MLP and Naïve approaches, regardless of merging degree. Both MLP and GBDT significantly perform more accurate for higher degrees of merging (4P and 5P) than the lower ones (2P and 3P). The primary reason is that, the lower degree of merging saves relatively low amount of execution-time, which is difficult to accurately predict. The maximum prediction accuracy is 93% when GBDT is employed in 4P.

Knowing that merging functions/tasks can be helpful in a serverless system, in the next section, we will explain how the merging can be implemented in MSC.

6.4   Function Aggregation in the Admission Control Unit of MSC

Admission Control unit in MSC is the front gate of the scheduling queue and it is in charge of performing merging arriving function calls (tasks) with the ones already in the queue. This is a more efficient approach than performing the merging in the scheduling queue (i.e., after the function admission), because in that case to find mergeable tasks, the entire queue has to be scanned and perform a pair-wise matching between the queued tasks, which implies a significant number of redundant comparisons.

The proposed merging mechanism, shown in Fig. 6.7, consists of three main components as follow: (a) Task similarity detector; (b) Merging appropriateness identifier; and (c) Task merger. **Task Similarity Detector** is a lightweight method based on hashing techniques to identify mergeable tasks. As detailed in Sect. 6.5, it maintains multiple hash tables to cover multiple levels of tasks' mergeability. If the arriving task is identified mergeable with an existing task, then the system employs the **Merge Appropriateness Identifier** to assess if performing the merge on the identified tasks can impact other tasks in the system or not. Merge appropriateness identifier has three cooperating modules. *Position Finder* locates the suitable position for merged tasks in the scheduling queue, such that the other tasks are not affected. To examine each position, Position finder consults with *Merge Impact Evaluator* to estimate which and how many tasks can potentially miss their deadlines as the result of merging. The task merging decision is made based on system oversubscription level obtained from *Workload Assessor* (see Sects. 6.6 and 6.7 for further details). Once the merging is confirmed as appropriate in a certain position of the batch queue, the **Task Merger** component carries out the merge operation on the two tasks.

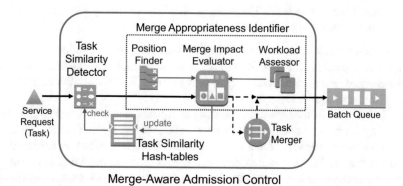

Fig. 6.7 Function aggregation mechanism inside Admission Control of MSC. Before adding the tasks of a function to the batch queue, it is checked if it is mergeable with any other queued tasks and whether or not the merging operation is appropriate to be achieved

6.5   Task Similarity Detection

6.5.1   Categories of Mergeable Tasks

Mergeability of two given tasks can be explained based on the amount of computation the two tasks share. In particular, mergeability of two or more tasks can be achieved in the following levels:

1. *Function/Task level*: This is when more than one invocation of a function occurs. In this case, the same processing tasks are present in the scheduling queue. Therefore, this level is also known as *Identical tasks* and can achieve maximum computational reusability. For instance, consider two viewers without personalized requirements stream the same video and need it to be transcoded with the same resolution to be displayed on compatible devices. As these function calls lead to identical video processing, merging them consumes the same resources required for only one task, hence, reducing both cost and processing delay.
2. *Data-and-Operation level*: This is when two or more functions perform the same operation on the same data but with different configurations (arguments). This level of merging results in a combined processing task for output equivalent to processing each task individually. Computational reusability can be achieved through the sharing of function loading overhead and common processing steps. For instance, consider two viewers who stream the same video with different resolutions. Without merging, the two tasks need to load the video, decode it, and encode it separately. However, by merging the two tasks, the loading and decoding operations can be shared, then the encoding operation is carried out separately.
3. *Data-only level*: This is when the only common sharing specification between two function calls is their data. Functions that share the same data can reduce the data retrieval overhead. This third tier function similarity level saves the least amount of processing time in comparison to other cases.

It is noteworthy that, although merging increases the execution time of the merged task (except in the function level), we will show that the execution time of the merged task is remarkably (up to 40%) shorter than the combined execution time of the unmerged tasks (see Sect. 6.2).

In MSC, the Admission Control component can achieve function/task level reusability for the same segments that need to be processed with the same function, but for different viewers. Data-and-Operation level reusability is achieved for segments that perform the same function, but with different configurations. Finally, Data-only reusability is achieved for the same segments that are served by different functions.

6.5.2 Detecting Tasks of Similar Functions

Assuming there are n tasks in the queue, for each arriving task, a naïve mergeable task detection method has the overhead of performing n comparisons to find the mergeable tasks. However, hashing techniques can be used to reduce the overhead. The general idea is to generate a hash key from the arriving task request signature (e.g., video segment id, function to perform, and its parameters). Then, the Admission Control finds mergeable tasks by searching for a matching key in the hash table of existing tasks in the scheduling queue.

The explained method can detect Function/Task level mergeability. We need to expand it to detect other levels of task mergeabilities. To maximize the computational reusability, an arriving task is first verified against Task level mergeability. If there is no match in the Task level, then the method proceeds with checking the next levels of mergeability, namely Data-and-operation level and Data-only level, respectively. To achieve the multi-level mergeability, we create three hash-tables—each covers one level of mergeability. The hash-keys in each level are constructed from the tasks' characteristics that are relevant in deciding mergeability at such level. For instance, keys in the hash-table that verifies task level mergeability are constructed from video segment id, processing type, and their parameters. While, keys in the hash-table that verifies Data-and-operation level mergeability are constructed from video segment id and processing type. Similarly, keys in the hash-table of Data-only level mergeability are constructed from segment id.

Each entry of the hash-tables includes a hash-key and a pointer to the corresponding task. Entries of the three hash-tables must be updated upon a task arrival and execution. The only exception is Task level merging, which does not require updating the hash-tables. Figure 6.8 shows the procedure for updating the hash-tables for a given task j.

When the system merges task j with existing task i, the merged task, denoted as $i + j$, is essentially the object of task i that is augmented with task information (e.g., processing parameters) of task j. In this case, as shown in Step (2) of this procedure, the system only adds an entry to each hash-table with hash-key of task j pointing to merged task $i + j$ as existing key for task i already pointed to task $i + j$. When task j is mergeable with existing task i, but the system decides to add task j to the batch queue without merging. In this case, task j has a higher likelihood of merging with other arriving tasks. The reason is that task i has not merged with task j, and it does not merge with other arriving tasks. Hence, as shown in Step (3) of the procedure, the matching entry pointing to task i is redirected and points to task j. It is worth noting that if the arriving task does not match with any of the existing tasks, as shown in Step (4), its hash-keys must be generated and added to the respective hash-tables. Also, when a task is served (processed), its corresponding entries are removed from the hash-tables.

Upon arrival of task j:

(1) if j merges with existing task i on Task level similarity:

   – No update on hash-table is required

(2) if j merges with existing task i on operation-and-data or Data-only level similarity:

   – Add an entry to each hash-table with hash-keys of task j and point them to merged task $i + j$

(3) if j matches with existing task i but the system chooses not to merge them:

   – Add an entry to each hash-table with hash-keys of task j and point them to task j

(4) if j does not match with any of the existing tasks:

   – Hash-keys of task j are added to the respective hash-tables

Upon task j completing execution (*i.e.,* dequeuing task j):

– Remove all entries pointing to task j from hash-tables

Fig. 6.8 The procedure to update hash-tables upon arrival or completion of tasks

6.6 Identifying Merging Appropriateness

6.6.1 Overview

Assume that arriving function call (task) j has Data-and-operation or Data-only similarity with existing task i. Also, assume that task i is scheduled ahead of at least one other task, denoted task k, in the scheduling queue. Merging task j with i either delays the execution of task k or task i. Such an imposed delay can potentially cause task k or i to miss their deadlines. Therefore, it is critical to assess the impact of merging tasks before performing the merge. The merge should be carried out only if it does not cause more QoS violations than it improves. It is noteworthy that Task level merging does not delay the execution of other tasks; thus, it always can be performed.

Accordingly, in this section, we first introduce Merge Impact Evaluator component whose job is to assess the impact of the merging arriving task on existing tasks. Later, we introduce Position Finder, whose job is to position the arriving task in the scheduling queue, either through merging with other tasks or as a new entry in the scheduling queue.

6.6.2 Evaluating the Impact of Merging

Ideally, task aggregation should be performed without causing deadline violations for other tasks. Accordingly, the impact of merging two or more tasks is evaluated based on the number of tasks missing their deadlines due to the merging. The evaluation requires the Time Estimator component (see Fig. 6.1) to estimate the execution time of the tasks (including their mean and standard deviation). To evaluate the impact of merging, a temporary structure, called *virtual queue*, is constructed that contains a copy of machine queues. Then, we assume the merging has taken place on the tasks in the batch queue and schedule them to the virtual queue according to the scheduling policy. This enables us to estimate the number of tasks missing their deadlines in the presence of merging.

To assure the minimal impact of the merging, by default, a worst-case analysis is performed on the completion time of the affected tasks to estimate the number of tasks missing their deadlines. For a given task i, we assume its execution time follows a Normal distribution [13, 16] and μ_i and σ_i represent the mean and standard deviation of its execution time. Let E_i be the estimated execution time of task i. In the worst-case analysis, we consider E_i to be large enough that with a high probability (97.7%), the real execution time is less than E_i. As such, E_i is formally defined based on Eq. (6.3).

$$E_i = \mu_i + \alpha \cdot \sigma_i \tag{6.3}$$

In this equation, α is the standard deviation coefficient and its value equals 2, such that with 97.7% chance task i is not affected by the merging. Note that to encourage more aggressive merging under oversubscription, we can relax the severity of the worst-case analysis by diminishing the value of α (see Sect. 6.7 for further details).

Once E_i is known, we can leverage it to estimate the completion of task i on a given machine m, denoted as C_i^m. We know that calculating C_i^m involves the summation of the following four factors: (a) current time, denoted τ; (b) estimated remaining time to complete the task currently executing on machine m, denoted e_r^m; (c) sum of the estimated execution times of N tasks that are pending in machine queue m, ahead of task i. This is calculated as $\sum_{p=1}^{N}(\mu_p + \alpha \cdot \sigma_p)$; (d) estimated execution time of task i. The formal definition of C_i^m is shown in Eq. (6.4),

$$C_i^m = \tau + e_r^m + \sum_{p=1}^{N}(\mu_p + \alpha \cdot \sigma_p) + (\mu_i + \alpha \cdot \sigma_i) \tag{6.4}$$

In the tie situation that the number of tasks missing their deadlines with and without merging is the same, we choose to perform merging to reduce the overall time of using cloud resources. However, one may argue an alternative approach to not perform the merging, because merging can marginally increase the chance of missing deadline for other tasks.

6.6.3 Positioning Aggregated Tasks in the Scheduling Queue

Once two tasks are detected as mergeable, the next question is: where should the merged task be placed in the batch queue? The number of possible answers depends on the scheduling policy of the underlying serverless computing platform. If manipulating the order of tasks in the batch queue is allowed, then the Position Finder examines possible locations for the merged tasks in the queue. For each location, it consults with the Merge Impact Evaluator component (see Fig. 6.7) to identify if the merge has potential side-effects on the involved tasks or not. Once Position Finder locates an appropriate position, it notifies Task Merger to construct the merged task.

Scheduling policies usually sort tasks in the batch queue based on a certain metric (known as the queuing policy). For instance, Earliest Deadline First [15] sorts the queued tasks based on their deadlines. This assumption restricts the number of positions can be identified for the merged tasks that in turn limits the performance gain of task merging. We investigate two main scenarios: (a) when the queuing policy is mandated, (elaborated in Sect. 6.6.3.1); (b) when the queuing policy is relaxed (elaborated in Sect. 6.6.3.2).

6.6.3.1   Task Positioning While Queuing Policy Is Maintained

Three commonly used queuing policies are studied: (a) First Come First Served (FCFS); (b) Earliest Deadline First (EDF); and (c) Max Urgency. While FCFS and EDF are known queuing policies, Max Urgency sorts the tasks in the queue based on tasks' deadline and execution time. More specifically, for task i, urgency is calculated as $U_i = 1/(\delta_i - E_i)$, where U_i is urgency score of task i, δ_i is its deadline, and E_i is its estimated execution time.

First Come First Served (FCFS)

Let j be the arriving task and i a matching task already exists in the queue. We can merge tasks by either augment task i with j's specification or cancel task i and reinsert $i + j$ into the queue. Therefore, the arrival time of the merged task $(i + j)$ can be either the arrival time of task i or task j. In the former case, $i + j$ delays completion time of all tasks located behind i. In the latter case, $i + j$ only delays completion time of i. In either case, the delayed task(s) can potentially miss their deadline(s) due to the merge operation. A compromise between these two extreme positions is possible and is described in Sect. 6.6.3.2.

Earliest Deadline First (EDF)

In this policy, tasks with an earlier deadline are positioned earlier in the queue. When two or more tasks are merged, each of them still keeps its individual deadline. However, only the earliest deadline is considered for the queuing policy. Assuming that task i has an earlier deadline than j, task $i + j$ can be only positioned in task i's spot.

Max Urgency

Recall that except in Task level merging, other levels of merging increase the execution time of the merged task. In this case, the urgency of $i + j$ is: $U_{i+j} = 1/(min(\delta_i, \delta_j) - E_{i+j})$. This means the urgency of the merged task is increased. Thus, the merged task can potentially move forward in the queue and get executed earlier. As such, tasks merging in max urgency queue can potentially cause missing the deadline of tasks located ahead of i in the scheduling queue as well.

6.6.3.2 Task Positioning While Queuing Policy Is Relaxed

Queuing policies mentioned in the previous part are not aware of task merging. Except for Max Urgency that moves the merged task forward in the queue due to the increase in the merged task urgency, other policies do not relocate the merged task. However, a more suitable position for the merged task can be found by relaxing the queuing policy. In this case, assuming there are n tasks in the batch queue, the merged task, $i + j$, has to be examined against $n + 1$ possible locations to find the position that maximizes the chance of all tasks meeting their deadlines. Examining each possible location implies evaluating the impact of merging, hence, calling the scheduling method. Assuming there are m available machines, each impacts evaluation costs $n \cdot m$ and performing such evaluation for all $n + 1$ possible locations implies $(n^2 + n) \cdot m$ complexity. This makes the time complexity of finding an optimal solution as approximately $O(n^3)$.

Such overhead itself is a burden to the system that is already oversubscribed. As such, in the rest of this section, we introduce two Position Finding heuristics and analyze them. The objectives of these heuristics are: first, not to allow the merged task to miss its deadline; and second, do not cause other tasks to miss their deadlines.

Logarithmic Probing Heuristic

This heuristic evaluates the impact of merging when $i + j$ is in the middle of the queue. The evaluation result dictates how to proceed with the probe as follows:

(1) The position neither causes deadline violation for other tasks nor for $i + j$.
    Therefore, the appropriate position is found.

(2) Task $i + j$ misses its deadline, but the number of other tasks missing their deadlines does not increase as a result of merging. This implies that $i + j$ should be executed earlier. Thus, the procedure continues to probe in the first half of the queue.

(3) Task $i + j$ meets its deadline, but the number of other tasks missing their deadlines increases as a result of merging. This implies that $i + j$ should be executed later to reduce merging impact on other tasks. Thus, the procedure continues to probe in the latter half of the queue.

(4) Task $i + j$ misses its deadline, and the number of other tasks missing their deadlines increases as a result of merging. Then, stop the procedure and cancel merging because the procedure cannot find an appropriate position for merging.

The aforementioned steps are repeated until it terminates or there is no position left to be examined in the batch queue. In the latter case, we stop the procedure and cancel merging.

Linear Probing Heuristic

In the FCFS policy, we know that the order of tasks in the batch queue implies the order of their execution. That is, placing a task in position p of the queue only delays tasks located behind p. That said, the *first* phase of this heuristic aims at finding the latest position for task $i + j$ in the batch queue so that it does not miss its deadline. The latest position for $i + j$ in the queue implies the minimum number of tasks are affected—those located behind the merged task.

To carry out the first phase, the procedure constructs virtual queues to find the latest position for $i + j$. For that purpose, it alternates the position of $i + j$ in the batch queue, starting from the head of the queue. In each position, the completion time of $i + j$ is calculated based on the tasks located ahead of it and is examined if $i + j$ misses its deadline. Once task $i + j$ misses its deadline, the previous position is the latest possible location for it not to miss its deadline.

Once we found the latest position for $i + j$, we need to verify if the insertion of $i + j$ causes any deadline violation for the tasks behind it or not. For that purpose, in the *second* phase, we only need to evaluate the merging (via Merging Impact Evaluator) once. If there is no impact, then the found position is confirmed. Otherwise, the merging is canceled.

It is noteworthy that this procedure is efficient because the virtual queue is created only once. Also, after each task assignment to the virtual queue, it simply adds one more checking to calculate $i + j$ completion time.

Analysis of the Heuristics

In this part, we analyze Logarithmic Probing and Linear Probing heuristics in terms of their complexity and optimality of the position they find.

Complexity Analysis   Phase one of Linear Probing Heuristic examines n tasks to be scheduled on m machines with an additional check if $i + j$ can be scheduled on time directly after each of the n tasks. That results in $n \cdot m$ complexity to provide a single position for Phase two to verify. Phase two is essentially evaluating the impact of merging, which again needs n tasks to be scheduled on m machines. The combined complexity of the two phases is $2 \cdot n \cdot m$. Alternatively, Logarithmic Probing Heuristic spends trivial computation of $O(1)$ to pick a position in the batch queue to verify the appropriateness. If the position identified as inappropriate, the search continues for up to $\log n$ positions. Since the complexity of evaluating each position is $n \cdot m$, the total complexity is $n \cdot m \cdot \log n$. As the complexity of evaluating impact of merging dominates the total complexity, the Linear Probing Heuristic which spends less time evaluating the position is more efficient.

Optimality Analysis   Assume that there are multiple appropriate positions for task $i + j$. Logarithmic Probing Heuristic returns the first position it finds and meets the criteria, thus, is not biased to any certain appropriate position for the merged task. Alternatively, Linear Probing Heuristic always finds the latest appropriate position in the batch queue for task $i + j$. This ensures that task $i + j$ has the least impact on other tasks' completion times. Being the last possible position, however, increases the likelihood of $i + j$ to miss its deadline. In addition, this makes it unlikely for other tasks to be scheduled in front of $i + j$, hence, limiting the chance of future merging operations.

6.7   Adapting Merging Based on the Oversubscription Level

6.7.1   Overview

In Sect. 6.6, we discussed the merge appropriateness of each task by considering a worst-case analysis to assure no task is affected by the merging. However, when the system is oversubscribed, we can compromise the worst-case analysis and make the system more permissive to task merging in order to mitigate the oversubscription. In fact, sacrificing a few tasks in favor of more merging can lighten the system oversubscription and ultimately cause fewer tasks missing their deadlines. For that purpose, in this section, we introduce the Workload Assessor component (see Fig. 6.7) that is in charge of assessing the oversubscription level of the system and accordingly adjusting the aggression level of applying the task merging.

6.7.2 Quantifying Oversubscription in the MSC Platform

Level of oversubscription in the system can be quantified based various factors, such as the rate of missing deadline and the task arrival rate. The quantification can be achieved in a reactive manner (i.e., from known metadata) or in a proactive manner (i.e., based on the factors that suggest the system is about to get oversubscribed in the near future). In this part, we introduce a method for Workload Assessor that uses decisive indicators of oversubscription to quantify the oversubscription level of MSC as a serverless computing system.

The first intuitive idea to quantify oversubscription is based on the (measured or expected) ratio of the task arrival rate to the processing rate [21]. In this case, a system is oversubscribed, only if it cannot process tasks as fast as it receives them. This idea has two main limitations: (a) It requires the knowledge of processing rate, which is difficult to accurately measure; (b) It is prone to report false negative in the oversubscription evaluation. In particular, it cannot discriminate between different circumstances that the ratio tends to one. Such a circumstance can occur when the tasks' arrival and processing rates are similar, however, the batch queue may be congested (i.e., the system is oversubscribed) or may not be (i.e., the system is not oversubscribed).

Another idea is to use the ratio of number of tasks missing their deadlines to the total number of tasks executed [21]. This is based on the fact that an oversubscribed system cannot complete all its tasks on time, thus, missing a high number of task deadlines suggests an oversubscribed situation. Although this idea has a good potential, yet it falls short in quantifying the degree of oversubscription. That is, it cannot discriminate between a system that completes tasks a short time after their deadlines versus the one that completes tasks a long time after their deadlines.

Improving on the shortcomings of the aforementioned methods, we propose to quantify the oversubscription level of the system in a given time window based on the *deadline miss severity ratio*. We define *waitable time* of task i, denoted W_i, as the maximum time it can wait in the queue without missing its deadline. Let A_i denote the arrival time of task i, then its waitable time is calculated as: $W_i = \delta_i - A_i - E_i$. To quantify the oversubscription level, denoted OSL, in the first place, we discard the contribution of infeasible tasks (i.e., those with $W_i < 0$) and those that can complete on time (i.e., the ones with $C_i^m \leq \delta_i$). Next, the tasks that complete after their deadlines contribute to the oversubscription level based on the severity of their deadline miss. For a given task i, this is calculated based on the proximity between its completion time and its deadline (i.e., $C_i^m - \delta_i$) and with respect to its waitable time (i.e., W_i). Equation (6.5) formally shows how OSL is calculated. Recall that C_i^m is estimated based on Eq. (6.4) to quantify the oversubscription in the current time window and N_a represents the total number of tasks across all the machine queues. To adapt Eq. (6.5) for quantifying the oversubscription of a past time window, we need to replace the estimated completion time with the observed completion time of the tasks.

$$OSL = \frac{1}{N_a} \sum_{i=1}^{N_a} \begin{cases} 0, & W_i \leq 0 \\ 0, & C_i^m \leq \delta_i \\ \frac{C_i^m - \delta_i}{W_i}, & C_i^m > \delta_i \end{cases} \qquad (6.5)$$

6.7.3 Adaptive Task Merging Aggressiveness

The method explained in Sect. 6.6 estimates the side-effect of merging on other tasks in a conservative manner to assure that the merging does not cause their deadlines violated. In the face of oversubscription, estimation of the side-effect can be relaxed from the worst-case analysis to allow more aggressive task merging, hence, mitigating the oversubscription and increasing the overall QoS.

To make the aggressiveness of task merging adaptive, based on the measured oversubscription level of the system, we modify the acceptable probability that a merge operation does not cause deadline violation on other tasks of the system. More specifically, for higher values of the oversubscription level, the acceptable probability that other tasks meet their deadlines should be diminished and vice versa. For that purpose, we set the acceptable probability of meeting deadline for the tasks affected by merging to vary in the range of [2.3%, 97.7%], depending on the oversubscription intensity. To this end, the coefficient of standard deviation (α) has to be in $[-2, 2]$ range. Specifically, to adapt the value of α based on the oversubscription level, we determine α as: $\alpha = 2 - 4 \cdot OSL$.

6.8 Summary and Discussion

In this chapter, we investigate the reusing computation of functions in MSC as a serverless multimedia processing cloud platform. This causes a more efficient use of resources and offers green and cost-efficient services via merging new function invocations with other (exact or similar) function calls in the system. In that regard, two challenges were investigated: *First*, how to identify tasks of identical and similar functions in an efficient manner? *Second*, how to perform (or not perform) merging to achieve the best QoS in the system? To address the first challenge, three levels of similarity were introduced to perform the merging. Then, a method to detect different levels of similarity within a constant time complexity was introduced. To address the second challenge, a method was introduced to determine how to perform the merge operation so that the deadlines of other tasks in the system are likely least affected. Experimental evaluations demonstrate that task merging can reduce the overall execution time of tasks by more than 9%. Hence, cloud resources can be deployed for a shorter time. Interestingly, this cost-saving comes with improving QoS of the users by up to 18% too. It is concluded that when the level of oversubscription in the system is high, merging tasks aggressively (i.e., without being considerate of the impact on other tasks) helps to improve the QoS. Conversely, with lower levels of oversubscription, merging should be carried out with consideration of the impact on other tasks, not to cause unnecessary impact on the QoS.

In the next chapter, we focus on how latency of streaming can be improved in the MSC context. Specifically, we explain how an edge/fog computing variation of the MSC platform can be developed to offer an uninterruptible multimedia streaming service.

References

1. Ali Alfayly, Is-Haka Mkwawa, Lingfen Sun, and Emmanuel Ifeachor. QoE-driven LTE downlink scheduling for VoIP application. In *Proceedings of the 12th Annual IEEE Consumer Communications and Networking Conference*, CCNC '12, pages 603–604, Jan 2015.
2. Ibrahim Rizqallah Alzahrani, Naeem Ramzan, and Abbes Amira. Impact of segment size on dynamic adaptive video streaming over HTTP (dash) over LAN network. In *Proceedings of the Real-Time Image and Video Processing Conference*, volume 10670 of *SPIE '18*, page 106700H, May 2018.
3. Xavier Andrade, Jorge Cedeno, Edwin Boza, Harold Aragon, Cristina Abad, and Jorge Murillo. Optimizing cloud caches for free: A case for autonomic systems with a serverless computing approach. In *Proceedings of the 4th IEEE International Workshops on Foundations and Applications of Self* Systems*, FAS* W '19, pages 140–145, Jun. 2019.
4. Emna Baccour, Aiman Erbad, Kashif Bilal, Amr Mohamed, Mohsen Guizani, and Mounir Hamdi. FacebookVideoLive18: A Live Video Streaming Dataset for Streams Metadata and Online Viewers Locations. In *Proceedings of the 10th International Conference on Internet of Things*, ICIOT '20, 2020.
5. Jing Bi, Haitao Yuan, Wei Tan, MengChu Zhou, Yushun Fan, Jia Zhang, and Jianqiang Li. Application-aware dynamic fine-grained resource provisioning in a virtualized cloud data center. *IEEE Transactions on Automation Science and Engineering*, 14(2):1172–1184, Apr 2017.
6. Israel Casas, Javid Taheri, Rajiv Ranjan, Lizhe Wang, and Albert Y Zomaya. A balanced scheduler with data reuse and replication for scientific workflows in cloud computing systems. *Future Generation Computer Systems*, 74:168–178, Sep 2017.
7. Chavit Denninnart and Mohsen Amini Salehi. Leveraging Computational Reuse to Enable Cost- and QoS-Efficient Serverless Cloud Computing. *submitted to IEEE Transactions on Parallel and Distributed Systems (TPDS)*, May 2020.
8. Chavit Denninnart, Mohsen Amini Salehi, Adel Nadjaran Toosi, and Xiangbo Li. Leveraging computational reuse for cost-and QoS-efficient task scheduling in clouds. In *International Conference on Service-Oriented Computing*, pages 828–836, Nov. 2018.
9. Godred Fairhurst and Bernhard Collini-Nocker. Unidirectional lightweight encapsulation (ULE) for transmission of ip datagrams over an MPEG-2 transport stream (TS). Technical report, RFC 4326, Dec. 2005.
10. Jerome H Friedman. Stochastic gradient boosting. *Computational statistics & data analysis*, 38(4):367–378, 2002.
11. Fengyu Guo, Long Yu, Shengwei Tian, and Jiong Yu. A workflow task scheduling algorithm based on the resources' fuzzy clustering in cloud computing environment. *International Journal of Communication Systems*, 28(6):1053–1067, Apr 2015.
12. I-Hong Hou and Ping-Chun Hsieh. QoE-Optimal Scheduling for On-Demand Video Streams over Unreliable Wireless Networks. In *Proceedings of the 16th ACM International Symposium on Mobile Ad Hoc Networking and Computing*, MobiHoc '15, pages 207–216, Jun 2015.

13. Razin Hussain, Mohsen Amini, Anna Kovalenko, Yin Feng, and Omid Semiari. Federated edge computing for disaster management in remote smart oil fields. In *Proceedings of the 21st IEEE International Conference on High Performance Computing and Communications*, HPCC'19, pages 929–936, Aug. 2019.

14. Sotiris B Kotsiantis.   Decision trees: a recent overview.   *Artificial Intelligence Review*, 39(4):261–283, 2013.

15. Xiangbo Li, Mohsen Amini Salehi, Magdy Bayoumi, and Rajkumar Buyya. CVSS: A Cost-Efficient and QoS-Aware Video Streaming Using Cloud Services. In *Proceedings of the 16th IEEE/ACM International Conference on Cluster Cloud and Grid Computing*, CCGrid '16, May 2016.

16. Xiangbo Li, Mohsen Amini Salehi, Magdy Bayoumi, Nian-Feng Tzeng, and Rajkumar Buyya. Cost-efficient and robust on-demand video stream transcoding using heterogeneous cloud services. *IEEE Transactions on Parallel and Distributed Systems (TPDS)*, 29(3):556–571, Mar. 2018.

17. Wei Ling, Lin Ma, Chen Tian, and Ziang Hu. Pigeon: A dynamic and efficient serverless and FaaS framework for private cloud. In *Proceedings of the 6th International Conference on Computational Science and Computational Intelligence*, CSCI '19, pages 1416–1421, Dec. 2019.

18. Shaowei Liu, Kaijun Ren, Kefeng Deng, and Junqiang Song. A dynamic resource allocation and task scheduling strategy with uncertain task runtime on IaaS clouds. In *Proceedings of the 6th International Conference on Information Science and Technology*, ICIST '16, pages 174–180, May 2016.

19. Wes Lloyd, Shruti Ramesh, Swetha Chinthalapati, Lan Ly, and Shrideep Pallickara. Serverless computing: An investigation of factors influencing microservice performance. In *Proceedings of the 2018 IEEE International Conference on Cloud Engineering*, (IC2E'18), pages 159–169, Apr. 2018.

20. David M Magerman. Statistical decision-tree models for parsing. In *Proceedings of the 33rd annual meeting on Association for Computational Linguistics*, pages 276–283, Jun. 1995.

21. Dharmendra Prasad Mahato and Ravi Shankar Singh. Reliability modeling and analysis for deadline-constrained grid service. In *Proceedings of the 32nd International Conference on Advanced Information Networking and Applications Workshops*, WAINA '18, pages 75–81, May 2018.

22. Darius Plonis, Andrius Katkevičius, Antanas Gurskas, Vytautas Urbanavičius, Rytis Maskeliūnas, and Robertas Damaševičius. Prediction of meander delay system parameters for internet-of-things devices using pareto-optimal artificial neural network and multiple linear regression. *IEEE Access*, 8:39525–39535, 2020.

23. Kochetov Vadim.   Overview of different approaches to solving problems of data mining. *Procedia computer science*, 123:234–239, 2018.

24. VideoLan. x264, the best h.264/avc encoder. Accessed on 2020 May 20.

25. YouTube, LLC. Youtube. Accessed on 2020 May 10.

26. Hongliang Yu, Dongdong Zheng, Ben Y Zhao, and Weimin Zheng. Understanding user behavior in large-scale video-on-demand systems. In *ACM SIGOPS Operating Systems Review*, volume 40, pages 333–344, 2006.

27. Hao Zhang, Bogdan Marius Tudor, Gang Chen, and Beng Chin Ooi. Efficient In-memory Data Management: An Analysis. *Proceedings of the VLDB Endowment*, 7(10):833–836, Jun 2014.

28. Jing Zhang, Gongqing Wu, Xuegang Hu, and Xindong Wu. A distributed cache for hadoop distributed file system in real-time cloud services. In *Proceedings of the 13th ACM/IEEE International Conference on Grid Computing*, GRID '12, pages 12–21, Sep 2012.

Chapter 7
Low-Latency Delivery Networks
for Multimedia Streaming

7.1 Overview

Beyond any feature, a multimedia streaming service provider and viewers expect a low-latency and uninterruptible streaming service from MSC. The primary practice to reduce the latency in current streaming service providers is to rely on content delivery networks (CDN) [1].

To elaborate on the reasons of multimedia streaming latency and the role of the CDN technology in overcoming it, we describe the workflow of operations to serve a streaming request, from the point it is issued by the viewer until it is served on the cloud and delivered to the viewers via CDN. Figure 7.1 provides a bird-eye view of such workflow for VOD and live-streaming cases.

According to Fig. 7.1a, VOD contents are uploaded by content providers (e.g., movie producer, UGC etc.) to origin cloud server, where the contents will transcoded, packaged and later stored on cloud storage (e.g., AWS S3¹). Whenever a viewer starts to play a given video, the player needs to fetch the master manifest for that video first, as mentioned in Sect. 2.4.3, it sends a manifest request to CDN. If the viewer is the unlucky one who is the first one requests the video, the player is not able to find the manifest in the CDN. In this case, CDN sends a request to cloud origin server where stores both the manifests and contents. After CDN retrieves the manifest, it responds to the player. Based on the video manifest, current network bandwidth and player buffer emptiness, player makes the decision to pick which video version, and starts to request video content segments. Unfortunately, if the player is the first one request that video segments, it has to go through the same request process as the manifest. On the bright side, the requested manifest and video segments will to cached at CDN side for a period of time, so the next viewers are able to retrieve them and start to playback quickly.

---

¹ https://aws.amazon.com/s3/.

© Springer Nature Switzerland AG 2021
M. A. Salehi, X. Li, *Multimedia Cloud Computing Systems*,
https://doi.org/10.1007/978-3-030-88451-2_7

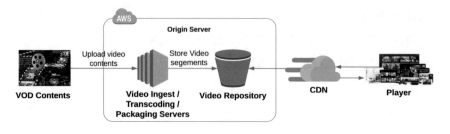

(a) Video On Demand (VOD)

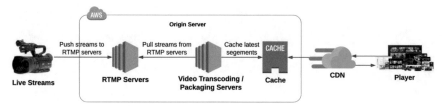

(b) Live Streaming

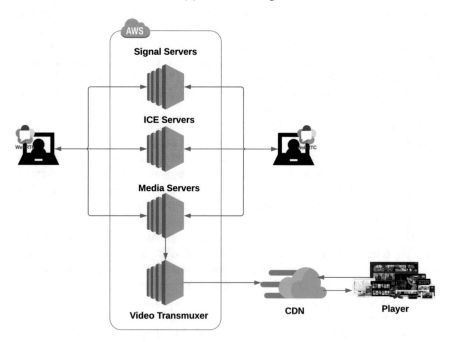

(c) WebRTC video conference and webinar

Fig. 7.1 A bird-eye view of the whole cloud-based multimedia streaming: from user's streaming request to processing and content delivery

For live streaming, as shown in Fig. 7.1b, the whole process is very similar. However, there are some fundamental difference between live and VOD. Origin server only cache the updated manifest and a few latest video segments, unless it is required to store videos for VOD purpose later on, because there is no point to watch older video contents when it is live. Another difference is live streaming needs a RTMP server [32] (commonly used in live platforms, which may be replaced by other protocol in the future), which serve the RTMP stream. Live camera push the live contents to RTMP server, video transcoder server pulls the stream from the RTMP server, transcodes and packages it to multiple versions.

Another popular video stream applications are video conferencing and webinar. WebRTC [37] has become one of most common protocols that used in these applications due to its sub-second low latency. The architecture of WebRTC based peer to peer (P2P) video conferencing is quite different from VOD and live streaming, as shown in Fig. 7.1c. Before trying to establish the connection, WebRTC application needs to check if the other peer is reachable or if it is willing to establish the connection. It sends an offer through signal server, and the peer must return an answer. To establish the network connection, WebRTC clients usually have to contact ICE servers (e.g., STUN, TURN [19]) to bypass the firewall or some protocol limitations. Normally, after network connection has been established, WebRTC clients can start peer to peer communication. However, if the client connects increases, each client will have to set up connection with each other, which faces complexity and bandwidth limitation. Media Servers like MCU [40] or SFU [8] are commonly placed between WedRTC peers. That means each client directly communicate to the media server, where the media content will be processed and distributed to its peers. Although, media server has its scaling limitation, when the viewers increase up to thousands or millions, it is better to transmux the video and use broadcasting protocols (e.g., DASH, HLS etc.), as what VOD and live streaming does. Webinar basically utilizes such architecture, to scale up to large audiences, while suffers longer delay in comparison to video conferencing.

More specifically, we can consider three tiers that collectively achieve low-latency multimedia streaming: (a) the processing cloud (a.k.a. encoding cloud) tier that is in charge of processing the multimedia contents based on the desired characteristics; (b) the storage cloud tier where the original video contents are stored; and (c) the edge tier, composed of geographically distributed servers close to the users, that are in charge of caching the multimedia contents [55]. Upon requesting a stream by a user, an HTTP request is sent to the CDN system to stream the content with specified characteristics (e.g., resolution and bitrate). Then, the following sequence of actions are taken within the CDN system: (1) The streaming request is redirected to the edge server that is closest to the user. (2) If the requested segment, with the specified characteristics, is available on the edge server, it is streamed to the user. Otherwise, the edge server fetches the streaming segment from the storage tier and then sends it to the user. (3) If the segment with the specified characteristics is not available on the storage tier, it sends processing (e.g., encoding) request to the processing cloud tier, where the original multimedia contents is processed based on the requested characteristics before sending it to the edge tier and subsequently to the end user.

Although using CDNs is the mainstream in reducing the streaming latency, an alternative approach called peer-to-peer streaming can be also used in certain contexts to reduce the latency. In this chapter, we first provide different possible approaches to reduce the latency. Then, we explain the protocols exist for this purpose, and finally we explain how interactive video streaming can be achieved by upgrading the CDN technology to the fog computing technology.

7.2 Content Delivery Networks (CDN)

The original goal of CDN technology was to reduce the network latency to access the web contents. CDNs replicate the contents across geographically distributed servers that are in the viewers' locality [42, 46]. Considering that the large size of multimedia contents usually takes a long transmission time, using CDNs to cache the multimedia contents close to viewers reduces the latency time dramatically. Netflix, as one of the largest stream providers, employ three different CDN providers (Akamai, LimeLight, and Level-3) to cover its viewers across different regions [4]. For that purpose, the processed (e.g., transcoded) and packaged video contents are replicated in all the three CDNs. Netflix also utilizes its Open Connect [12] technology within Internet Service Providers (ISPs) in numerous geographical locations to minimize the video streaming latency.

Clouds are known for their centrality and high latency communication to users [26]. To reduce the network latency and to reduce the load of requests from the servers, video contents are normally cached in the Content Delivery Networks (CDN) such as Akamai. The CDNs are distributed and located geographically close to viewers. CDNs that are offered in form of a cloud service are known as cloud CDN. Compared to traditional CDNs, cloud CDNs are cost-effective and offer low latency services to content providers without having their own infrastructure. The users are generally charged based on the bandwidth consumption and storage cost [13].

A large body of research has been undertaken on the efficient use of CDNs for video streaming [9, 11, 15, 49]. Cranor et al. [15] proposed the PRISM architecture for distributing, storing, and delivering high-quality streaming content over IP networks. They design a framework to support VOD streaming content via distribution networks services (i.e., CDNs). Wee et al. [49] presented an architecture for mobile streaming CDN which was designed to fit the mobility and scaling requirements. Apostolopoulos et al. [9] proposed multiple paths between nearby edge servers and clients in order to reduce the latency and deliver high-quality streaming. Benkacem et al. [11] developed a system to offer CDN slices through multiple administrative cloud domains. Al-Abbasi et al. [7] proposed a model for video streaming, typically composed of a centralized origin server, several CDN sites, and edge-caches located closer to the end users. Their proposed approach focused on minimizing a performance metric, called stall duration tail probability (SDTP), and present a novel and efficient algorithm that can significantly improve the SDTP metric. Configuring CDN for Live streaming has some nuances with respect to scalability, latency quality, and reliability that are discussed in [30, 38, 53].

Hu et al. [24] presented an approach using the cloud CDN to minimize the cost of system operation while maintaining the service latency. Based on viewing behavior prediction, Hu et al. [25] investigated the community-driven video distribution problem under cloud CDN and proposed a dynamic algorithm to trade-off between the incurred monetary cost and QoS. Their results came with less operational cost while satisfying the QoS requirement. Jin et al. [28] proposed a scheme that offers the service of on-demand virtual content delivery for user-generated content providers to deliver their contents to viewers. The proposed approach was developed using a hybrid cloud. Their scheme offered elasticity and privacy by using virtual content delivery service with keeping the QoE to user-generated content providers.

Beyond the many advantages and popularity of using the CDN technology for low-latency streaming, there are a few issues about CDNs that have to be considered. Importantly, the high cost, lack of processing ability, and low scalability are some of these issues.

7.3 Peer to Peer (P2P) Networks

P2P networks enable direct sharing of computing resources (e.g., CPU cycles, storage, and content) among peer nodes in a network [41]. P2P networks are designed for both clients and servers to act as peers. They can download data from the same nodes and upload them to other nodes in the network. P2P networks can disseminate data files among users within a short period of time. Although P2P networks are not designed for multimedia streaming, they are utilized for this purpose too.

P2P streaming is categorized into two types, namely tree-based and mesh-based. Tree-based P2P structure distributes multimedia streams by sending data from one peer to its children. In the mesh-based P2P structure, the peers do not follow a specific topology, instead, they function based on the content and bandwidth availability of the peers [36]. One drawback of using tree-based P2P streaming is the vulnerability to the peers' churn. The drawback of deploying mesh-based P2P streaming is the playback quality degradation, ranging from low video bit rates and long startup delays, to frequent playback freezes. Golchi et al. [21] proposed a method for streaming video in P2P networks. Their approach uses the algorithm of improved particle swarm optimization(IPSO) to determine the appropriate way for transmitting data that ensures service quality parameters. They showed that the proposed approach works efficiently more than the other methods. P2P-based streaming systems are highly scalable, low cost, and robust against churns.

Figure 7.2 shows two popular variations of tree-based P2P structure, namely single tree-based and multi-tree based structures. In *Single Tree-based streaming*,

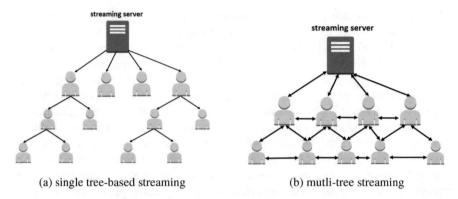

(a) single tree-based streaming   (b) mutli-tree streaming

Fig. 7.2 Peer-to-peer (P2P) approaches for low-latency video streaming

shown in Fig. 7.2a, video streaming is carried out at the application layer and the
streaming tree is formed by the participating users. Each viewer joins the tree at a
certain level and receives the video content from its parent peer at the above level.
Then, it forwards the received video to its children peers at the below level [14, 27].

In *Multi-Tree Streaming* (a.k.a. mesh-tree), shown in Fig. 7.2b, a peer develops
the peering connection with other close peers. Then, the peer can potentially
download/upload video contents from/to multiple close peers simultaneously. If a
peer loses the network connection, the receiving peer could still download video
from remaining nearby peers. Meanwhile, the peer can locate new peers to maintain
the required level of connectivity. The strong peering in mesh-based streaming
systems supports them to be robust against peer churns [39, 47]. Ahmed et al. [6]
proposed a multi-level multi-overlay hybrid peer-to-peer live video system that
offers to the Online Games players the way of streaming the video simultaneously
and enables to watch the game videos of other players. Their approach aimed to
reduce the transmission rate while increasing the number of peers and the delivery
and reliability of data are guaranteed on time.

Tree-based P2P VOD streaming shares the video stream on the network and
achieves fast streaming. The video stream is divided into small size data block.
The server disperses the data blocks to different nodes. The nodes download their
missing blocks from their neighboring peers [48]. Guo et al. [22] proposed an
architecture that uses the P2P approach to cooperatively stream video by only
relying on unicast connections among peers. Xu et al. [50] proposed an approach
based on binary tree strategy to distribute VOD P2P networks. Their approach
divides the videos into segments to be fetched from several peers. Yiu et al. [54]
proposed VMesh distributed P2P VOD streaming approach. In their approach,
videos are split into segments and then stored at the storage of the peers. Xu
et al. [52] proposed a scheme based tree to make user interacting in the P2P
streaming. The proposed scheme presents an advantage to support the users requests
asynchronously while maintaining a high resilience.

The main advantages of P2P are low cost and scalability, however, it suffers form unstable QoS. Therefore, researchers proposed to combine the advantages of both CDN and P2P in one system. Accordingly, several hybrid systems were developed to combine P2P and CDN for content streaming. Afergan et al. [5] proposed an approach which utilizes CDN to build CDN-P2P streaming. In their method, they dynamically determine the number and locations of replicas for P2P service. Xu et al. [51] presented a scheme that is formed by both CDN and P2P streaming. They showed the efficiency of their approach by reducing the cost of CDN without impacting the quality of the delivered videos.

7.4   Fog Delivery Networks (FDN) Versus Content Delivery Networks (CDN)

As mentioned earlier, multimedia stream providers use CDNs to cache part of the multimedia repository into their edge locations that are physically close to viewers, hence, resulting in a lower latency compared to accessing from a more centrally located cloud server. The problem is that the large and fast-growing repository size of streaming providers has made it infeasible to cache a large portion of the overall content on their CDNs. In addition, caching on CDNs is less effective because of the fact that streaming providers have to maintain multiple versions of the same content to be able to support different services on them (e.g., to support heterogeneous display devices and network conditions [33]). As such, instead of pre-processing and maintaining multimedia contents into multiple versions, mechanisms for on-demand processing (e.g., on-demand transcoding [33]) of multimedia contents is becoming a common practice [34, 35]. However, the challenge is that on-demand video processing cannot be performed on CDNs since they are predominantly used for caching purposes [1].

These limitations lead to frequent pulling the content directly from central cloud servers, which increases streaming latency, thus, decreasing viewers' QoS, particularly, in distant areas [29]. To overcome these limitations, Fog Delivery Network (FDN) that leverages the computing ability of fog systems is introduced to carry out on-demand processing of the multimedia content at the edge level. Importantly, Federated FDN, a.k.a. F-FDN, that is composed of several Fog Delivery Networks (FDN) that can exchange multimedia contents (segments) and collaboratively stream the multimedia contents to viewers are introduced. F-FDN can be particularly effective for low-latency streaming in remote areas.

Using F-FDN, multimedia streaming providers only need to cache a base version of a multimedia content in an edge (fog) and process them to match the characteristics of the viewers' devices in an on-demand manner. More importantly, F-FDN can achieve location-aware caching (i.e., pre-processing) of multimedia streams. That is, multimedia streams that are popular (i.e., hot) in a certain region are pre-processed and cached only in that region. Due to resource limitations of FDN, often only the hot portions of multimedia contents are pre-processed [16] and the remaining portions are processed in an on-demand manner. To alleviate the on-demand processing load in an FDN, the distributed nature of F-FDN can be leveraged to reuse the pre-processed multimedia contents on the neighboring FDNs. This allows different portions of a multimedia content be streamed from multiple sources (i.e., FDNs), and subsequently, increasing viewers' QoE.

In summary, F-FDN can improve the QoE of viewers located in distant areas. A method within each FDN is used to achieve multimedia streaming from multiple FDNs simultaneously.

7.4.1   Federated Fog Delivery Networks (F-FDN)

Overview
The aim of F-FDN is to deliver the highest possible QoE to viewers, independent of their geographical location. One of the most differentiating qualities of F-FDN compared to other multimedia streaming systems is the ability to evaluate on a segment by segment basis how to stream a multimedia content. It is worth noting that, in CDNs, the entire content is always streamed from the same CDN server as long as a connection is maintained with the viewer [44].

F-FDN is composed of several connected, peer Fog Delivery Networks (FDNs) that are also connected to a central cloud server. An FDN caches pre-processed segments for the multimedia contents that are hot in a certain region. This results in each FDN having varied pre-processed contents that are optimized to the viewers local to that FDN. Upon arrival of a streaming request, the viewer (i.e., requester) is connected to its most local FDN. As the contents are being streamed, decisions are made on a segment by segment basis as to how the GOP is delivered to the viewer, so that the likelihood of meeting the segment's deadline is maximized. The process in making these decisions is described in detail in Sect. 7.4.2.

An example of a video being streamed to a viewer from multiple sources can be observed in Fig. 7.3. As we can see in the figure, using F-FDN, a video segment can be streamed to a viewer in three different ways:

1. FDN Local Cache: the FDN local to the viewer already has the requested video segment in it's cache and streams the segment to the viewer.
2. Processed On-demand: the local FDN processes the missing (i.e., non-cached) segments according to the characteristics of the request and then stream them to the viewer.
3. Neighboring FDN's Cache: the missing segments exist in the cache of a neighboring FDN, the segment is then transferred to the local FDN and then streamed to the viewer.

At a high level, F-FDN is composed of two main components, namely a Central Cloud and a distributed network of FDNs. Figure 7.4 shows the internals of the Central Cloud and each FDN. Details of each component is elaborated in the next subsections.

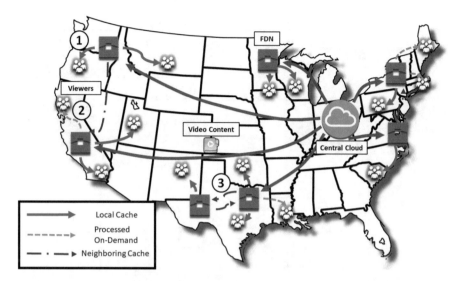

Fig. 7.3 High level view of the F-FDN architecture. Note the viewers who are receiving multimedia contents from multiple FDNs. (1) shows multimedia contents coming from FDN local cache; (2) shows multimedia contents being processed on-demand; and (3) shows multimedia contents coming from a neighboring FDN's cache

Central Cloud

The Central Cloud, with virtually unlimited storage and processing capabilities, is where all streaming requests are initially ingested and where all the FDNs in the system are managed. As it is seen in Fig. 7.4, Central Cloud consists of four main components:

- Ingestion Processor—handles all the incoming stream requests made by viewers. It determines which FDN is the most local to the viewer in order to start the streaming process. The FDN that is selected is the one that determines the way each segment is streamed to the viewer.
- Metadata Manager—keeps track of all the cached segments contained throughout the FDNs. In addition, it keeps track of other metadata, such as file size and network latency between neighboring FDNs. In Sect. 7.4.2, we explain how this metadata helps in determining the way to stream a content to the viewer.
- Fog Monitor—keeps track of the availability of FDNs via sending heartbeat pings to them. Also, it evaluates network latency between the FDNs which is then communicated to the Metadata Manager to maintain up-to-date information.
- Video Repository—contains a repository of all multimedia contents, pre-processed in multiple versions. This is where any cached content on FDNs originates from. In the event that one or more segments are missing in a local FDN, one decision can be fetching the segments from the multimedia repository of the Central Cloud.

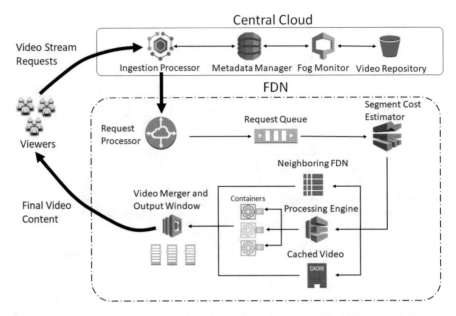

Fig. 7.4 System Components of the F-FDN architecture. It is composed of a centrally located cloud and a federation of multiple Fog Delivery Networks (FDNs)

Fog Delivery Network (FDN)

Each FDN consists of six components, as shown in Fig. 7.4 and explained below.

- Request Processor—receives streaming requests from the Central Cloud and put them into a request queue.
- Segment Cost Estimator—makes the decision as to how each segment in a stream request should be sent to viewers with the minimum possible latency (i.e., maximum likelihood of meeting the segment's deadline). For a given segment, it is determined whether the segment should be streamed from the local FDN's cache, processed on-demand by the local FDN, or retrieved from a neighboring FDN's cache and then streamed by the local FDN. The process by which these decisions are made is explained in Sect. 7.4.2.
- Neighboring FDN Metadata—contains knowledge of all cached segments on other FDNs and the network latency for accessing them. It is worth noting that the latency of accessing Central Cloud is also maintained by this component.
- On-demand Processing Engine—is in charge of on-demand processing of the streams. The engine uses multiple worker Virtual Machines (VMs) and enable the FDN to process incoming segments based on the characteristics of the viewer's device.
- Cached Video Segments—multimedia segments that are determined to be hot [16] in a region are pre-processed and cached by the FDN. For a given streaming request, if some of its segments are locally cached, they impose the minimum network latency and cause a higher QoE for the viewer.

- Video Merger and Output Window—where the segments of the multimedia stream are put in the correct order and then streamed to the viewer.

7.4.2 Efficient Operation of F-FDN

The distributed nature of F-FDN provides multiple options (sources) to stream a single video segment. To minimize missing presentation deadline of a multimedia segment, it should be streamed from the source that imposes the minimum streaming latency, hence, offering the maximum probability to meet the segment's deadline.

The streaming latency is affected by two main factors, namely *segment processing time* and *segment transfer time* across the network. In particular, both of these factors have a stochastic nature [43]. An ideal method to stream multimedia contents in F-FDN should be robust against these stochastic factors. That is, the method should maintain its performance, in terms of meeting the deadlines of streaming tasks, even in the presence of these uncertainties. In this part, we explain a method within FDNs that accounts for the uncertainties and maximizes the probability of meeting deadline for a given streaming segment, hence, minimizing the likelihood of any interruption in the streaming process. This method is utilized within the Segment Cost Estimator component of FDN and makes the FDN robust. The symbols used in this part are summarized in Table 7.1.

Network Latency of Streaming a Segment in FDN
For a given segment i, the latency probability distribution of transferring it between two points can be obtained based on the segment size (denoted s_i) and the amount of data that can be transferred within a time unit between the two points (i.e., the network throughput). Prior studies show that the latency probability distribution to transfer segment i follows a normal distribution (denoted N_i^τ) [23, 34]. The two points can be between two FDNs or an FDN and a viewer.

Robust and Low-Latency Multimedia Delivery Using F-FDN
Robustness of segment i, denoted r_i, is formally defined as the probability that segment i is delivered to the viewer's device before or at its deadline δ_i.

As mentioned earlier, each segment can be retrieved using one of the following choices: (a) from the FDN's local cache; (b) processing it on-demand in the

Table 7.1 Important symbols used in Sect. 7.4.2

Symbol	Description
s_i	Size of segment i
r_i	Probability of processing segment i on time (robustness)
$N_i^C(\mu_i, \sigma_i)$	Overall delivery distribution (end-to-end latency) for segment i
$N_i^\tau(\mu_{jv}, \sigma_{jv})$	Distribution of network throughput between two points for a given segment i
$N_i^E(\mu_{ij}, \sigma_{ij})$	Processing time distribution for segment i

local FDN; (c) from a neighboring FDN's cache. In choice (a), the robustness of delivering segment i is obtained from the segment latency probability distribution between local FDN j and viewer's device v. As such, the probability distribution for delivering a segment to the viewer, denoted $N_i^C(\mu_i, \sigma_i)$, for choice (a) is determined using Eq. (7.1).

$$N_i^C(\mu_i, \sigma_i) = N_i^\tau(\mu_{jv}, \sigma_{jv}) \tag{7.1}$$

In choice (b), the latency is impacted not only by the segment latency probability distribution between FDN j and the viewer's device v, but also by the time to process the segment in FDN j. The processing times of a video segment can be estimated based on a probability distribution. This distribution is obtained from historical execution times of a particular function (e.g., bit-rate transcoding) for a segment. It has been shown that the processing time of a segment exhibits a normal distribution [34]. Let $N_i^E(\mu_{ij}, \sigma_{ij})$ be the probability distribution of completing the processing of segment i on FDN j; also let $N_i^T(\mu_{jv}, \sigma_{jv})$ be a normal distribution representing latency to deliver segment i from the local FDN j to the viewer's device v. Then, the probability distribution of delivering segment i to the viewer is calculated by convolving the two distributions as shown in Eq. (7.2).

$$N_i^C(\mu_i, \sigma_i) = N_i^E(\mu_{ij}, \sigma_{ij}) * N_i^\tau(\mu_{jv}, \sigma_{jv}) \tag{7.2}$$

Similarly, the latency for choice (c) is impacted by two factors, the latency distribution for retrieving a segment from a neighboring FDN k to the local FDN j, denoted $N_i^T(\mu_{kj}, \sigma_{kj})$, and the segment latency distribution between FDN j and viewer's device v, denoted $N_i^\tau(\mu_{jv}, \sigma_{jv})$. Therefore, to obtain the probability distribution of delivering segment i, these two probability distributions are convolved as shown in Eq. (7.3).

$$N_i^C(\mu_i, \sigma_i) = N_i^\tau(\mu_{kj}, \sigma_{kj}) * N_i^\tau(\mu_{jv}, \sigma_{jv}) \tag{7.3}$$

Once we have the final distribution, $N_i^C(\mu_i, \sigma_i)$ the robustness of segment i can be measured using its deadline δ_i based on Eq. (7.4). In fact, in this case the likelihood that segment i can be delivered before δ_i is the cumulative probability for a random variable X to be less than or equal to δ_i, which is the robustness of segment i.

$$r_i = P(X \leq \delta_i) \tag{7.4}$$

The algorithm for the Segment Cost Estimator (shown in Fig. 7.5) utilizes the robustness for each segment of a video stream to determine how to fetch that segment, hence, assuring a high quality and uninterruptible video streaming experience for viewers. The algorithm first checks if segment i exists in the local cache of FDN j to be streamed to the viewer (Step 1). If it does not exist locally, then a list of all neighboring FDNs containing segment i is retrieved from the

Upon receiving a multimedia streaming request m, at FDN_j:
For every segment i in the stream request m:

(1) if i exists in FDN_j's local cache, stream i to viewer
(2) else if i is available in neighboring FDNs or in central cloud:

    (3) retrieve list of metadata of all remote locations that match segment i
    (4) For each metadata item l in the metadata list:
        (5) calculate the cumulative probability of the transfer time from l using the presentation time of i
        (6) track which FDN l offers the highest probability of success
    (7) convolve processing and transfer time distributions for segment i in FDN_j and calculate its cumulative probability
    (8) compare the probability of processing i on-demand with the probability of streaming i from FDN offers the highest probability of success
    (9) stream segment i from the option with the highest probability of satisfying $i's$ deadline

Fig. 7.5 Procedure followed by Segment Cost Estimator

Metadata Manager and their respective robustness values are calculated (Steps 2–7). The robustness of on-demand processing segment i is also calculated and compared against the neighboring FDN that has segment i with the highest robustness (Steps 8–9). Finally, in Step 10, the option with the highest robustness is chosen to provide segment i.

7.4.3 Introducing Different Streaming Delivery Methods for Evaluation

In this section, we explain alternative methods for stream delivery. Table 7.2 provides an overview for the various methods we implemented and highlights differences in their characteristics. These methods encompass current practices for multimedia streaming (namely, CDN and Central Cloud) and baseline methods (namely, F-CDN, Isolated FDN, and Deterministic F-FDN) that focus on various aspects of the F-FDN platform in isolation. Finally, the *Robust F-FDN* is the streaming delivery method operating based on the theory developed in Sect. 7.4.2. It is noteworthy that these methods are implemented within the *Segment Cost Estimator* component of the FDN (see Fig. 7.4). The rest of this section further elaborates on the characteristics of the implemented methods that are used in the experiment section.

Table 7.2 Characteristics of various methods implemented to examine the performance of the F-FDN platform

Methods	Characteristics			
	Caching at edge	Federated	On-demand processing	Robustness consideration
Central cloud	No	No	No	No
CDN	Yes	No	No	No
Federated CDN (F-CDN)	Yes	Yes	No	Yes
Isolated FDN (I-FDN)	Yes	No	Yes	Yes
Deterministic F-FDN	Yes	Yes	Yes	No
Robust F-FDN	Yes	Yes	Yes	Yes

Central Cloud This method considers only the central cloud where all the video contents are available in the main video repository. Every video segment is streamed directly from the cloud and no geographically spread FDN or CDN are considered to reduce the streaming latency.

CDN Due to popularity of the CDN approach in the streaming industry, we consider it in our evaluations. Our simulated CDN consists of a central cloud that holds the same characteristics as the previously described system and CDN servers which have 75% of the requested videos cached, which is a realistic level for CDN caching [17]. As CDNs are located close to viewers, any segments streamed from them have a lower latency compared to the central cloud. It is noteworthy that CDN servers do not perform any computation and caches the entirety of a video, rather than only a portion. Also, any segment that is not found in a CDN, is streamed from the central cloud.

Federated CDN The Federated CDN (F-CDN) includes a central cloud and CDN servers in its system. The key difference of F-CDN with CDN is partial segment caching. In F-CDN, it is possible to cache only few segments of a stream, rather than the entirety of the multimedia content. Owing to the federated nature, in F-CDN, segments can be streamed from the local CDN, a neighboring CDN, or from the central cloud. The rationale of implementing this method is to observe the impact of federation of cached contents, without the ability to process multimedia content on-demand. This method makes use of the robustness definition, introduced in Sect. 7.4.2, to stream a given segment from the CDN that offers the highest probability to meet the deadline of that segment.

Isolated FDN (I-FDN) The Isolated FDN method includes a central cloud and a single FDN. In this system, the FDN node performs on-demand processing of segments, in addition to caching. However, it does not consider retrieving segments from neighboring FDNs. That is, the segments are streamed only from the FDN's cache, processed on-demand, or from the central cloud. The streaming decisions for each segment is made between the local FDN and central cloud based on the robustness definition (see Sect. 7.4.2). The rationale of implementing this method is to study the impact of lack of federation on the streaming QoE.

Deterministic F-FDN The Deterministic F-FDN method consists of a central cloud and a federation of FDNs. While each FDN can perform caching and on-demand processing, the federation enables the option to stream cached segments from neighboring FDNs as well. In the Deterministic F-FDN, for each segment, streaming decisions are only made based on expected transmission and processing times, i.e., it ignores the stochastic nature that exists in the F-FDN environment. This method demonstrates the impact of ignoring uncertainties that exist in the system on the overall streaming QoE.

Robust F-FDN Unlike Deterministic F-FDN, the Robust F-FDN operation takes into account the stochastic nature that exists in both communication and computation of the F-FDN platform. The more informed decision making is expected to have more streaming tasks meeting their deadlines, resulting in a more robust streaming service, regardless of the viewers' geographical location. It is, in fact, the implementation of the theory developed in Sect. 7.4.2 and the method described in the algorithm of Fig. 7.5.

7.4.4   Evaluation of Stream Delivery Methods

Experimental Setup
We conducted an emulation study using the MSC platform to understand the behavior of the F-FDN platform. Within MSC, we simulated three worker VMs that are modeled after the Amazon GPU (`g2.2xlarge`) VM to perform the video processing. The reason we considered GPU-based VMs is that in [34] it is shown that these VM types fit the best for multimedia processing tasks. The experiments are conducted by using three FDNs in the system, in addition to a central cloud server. The streaming requests arrive to one of these FDNs and we measure the performance metrics obtained in that FDN. The other two FDNs serve as neighbors, caching a portion of video segments.

Different workload traces of video stream requests are generated to examine the system behavior under various workload conditions and streaming methods. The workloads used in the experiments are created using a set of benchmark videos that contain different lengths and content types. The benchmark videos are publicly available for reproducibility purposes at https://goo.gl/TE5iJ5. For each video segment in the workload traces, there is an associated processing (i.e., execution) time, which is obtained from the mean of 30 times execution of that segment on Amazon GPU VM. For the sake of accuracy and to remove uncertainty in the results, we generated 30 different workload traces. Each workload trace simulates 3 min of video stream request arrivals. The arrival time of each streaming request is determined by uniformly sampling within the time period. All segments of the same video have the same arrival time but different deadlines (i.e., presentation times). Accordingly, each experiment is conducted with the 30 workload traces and the mean and 95% confidence interval of the results are reported.

We track the number of deadlines that are missed, which indicates the robustness of the system. A deadline is considered missed due to a segment being streamed after its associated presentation time. The presentation time of a segment is based on the order of the segment's appearance in a video. As the experiments consider the use case of video on-demand (VOD) streaming service, even if a segment misses its deadline, it still must complete its execution and is streamed to the viewer.

To consider bandwidth usage in the evaluations, we have a limited bandwidth value from the local FDN to the viewer, and from the local FDN to other neighboring FDN. This bandwidth value becomes more congested as segments are initially streamed and less congested as segments finish streaming. Each node also has an associated latency value. The network latency values used for the edge servers and the central cloud server were taken from [2, 3]. The average bandwidth was set on 1 Gbps.

Examining the Suitable Cache Size for FDNs

In the first experiment, we intend to find the minimum percentage of video contents that needs be cached within an FDN, so that a high level of QoE is maintained for viewers. Recall that the QoE is measured in terms of percentage of segments missing their presentation deadline. We evaluate variations of FDNs (namely, F-CDN, I-FDN, Deterministic F-FDN, and Robust F-FDN) to understand how different methods take advantage of the caching feature. For that purpose, as shown in Fig. 7.6, the percentage of segments that are cached in each FDN (horizontal axis) is increased and the percentage of video segments that miss their deadlines (vertical

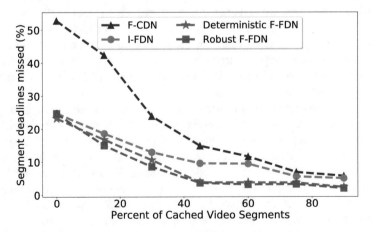

Fig. 7.6 Deadline miss rate of different streaming methods as the caching level is increased. The simulations are run using a workload of 3500 segments

axis) is measured. In this experiment, workload traces consisting of 3500 segments being streamed to viewers were used.

We observe that as the percentage of cached segments is increased, the deadline miss rate drops remarkably across all methods—from approximately 53% to around 2%. Specifically, when the total cached video content is at 0%, we are able to see a major difference between F-CDN and the other three systems. Zero percent caching for F-CDN, in fact, shows the case of streaming only from the central cloud. However, we can observe that other methods with the ability to process segments at the fog (FDN) level, in addition to streaming segments from cloud, can dramatically reduce deadline miss rate (approximately 52% improvement).

As the level of cached video content is increased, we observe the benefit of streaming video segments from neighboring FDNs. For instance, comparing the I-FDN and Deterministic F-FDN shows that at 30% caching, deadline miss rate is reduced by 2.3% (denoting 18% improvement), whereas at 90% caching, the deadline miss rate of Deterministic F-FDN is 2.7% lower than I-FDN (denoting 53% improvement). We can conclude that the streaming of video segments from neighboring FDNs unburdens the on-demand processing of the local FDN to the point where missing a deadline becomes significantly less likely.

Based on our observation and analysis in this experiment, 30% caching level is used for the FDN systems in the next experiments. We believe that this caching level provides a sustainable trade-off between the cache size and streaming QoE.

Analyzing the Impact of Oversubscription
In this experiment, the goal is to study the robustness of the F-FDN platform against increasing workload intensity (a.k.a. oversubscription) and compare it against alternative methods. For that purpose, we vary the number of arriving video segments from 3000 to 4500 (with increments of 500) within the same time interval and measure the percentage of segments missing their deadlines. In this experiment, FDN-based methods cache 30% and the CDN method caches 75% (for practical reasons [17]) of video segments, while Central Cloud stores all the video contents.

Figure 7.7 demonstrates the performance of different methods as the workload size increases (horizontal axis). We observe that as the number of arriving requests increases, the percentage of segments missing their deadlines increases too. In particular, in comparing the CDN and Central Cloud methods, we see the benefit of a viewer being able to access a CDN server that is much closer to them geographically. Across all workloads, the CDN method misses an average of 54% less deadlines than the Central Cloud method. With the presence of on-demand processing in the I-FDN compared to CDN, there is an average of a 17% deadline miss rate improvement. Performance is shown to further increase upon adding the federation of FDNs for streaming, as is present in the Deterministic and Robust F-FDN methods. Compared to the I-FDN, the Deterministic F-FDN has an average of 34% less deadlines missed.

Comparing the performance of the Deterministic F-FDN and the Robust F-FDN methods, we observe a further improvement of deadline miss rate. Across all workloads, the Robust F-FDN performs an average of 28% better than the

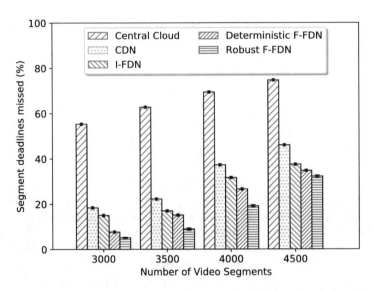

Fig. 7.7 Deadline miss rate at increasing workload intensity. FDN-based methods cache 30% of segments while CDN has 75% of videos cached

Deterministic F-FDN. This is due to capturing the stochastic factors (related to communication and computation) present in Robust F-FDN and absent in the Deterministic F-FDN.

Analyzing the Impact of Network Latency
The goal of this experiment is to evaluate the robustness of the explored methods against viewers' geographical locations. This is particularly important for viewers located in distant areas, where the quality of the edge network commonly fluctuates and is highly uncertain. For that purpose, we study the performance of different methods where the uncertainty in the network latency between the viewer and FDNs and between FDNs is steadily increased.

The result of this experiment is shown in Fig. 7.8. The horizontal axis shows the average latency to receive a cached video segment and the vertical axis shows the percentage of segments that missed their deadlines. We evaluated CDN, I-FDN, Deterministic F-FDN, and Robust F-FDN methods. Because our focus is on the edge network, we do not consider the Central Cloud method. This experiment is conducted with 3500 segments and 30% of video segments are cached in each FDN, except CDN that caches 75% of all videos.

We observe that all methods result in a higher deadline miss rate as the network latency is increased. However, we observe that CDN deadline miss rate is increased at a greater rate than that of the other methods. When comparing the CDN and I-FDN system at an average network latency of 1000 ms the deadline miss rate is at a difference of 20.2%. Nonetheless, when the average network latency is increased to 4000 ms, the difference in deadline misses maintains at 20.4%. For the CDN

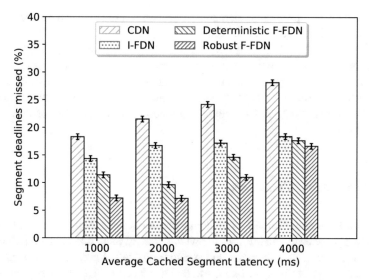

Fig. 7.8 Deadline miss rate with increasing latency of the edge network. The experiments are conducted using 3500 video segments. FDN-based methods contain 30% and CDN has 75% cached video contents

method, all segments that are not cached must be streamed from the central cloud. When the latency for streaming from the CDN is not ideal, more segments are streamed from the central cloud. Since I-FDN can perform on-demand processing for segments that are not cached, there is less of a reliance on the central cloud. This explains the consistently better performance of I-FDN as the average network latency is increased when compared to the CDN method.

In comparing I-FDN to Deterministic F-FDN, we notice that the difference of deadline miss rate decreases between the two methods, as the network latency increases. Particularly, at an 1000 ms network latency, the Deterministic F-FDN performs 64% better than I-FDN. However, when the network latency is increased to 4000 ms, there is only a 7.6% difference in deadline miss rate between the two methods. This decrease in difference of deadline miss rates can be explained by the Deterministic F-FDN choosing to stream segments from neighboring FDNs less, instead, processing those segments in an on-demand manner. The same phenomenon can be observed when comparing I-FDN and Robust F-FDN. At 1000 ms network latency, the deadline miss rate difference is 97% and at 4000 ms network latency, the difference is only 15.4%. This observation shows the adaptability that is inherent to our system.

In general, we observe that Robust F-FDN outperforms other methods. However, the difference between Deterministic F-FDN and Robust F-FDN becomes less prominent, when the network latency at the edge is at the highest we tested (4000 ms). The reason for outperformance is capturing stochasticity in the network latency. However, the reason for similar performance at 4000 latency is that both methods choose to process on-demand, as opposed to relying on a highly uncertain network and fetch segments from neighboring FDNs.

It can be concluded that F-FDN platform, in general, can remarkably improve the performance of streaming compared to traditional CDN-based methods. Interestingly, the improvement becomes more significant, as the network becomes more uncertain. Among the FDN-based methods, Robust F-FDN can capture the stochasticity that exists in the network to a certain level and further improve the performance.

7.5 Streaming Protocols

To reduce latency, multimedia streaming protocols have evolved dramatically. In the early days, viewers had to wait the whole content to be downloaded before they can begin to watch it. This method of streaming is called *progressive downloading* and its latency is remarkable. Later, Adobe introduced RTMP streaming server that basically splits the video to smaller chunks, so that the player can begin playing, once a chunk is downloaded, as opposed to waiting for the whole video. Low latency and playback flexibility made the RTMP a popular streaming protocol for a some time. However, RTMP has/had its own bottlenecks. For instance, it requires a dedicated streaming server and its connection can be blocked by a firewall because its port number is different from the popular HTTP.

Adaptive bitrate streaming (ABR) starts to take over the streaming world in the past few years. The most common protocols under this approach are Apple's HLS, MPEG group's DASH, and Microsoft's Smooth. These protocols are based on HTTP that solves the firewall configuration problem and uses web server directly, instead of using a separate dedicated streaming server. With regards to the latency, ABR protocols make use of the RTMP approach, which splits the multimedia contents into segments. Each segment can be as small as a Group of Pictures (GOP). However, the small segment size leads to a higher HTTP request traffic that in turn can cause a higher latency. Therefore, the segment size should be chosen carefully and by considering all aspects. The HLS protocol recommends 10s as the segment size whereas DASH recommends 6s.

Even though the typical ABR protocol could reduce the streaming latency substantially in compare to the original progressive download, the latency could still reach to around 30s, which is not acceptable for live streaming use cases. Recently, low-latency ABR protocols, such as Low-Latency HLS (LLHLS) [18], CMAF [31], and WebRTC [37], have been proposed. Both LLHLS and CMAF split the multimedia segments into even smaller chunks, which can be just a few frames, and use the chunk transfer encoding technology [45] to encode and deliver the frames. However, these protocols need support from the stream player end. Once the player receives a small chunk, it can begin playing without waiting for the whole segment to be downloaded. LLHLS and CMAF can reduce the streaming latency to less than 5s.

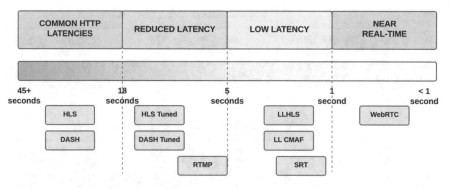

Fig. 7.9 Low latency streaming protocols

The latest and fastest streaming protocol is WebRTC [37], which operates based on the UDP transport protocol. It can stream the video contents with only 1s latency. The protocol is widely used in the video conferencing or other peer to peer applications. Figure 7.9 gives a brief comparison among the latency of the streaming protocols.

7.6 Case-Study: Low-Latency Streaming in Practice

To achieve low latency broadcasting, scalability is as important as latency. While WebRTC offers the lowest latency, it is difficult to scale up to handle millions of concurrent viewers. Nowadays, the most commonly used low latency broadcasting protocols are CMAF, LHLS, and LL-HLS.

Will [31] from Akamai presented an ultra low latency streaming approach using chunked transferred encoding with CMAF. In considering of delivery efficiency and cost, video and audio tracks are usually split into segments (e.g., 10s) or fragments (e.g., 2s). Larger size of video segment means less segment requests needed, but also causes high latency. With CMAF, the video and audio fragments can be split further into multiple smaller chunks. The chunk size can as small as one frame, and the first chunk contains the instantaneous decoder refresh (IDR) frame, as shown in Fig. 7.10.

Smaller video chunk usually means higher number of requests, which cause higher bandwidth waste. To address this issue, low latency CMAF has adopted two technologies: chunked transfer encoding (CTE) [45] and Hypertext Transfer Protocol (HTTP/1.1) push [20].

Normally, segment is only produced once all frames inside that segment are transcoded, and then it will be cached at the edge CDN, where the players can download. Depends on the segment size, which can incurs large latency while waiting the transcode complete. On the other hand, the player usually needs to buffer

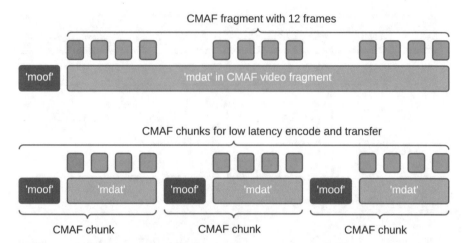

Fig. 7.10 Chunked encoding of a CMAF segment

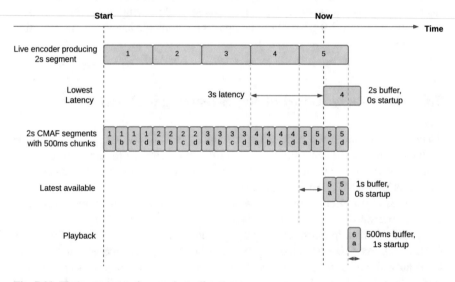

Fig. 7.11 Player startup options against a live stream

a few segments (e.g., 30s) before it can start to play, which adds more latency before the video becomes viewable.

Instead of generating a whole segment, what if the transcoder produces smaller chunks (can be as small as one frame) whenever they are ready. As long as the player receive those chunks, it can start decoding and playing without waiting for the whole segment downloaded. As a result, it lowers the latency to even under 500 ms, as shown in Fig. 7.11. This solution is called chunked transfer encoding (CTE) [31].

One of the main concerns for CTE is the increasing request numbers for smaller chunks for. HTTP/1.1 push has been used to resolve this issue. With push mechanism, the player only needs to send one request for a segment, CDN will push all chunks belong to the requested segment to the player once they are ready. This approach lowers both bandwidth and latency.

Twitch[2] uses similar approach for their low latency live streaming delivery. John [10] customizes HLS spec with special tags (e.g., #EXT-X-PREFETCH) to request a segment which is not ready yet. The connection will be kept alive, whenever any chunks inside that segment are ready, they will be pushed to player. It is noteworthy that Twitch's HLS manifest does not present chunks, so it basically looks like a normal HLS manifest with some custom tags.

Unfortunately, Apple did not incorporate such hacking into HLS spec. Instead, it comes up with its own LL-HLS, which does not even use CTE. To achieve low latency, as we mentioned before, the simplest thing we can do is make the segment smaller. LL-HLS recommend split video to smaller parts, each part's url will be presented in the manifest as well. To avoid high request rate, Apple has adopted HTTP2 push mechanism. However, in addition to pushing the parts to the player, the server also need to update the manifest after each part, and push the latest manifest before the video part.

In comparison of the previous two, the benefit of LL-HLS is that we know which part has the IDR, so when player switches versions much faster. While there are much more bottlenecks that makes LL-HLS much harder to be used, namely bandwidth waste because extra manifest delivery, HTTP2 push support from CDN providers etc.

7.7 Summary

In this chapter, we covered the latency aspect of the multimedia streaming within the MSC context. As the technology resembles CDN, we called FDN. Then, we developed a variation of the MSC platform for FDN that can handle both caching and on-demand processing of the multimedia content. To improve the latency, particularly in remote areas, we proposed a federation of fog computing systems where the MSC platforms are federated to collaboratively stream the multimedia contents from multiple sources.

In the next chapter, we cover other important aspects of the multimedia streaming, such as storage, security, and networking.

---

[2] www.twitch.tv.

References

1. Content Delivery Network (CDN) Caching. www.aws.amazon.com/caching/cdn/, accessed on Aug. 06, 2018.
2. CDN Network Test. www.cloudharmony.com/speedtest-for-cdn, accessed on Aug. 07, 2018.
3. CDN Performance. www.cloudflare.com/learning/cdn/performance/, accessed on Aug. 07, 2018.
4. Vijay Kumar Adhikari, Yang Guo, Fang Hao, Matteo Varvello, Volker Hilt, Moritz Steiner, and Zhi-Li Zhang. Unreeling netflix: Understanding and improving multi-cdn movie delivery. In *Proceedings of the IEEE International Conference on Computer Communications*, INFOCOM '12, pages 1620–1628, 2012.
5. Michael M Afergan, F Thomson Leighton, and Jay G Parikh. Hybrid content delivery network (cdn) and peer-to-peer (p2p) network, Dec. 2012. US Patent 8,332,484.
6. Shakeel Ahmad, Christos Bouras, Eliya Buyukkaya, Muneeb Dawood, Raouf Hamzaoui, Vaggelis Kapoulas, Andreas Papazois, and Gwendal Simon. Peer-to-peer live video streaming with rateless codes for massively multiplayer online games. *Peer-to-Peer Networking and Applications*, 11(1):44–62, 2018.
7. Abubakr O Al-Abbasi and Vaneet Aggarwal. Edgecache: An optimized algorithm for cdn-based over-the-top video streaming services. In *Proceedings of the IEEE Conference on Computer Communications Workshops (INFOCOM WKSHPS)*, pages 202–207. IEEE, 2018.
8. Emmanuel André, Nicolas Le Breton, Augustin Lemesle, Ludovic Roux, and Alexandre Gouaillard. Comparative study of webRTC open source SFUs for video conferencing. In *2018 Principles, Systems and Applications of IP Telecommunications (IPTComm)*, pages 1–8. IEEE, 2018.
9. John Apostolopoulos, Tina Wong, Wai-tian Tan, and Susie Wee. On multiple description streaming with content delivery networks. In *Proceedings of the 21st Annual Joint Conference of the IEEE Computer and Communications Societies*, volume 3, pages 1736–1745, 2002.
10. John Bartos. Why hls.js is standardizing low-latency streaming, https://www.twitch.tv/demuxed/video/326087400?collection=u1vmyymiybxvlq&filter=all&sort=time. Accessed June. 16, 2021.
11. Ilias Benkacem, Tarik Taleb, Miloud Bagaa, and Hannu Flinck. Performance benchmark of transcoding as a virtual network function in cdn as a service slicing. In *Proceedings of the IEEE Conference on Wireless Communications and Networking (WCNC)*, 2018.
12. Timm Böttger, Felix Cuadrado, Gareth Tyson, Ignacio Castro, and Steve Uhlig. Open connect everywhere: A glimpse at the internet ecosystem through the lens of the netflix cdn. *ACM SIGCOMM Computer Communication Review*, 48(1):28–34, Apr. 2018.
13. Fangfei Chen, Katherine Guo, John Lin, and Thomas La Porta. Intra-cloud lightning: Building CDNs in the cloud. In *Proceedings of the IEEE Conference INFOCOM*, pages 433–441. IEEE, 2012.
14. Yang-hua Chu, Sanjay G Rao, and Hui Zhang. A case for end system multicast (keynote address). In *ACM SIGMETRICS Performance Evaluation Review*, volume 28, pages 1–12. ACM, 2000.
15. Charles D Cranor, Matthew Green, Chuck Kalmanek, David Shur, Sandeep Sibal, Jacobus E Van der Merwe, and Cormac J Sreenan. Enhanced streaming services in a content distribution network. *IEEE Internet Computing*, 5(4):66–75, 2001.
16. Mahmoud Darwich, Mohsen Amini Salehi, Ege Beyazit, and Magdy Bayoumi. Cost-efficient cloud-based video streaming through measuring hotness. *The Computer Journal*, Jun. 2018.
17. Stefan Dernbach, Nina Taft, Jim Kurose, Udi Weinsberg, Christophe Diot, and Azin Ashkan. Cache content-selection policies for streaming video services. In *Proceedings of the 35th Annual IEEE International Conference on Computer Communications*, INFOCOM '16, pages 1–9, Apr. 2016.
18. Kerem Durak, Mehmet N Akcay, Yigit K Erinc, Boran Pekel, and Ali C Begen. Evaluating the performance of apple's low-latency HLS. In *2020 IEEE 22nd International Workshop on Multimedia Signal Processing (MMSP)*, pages 1–6. IEEE, 2020.

19. Sam Dutton. Webrtc in the real world: Stun, turn and signaling. *Google, Nov*, 2013.
20. Roy Fielding, Jim Gettys, Jeffrey Mogul, Henrik Frystyk, Larry Masinter, Paul Leach, and Tim Berners-Lee. Hypertext transfer protocol–http/1.1, 1999.
21. Mahya Mohammadi Golchi and Homayun Motameni. Evaluation of the improved particle swarm optimization algorithm efficiency inward peer to peer video streaming. *Computer Networks*, 2018.
22. Yang Guo, Kyoungwon Suh, Jim Kurose, and Don Towsley. P2cast: peer-to-peer patching scheme for VoD service. In *Proceedings of the 12th international conference on World Wide Web*, pages 301–309, 2003.
23. Torsten Hoefler and Roberto Belli. Scientific benchmarking of parallel computing systems: twelve ways to tell the masses when reporting performance results. In *The International Conference for High Performance Computing, Networking, Storage, and Analysis*, SC '15, page 73, Nov. 2015.
24. Han Hu, Yonggang Wen, Tat-Seng Chua, Jian Huang, Wenwu Zhu, and Xuelong Li. Joint content replication and request routing for social video distribution over cloud CDN: A community clustering method. *IEEE transactions on circuits and systems for video technology*, 26(7):1320–1333, 2016.
25. Han Hu, Yonggang Wen, Tat-Seng Chua, Zhi Wang, Jian Huang, Wenwu Zhu, and Di Wu. Community based effective social video contents placement in cloud centric CDN network. In *Proceeding of the IEEE International Conference on Multimedia and Expo*, ICME '14, pages 1–6, 2014.
26. Razin Hussain, Mohsen Amini Salehi, Anna Kovalenko, Omid Semiari, and Saeed Salehi. Robust resource allocation using edge computing for smart oil field. In *Proceedings of the 24th International Conference on Parallel and Distributed Processing Techniques and Applications*, PDPTA '18, pages 495–503, July 2018.
27. John Jannotti, David K Gifford, Kirk L Johnson, M Frans Kaashoek, et al. Overcast: reliable multicasting with on overlay network. In *Proceedings of the 4th Conference on Symposium on Operating System Design & Implementation-Volume 4*, page 14. USENIX Association, 2000.
28. Yichao Jin, Yonggang Wen, Guangyu Shi, Guoqiang Wang, and Athanasios V Vasilakos. Codaas: An experimental cloud-centric content delivery platform for user-generated contents. In *Proceedings of the International Conference on Computing, Networking and Communications*, ICNC '12, pages 934–938. IEEE, 2012.
29. Shoaib Khan, Rüdiger Schollmeier, and Eckehard Steinbach. A performance comparison of multiple description video streaming in peer-to-peer and content delivery networks. In *Proceedings of the IEEE International Conference on Multimedia and Expo*, volume 1 of *ICME '04*, pages 503–506, Jun. 2004.
30. Leonidas Kontothanassis, Ramesh Sitaraman, Joel Wein, Duke Hong, Robert Kleinberg, Brian Mancuso, David Shaw, and Daniel Stodolsky. A transport layer for live streaming in a content delivery network. *Proceedings of the IEEE*, 92(9):1408–1419, 2004.
31. Will Law. Ultra-low-latency streaming using chunked-encoded and chunked-transferred CMAF. Technical report, Akamai, 2018.
32. Xiaohua Lei, Xiuhua Jiang, and Caihong Wang. Design and implementation of streaming media processing software based on RTMP. In *2012 5th International Congress on Image and Signal Processing*, pages 192–196. IEEE, 2012.
33. Xiangbo Li, Mohsen Amini Salehi, Magdy Bayoumi, and Rajikumar Buyya. CVSS: A Cost-Efficient and QoS-Aware Video Streaming Using Cloud Services. In *Proceedings of the 16th IEEE/ACM International Symposium on Cluster, Cloud, and Grid Computing*, CCGrid '16, May 2016.
34. Xiangbo Li, Mohsen Amini Salehi, Yamini Joshi, Mahmoud Darwich, Landreneau Brad, and Magdi Bayoumi. Performance Analysis and Modelling of Video Stream Transcoding Using Heterogeneous Cloud Services. *IEEE Transactions on Parallel and Distributed Systems (TPDS)*, Sep. 2018. doi: https://doi.org/10.1109/TPDS.2018.2870651.
35. Xiangbo Li, Mohsen Amini Salehi, Magdy Bayoumi, Nian-Feng Tzeng, and Rajkumar Buyya. Cost-Efficient and Robust On-Demand Video Stream Transcoding Using Heterogeneous Cloud

Services. *IEEE Transactions on Parallel and Distributed Systems (TPDS)*, 29(3):556–571, Mar. 2018.

36. Yong Liu, Yang Guo, and Chao Liang. A survey on peer-to-peer video streaming systems. *Peer-to-peer Networking and Applications*, 1(1):18–28, 2008.

37. Salvatore Loreto and Simon Pietro Romano. *Real-time communication with WebRTC: peer-to-peer in the browser*. O'Reilly Media, Inc., 2014.

38. Zhi Hui Lu, Xiao Hong Gao, Si Jia Huang, and Yi Huang. Scalable and reliable live streaming service through coordinating cdn and p2p. In *Proceedings of the IEEE 17th International Conference on Parallel and Distributed Systems*, ICPADS '11, pages 581–588, 2011.

39. Nazanin Magharei, Reza Rejaie, and Yang Guo. Mesh or multiple-tree: A comparative study of live p2p streaming approaches. In *Proceedings of the 26th IEEE International Conference on Computer Communications*, INFOCOM '07, pages 1424–1432, 2007.

40. Kwok-Fai Ng, Man-Yan Ching, Yang Liu, Tao Cai, Li Li, and Wu Chou. A P2P-MCU approach to multi-party video conference with WebRTC. *International Journal of Future Computer and Communication*, 3(5):319, 2014.

41. Naeem Ramzan, Hyunggon Park, and Ebroul Izquierdo. Video streaming over p2p networks: Challenges and opportunities. *Signal Processing: Image Communication*, 27(5):401–411, 2012.

42. Stefan Saroiu, Krishna P. Gummadi, Richard J. Dunn, Steven D. Gribble, and Henry M. Levy. An analysis of internet content delivery systems. *SIGOPS Oper. Syst. Rev.*, 36(SI):315–327, December 2002.

43. Arman Shojaeifard, Kai-Kit Wong, Wei Yu, Gan Zheng, and Jie Tang. Full-duplex cloud radio access network: Stochastic design and analysis. *IEEE Transactions on Wireless Communications*, 17(11):7190–7207, Nov. 2018.

44. Volker Stocker, Georgios Smaragdakis, William Lehr, and Steven Bauer. The growing complexity of content delivery networks: Challenges and implications for the internet ecosystem. *Telecommunications Policy*, 41(10):1003–1016, Nov. 2017.

45. Viswanathan Swaminathan and Sheng Wei. Low latency live video streaming using http chunked encoding. In *2011 IEEE 13th International Workshop on Multimedia Signal Processing*, pages 1–6. IEEE, 2011.

46. A. Vakali and G. Pallis. Content delivery networks: status and trends. *IEEE Internet Computing*, 7(6):68–74, Nov 2003.

47. Vidhyashankar Venkataraman, Kaouru Yoshida, and Paul Francis. Chunkyspread: Heterogeneous unstructured tree-based peer-to-peer multicast. In *Proceedings of the 2006 14th IEEE International Conference on Network Protocols*, ICNP '06, pages 2–11, 2006.

48. Aggelos Vlavianos, Marios Iliofotou, and Michalis Faloutsos. BiToS: Enhancing BitTorrent for supporting streaming applications. In *Proceedings of the 25th IEEE International Conference on Computer Communications*, INFOCOM '06, pages 1–6, 2006.

49. Susie Wee, John Apostolopoulos, Wai-tian Tan, and Sumit Roy. Research and design of a mobile streaming media content delivery network. In *Proceedings of the International Conference on Multimedia and Expo*, volume 1 of *ICME '03*, pages I–5, 2003.

50. Changqiao Xu, G-M Muntean, Enda Fallon, and Austin Hanley. A balanced tree-based strategy for unstructured media distribution in P2P networks. In *Proceedings of the IEEE International Conference on Communications*, ICC '08, pages 1797–1801, 2008.

51. Dongyan Xu, Sunil Suresh Kulkarni, Catherine Rosenberg, and Heung-Keung Chai. Analysis of a CDN–P2P hybrid architecture for cost-effective streaming media distribution. *Multimedia Systems*, 11(4):383–399, 2006.

52. Tianyin Xu, Jianzhong Chen, Wenzhong Li, Sanglu Lu, Yang Guo, and Mounir Hamdi. Supporting VCR-like operations in derivative tree-based P2P streaming systems. In *Proceedings of the IEEE International Conference on Communications*, ICC '09, pages 1–5, 2009.

53. Hao Yin, Xuening Liu, Tongyu Zhan, Vyas Sekar, Feng Qiu, Chuang Lin, Hui Zhang, and Bo Li. Design and deployment of a hybrid CDN-P2P system for live video streaming: experiences with livesky. In *Proceedings of the 17th ACM international conference on Multimedia*, pages 25–34. ACM, 2009.

54. W-P Ken Yiu, Xing Jin, and S-H Gary Chan. Vmesh: Distributed segment storage for peer-to-peer interactive video streaming. *IEEE journal on selected areas in communications*, 25(9), 2007.
55. M. Zink, R. Sitaraman, and K. Nahrstedt. Scalable 360 video stream delivery: Challenges, solutions, and opportunities. *Proceedings of the IEEE*, 107(4):639–650, April 2019.

Chapter 8
Other Aspects of Multimedia Clouds

8.1 Domain-Specific Billing

Designing a billing policy for any type of service is a trade-off between simplicity and accuracy. Too simple billing models often make users feel unfair, whereas, too complicated (and accurate) ones make users puzzled. A well-designed billing policy should also incentivize user's interaction with the system. For instance, a buffet model makes users watch more media than they really require. This was a preferred model in the past, as people were mostly watching the broadcasts. However, as we transition into the on-demand multimedia streaming, wasteful usage implies a higher Internet cost that can be avoided by charging users only for what (or how) they watch. For instance, streaming a high-resolution movie to users that only listen to it should not happen when watching at different resolutions cost differently.

The simplest billing policy for multimedia streaming services is to pay a flat rate for monthly access and gain an unlimited access to the contents. This payment plan is also the earliest form of payment model for multimedia service. This model made perfect sense back in the age of cable TV. Back then, multimedia are broadcasted rather than streaming on-demand, and therefore, there is no difference in broadcasting price whether the subscriber is watching the content or not. This pricing model has similar pros and cons as the buffet (all you can eat) model at the restaurants. On the one hand, it encourages users to pay more and access more content than they would otherwise do in other pricing models. On the other hand, this pricing model is highly unfair to people who do not access much content but have to pay the same price. Recently, people are more aware of the danger of over-eating and spend too much screen time and hence, prefer to avoid such buffet paying scheme when possible. Therefore, another pricing model should be offered in conjunction with the buffet pricing model.

With the advancement of DRM and data logging technologies, a more granular billing policy has become a common practice. Subscribers pay for the access of each content they access, either as the number of content or based on the time they

© Springer Nature Switzerland AG 2021
M. A. Salehi, X. Li, *Multimedia Cloud Computing Systems*,
https://doi.org/10.1007/978-3-030-88451-2_8

spend watching the content. On a high-level view, this pricing model seems to strike a perfect balance between simplicity and accuracy of the actual cost involved to stream the media contents. However, considering expensive content has a higher cost to grant the access and stream, streaming companies tend to vary the content costs into multiple price categories. For example, each movie costs differently; and for the same movie, the high-resolution one costs more than the lower resolution one.

Consider a case where a subscriber originally purchases the HD access to a live stream. Later, the internet connection drops and the subscriber cannot watch in the HD quality anymore. As such, the stream bit rate should be reduced and the subscriber is not getting what she paid for. Thus, a more granular payment model should be developed. We believe a billing policy for on-demand multimedia streaming should not incentivize wasteful streaming. Therefore, the payment should reflect the actual resource usage. Considering a high resolution and low resolution streaming require a vastly different amount of workload on the steaming engine, a fair pricing model should charge different prices accordingly. Similarly, in an interactive video streaming system, a user that requires more task processing services on their media should pay extra for such service.

This pricing model brings about several incentives toward more efficient interactive streaming systems. First, it encourages the content generators to create concise and engaging content that subscribers are less likely to skip the boring parts. This can improve the quality of the content and reduce the duration of the media segment in the system. Second, it reduces the amount of on-demand processing to personalize the content for each user to the minimum required. Finally, The pricing of each content can be dynamically adjusted based on the content availability. Considering video A is cached in a local CDN in the HD version and video B is not cached. There is no pricing incentive for users to watch video A over video B on traditional content-based pricing. Moreover, normally the non-HD version is cheaper than the HD one, so price-sensitive viewers are more likely to request a lower resolution of the video that needs extra processing from a higher resolution one. In the per-resource usage payment, since video A in HD is cached in the local CDN, a pricing model that calculates based on actual resource usage can incentivize more users to watch the cached version over other options that are more costly.

8.2 Networking of the Multimedia Streaming Clouds

One of the challenges for using cloud to deliver multimedia contents is the network limitations. To provide a high service availability and error resilience, cloud servers are distributed in multiple regions, and even multiple zones in each region. The latency for crossing these regions can be high. Therefore, efficient network routing is essential for both performance and expense purpose. Unfortunately, cloud providers usually don't provide control for network routing, so customers have to count on such routing and its implications.

For VOD streaming, the service availability is more important than the latency, therefore, this form of streaming gains the most benefit from the cloud services. In contrast, the latency is one of the most critical factors for live streaming, therefore, network routing plays a significant role in increasing/decreasing the latency. In order to provide low-latency live streaming, live streaming platforms, such as Twitch, have to manage their own infrastructures and network servers, so that they can put the frequently communicating servers in the same or close locations. To take advantage of cloud services, live streaming platforms usually utilize a hybrid approach, that means some services are executed on the bare metal server (e.g., ingest, transcode, and distribute) and other non-computing intensive services (e.g., state management, catalog, etc.) are performed in the cloud. Luckily, cloud providers do support such hybrid approach with some fast network communication solutions (e.g., AWS Direct Connet,[1] PrivateLink[2] etc.), which can directly connect multimedia customer's bare metal servers to cloud servers with physical network cables.

Another networking concern in multimedia streaming is the bandwidth cost. In fact, each request and response going through the cloud network is not free of charge. Multimedia contents bandwidth intensive, thus, avoiding duplicated content requests to the cloud servers can significantly save the costs. To achieve this, multiple layers of caching servers (or CDNs) are commonly used by the streaming service providers, so that if the player cannot locate the contents in the edge CDN, it will look it in a upper layer caching server instead of directly hitting cloud server. However, even the CDN bandwidth is costly. Actually, the CDN bandwidth cost usually accounts for large amount of the operational costs of the stream providers. There are some researches have been conducted [4] to reduce the bandwidth waste at the client side.

8.3 Security of Multimedia Streaming

8.3.1 Privacy

With the ubiquity of video streaming on a wide range of display devices, the privacy of the video contents has become a major concern. In particular, live contents either in form of video surveillance or user-based live-streaming capture places and record many unwanted/unrelated contents. For instance, a person who live-streams from a street, unintentionally may capture plate number of vehicles passing that location. Therefore, video streaming systems can easily compromise the privacy of people (e.g., faces and vehicles tags). Various techniques have been developed to protect the privacy of live video contents.

---

[1] https://aws.amazon.com/directconnect.

[2] https://aws.amazon.com/privatelink.

Dufeaux et al. [7] introduced two techniques to obscure the regions of interests while video surveillance systems are running. Their techniques are based on transform-domain or codestream-domain scrambling. In the first technique, the sign of selected transform coefficients is pseudorandomly flipped during encoding. In the second technique, some bits of the codestream are pseudorandomly inverted. Their proposed techniques demonstrate how to efficiently hide private data in regions of interest while surveillance remains comprehensible. Zhang et al. [19] came up with a framework to store the privacy information of a video surveillance system in form of a watermark. The proposed model embeds a signature into the header of the video. Moreover, it embeds the authorized personal information into the video that can be retrieved only with a secret key. Another research, conducted by Carrillo et al. [3], introduces a compression algorithm for video surveillance system, which is based on the encryption concept. The proposed algorithm protects the privacy by hiding the identity revealing features of the objects and human. Such objects and human identity could be decrypted with decryption keys when an investigation is requested.

Live video contents commonly are transmitted via wireless media which can be easily intercepted and altered. Moreover, DOS attacks can be launched on the live video traffics [1]. As such, in [2, 9] algorithms are provided to distinguish between packets that were damaged because of noise or an attack. In the former case, the errors must be fixed while in the latter the packet must be resent. The algorithm counts the number of 1s or 0s in a packet before the packet is sent and uses that count to generate a message authentication code (MAC). The MAC is appended to the end of the packet and sent over the network. When the packet is received, the MAC is calculated again, and the two codes are compared. If the differences in MACs passes a certain threshold, it is marked as malicious and discarded. Because the MAC is also sent over the network, the algorithm will detect bit errors in both the packet and the MAC.

8.3.2   Digital Rights Management

Another security aspect in video streaming is the copyright issue. This is particularly prominent for subscription-based video streaming services (such as Netflix) and large sponsored live event. Digital Rights Management (DRM) is the practice of securing digital contents, including video streams, to prevent unlawful copying and distribution of the protected material. Specifically, its goals are typically centered around controlling access to the content, enforcing rules about usage, and identifying and authenticating the content source. As such, contents protected with DRM are typically sold as a license to use the contents, rather than the content itself. DRM solutions to meet these goals often incorporate tools such as encryption, watermarking, and cryptographic hashing [17].

The process of DRM starts with encryption, video contents are encrypted and stored in the video repository and DRM providers keep the secret keys. Figure 8.1 summarizes the steps to stream a video protected with DRM. Upon request to stream

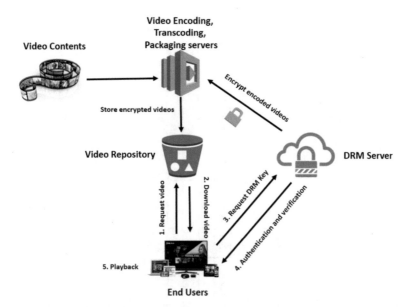

Fig. 8.1 Workflow of Digital Right Management (DRM) to support of video streaming security

an encrypted video, after downloading it, the secret key is requested from the DRM provider server to decrypt the video.

Currently, there are three major DRM technologies, namely Apple's Fairplay [16], Microsoft's PlayReady [12] and Google's Widevine [12]. These technologies are able to serve most of the devices and platforms in the market. To cover all devices, streaming service providers have to encrypt the every video content with three different DRM technologies and store them in the repository. The three DRM technologies supported platforms are shown in Table 8.1.

With the increasing demand to stream DRM-protected VOD, an offline application-driven DRM interceptor has been proposed in [6] that is the awareness of the network connection status of the client device. In this case, if the interceptor application decides that the client device is offline, it requests the license/key for the protected content. The license/key is controlled by the interceptor application. Accordingly, the requests of license/key are handled by the interceptor application that retrieves them from a locally data-store, and then send the key/license to the DRM module.

8.4 Storage Service for Multimedia Contents

Video streaming repositories are growing in size, due to the increasing number of content creation sources, diversity of display devices, and the high qualities viewers desire. This rapid increase in the size of repositories implies several challenges for

Table 8.1 DRM supported platforms

	Chrome	FireFox	IE 11	Safari	Android	iOS	Windows Phone	ChromeCast	Roku	Apple TV	Xbox
Fairplay				✓		✓				✓	
PlayReady		✓	✓	✓			✓	✓	✓		✓
Widevine	✓	✓			✓			✓			

multimedia storage systems. In particular, video streaming storage challenges are threefold: capacity, throughput, and fault tolerance.

One of the main reasons to have a challenge in video streaming storage capacity is the diversity of viewers' devices. To cover increasingly diverse display devices, multiple (more than 90) versions of a single video should be generated and stored. However, storing several formats of the same video implies a large-scale storage system. Previous studies provide techniques to overcome storage issues of video streaming. Miao et al. [13] proposed techniques to store some frames of a video on the proxy cache. Their proposed technique reduces the network bandwidth costs and increases the robustness of streaming video on poor network conditions.

When a multimedia content is stored on a disk, concurrent accesses to that content are limited by the throughput of the disk. This restricts the number of simultaneous viewers for a multimedia content. To address the throughput issue, several research studies have been undertaken. Provided that storing video streams on a single disk has a low throughput, multiple disk storage are configured to increase the throughput. Shenoy et al. [15] propose data stripping where a video is segmented and saved across multiple storage disks to increase the storage throughput. Video streams are segmented into blocks before they are stored. The blocks can be stored one after another (i.e., contiguously) or scattered over several storage disks. Although contiguous storage method is simple to implement, it suffers from the fragmentation problem. The scattered method, however, eliminates the fragmentation problem with the cost of more complicated implementation.

Scattering video streams across multiple disks and implementing data striping and data interleaving methods improves reliability and fault tolerance of video streaming storage systems [18].

8.4.1 Cloud Storage for Multimedia Streaming

The rapid growth of video streaming usage in various applications, such as e-learning, video surveillance and situational awareness, and on various forms of devices (e.g., smart-phones, tablets, laptops) has created the problem of *big multimedia data* [8]. The fast growth of multimedia contents on the Internet requires massive storage facilities. However, the current storage servers face scalability and reliability issues, in addition to the high maintenance and administration cost for storage hardware. The cloud storage services provide a solution for scalability, reliability, and fault tolerance [14]. As such, major streaming service providers (e.g., Netflix and Hulu) have relied entirely on cloud storage services for their video storage demands.

Table 8.2 provides a comparison of different storage solutions for video streaming in terms of accessibility of viewers to the same video stream, available capacity (storage space), scalability, reliability, incurred cost, and QoS. It is worth noting that although CDN is not a storage solution, but it can be used to reduce the storage

Table 8.2 Comparison of different technologies for storing video stream

	Accessibility	Capacity	Scalability	Reliability	Cost	QoE
In house storage	Limited	Large	No	No	High	High
Cloud storage (Outsourcing)	High	Large	Yes	Yes	Low	Low
Content delivery network (CDN)	High	Small	No	Yes	High	High
Peer 2 Peer	High	Large	Yes	Yes	Low	Low
Hybrid CDN-P2P	High	Small	Yes	Yes	Low	High

cost by caching temporally hot video streams. Therefore, we consider it in our comparison table.

On-demand processing of video streaming that the MSC platform enables is one effective way to reduce the storage volume and cost. This is particularly important when the long-tail access pattern to video streams is taken into consideration [5]. That is, except for a small portion of video streams that are hot the rest of videos are rarely accessed. Gao et al. [10] propose an approach that partially pre-transcodes video contents in the Cloud. Their approach pre-transcodes the beginning segments of video stream and which are more frequently accessed, while transcoding the remaining contents video stream upon request, this results to a reduction of storage cost. Their system model is based on a partial transcoding of video segments and a dynamic storing system that is adapted to the video access rate change. They designed an online algorithm to optimize the performance of their scheme. They stated that the viewers play 20% of the video duration. They adopted the video access pattern by implementing the truncated exponential distribution to represent the video view rate. They demonstrated that their approach reduces 30% of the cost compared to pre-transcoding the whole contents of video stream.

Darwich et al. [5] proposed a storage and cost-efficient method for cloud-based video streaming repositories based on the long-tail access patterns. They proposed both repository and video level solutions. In the video level, they consider access patterns in two cases, (a) when it follows a long-tail distribution; and (b) when the video has random (i.e., non-long-tail) access pattern. They define the cost-benefit of pre-transcoding for each GOP and determine the GOPs that need to be pre-processed and the ones that should be processed in an on-demand manner.

Krishnappa et al. [11] proposed strategies to transcode the segments of a video stream requested by users. To keep a minimized startup delay of video streams when applying online strategies on video, they came up with an approach to predict the next video segment that is requested by the user. They carried out their prediction approach by implementing Markov theory. Their proposed strategy results a significant reduction in the cost of using the cloud storage with high accuracy.

8.5 Summary

In this section, we covered several aspects of multimedia streaming. Importantly, we discussed billing of the multimedia streaming in MSC, storage of multimedia contents, and finally security and privacy of the multimedia contents and streams. In the next chapter, we explain a prototype implementation of the MSC platform where some of the main features explained in this book are implemented and evaluated.

References

1. Ekbal M. Al-Hurani and Hussein R. Al-Zoubi. Mitigation of dos attacks on video traffic in wireless networks for better QoS. In *Proceedings of the 8th International Conference on Computer Modeling and Simulation*, ICCMS '17, pages 166–169, 2017.
2. Mohammad A. Alsmirat, Islam Obaidat, Yaser Jararweh, and Mohammed Al-Saleh. A security framework for cloud-based video surveillance system. *Multimedia Tools and Applications*, 76(21):22787–22802, Nov. 2017.
3. Paula Carrillo, Hari Kalva, and Spyros Magliveras. Compression independent object encryption for ensuring privacy in video surveillance. In *proceedings of the IEEE International Conference on Multimedia and Expo, 2008*, pages 273–276, 2008.
4. Mahmoud Darwich, Ege Beyazit, Mohsen Amini Salehi, and Magdy Bayoumi. Cost efficient repository management for cloud-based on-demand video streaming. In *2017 5th IEEE International Conference on Mobile Cloud Computing, Services, and Engineering (MobileCloud)*, pages 39–44. IEEE, 2017.
5. Mahmoud Darwich, Mohsen Amini Salehi, Ege Beyazit, and Magdy Bayoumi. Cost efficient cloud-based video streaming based on quantifying video stream hotness. *The Computer Journal*, pages 1085–1092, June 2018.
6. David Kimbal Dorwin. Application-driven playback of offline encrypted content with unaware DRM module, August 18 2015. US Patent 9,110,902.
7. Frederic Dufaux and Touradj Ebrahimi. Scrambling for privacy protection in video surveillance systems. *IEEE Transactions on Circuits and Systems for Video Technology*, 18(8):1168–1174, 2008.
8. J. Edstrom, D. Chen, Y. Gong, J. Wang, and N. Gong. Data-pattern enabled self-recovery low-power storage system for big video data. *IEEE Transactions on Big Data*, Sep. 2018.
9. Gábor Fehér. Enhancing wireless video streaming using lightweight approximate authentication. In *Proceedings of the 2nd ACM International Workshop on Quality of Service & Security for Wireless and Mobile Networks*, Q2SWinet '06, pages 9–16, 2006.
10. G. Gao, W. Zhang, Y. Wen, Z. Wang, and W. Zhu. Towards cost-efficient video transcoding in media cloud: Insights learned from user viewing patterns. *IEEE Transactions on Multimedia*, 17(8):1286–1296, Aug 2015.
11. Dilip Kumar Krishnappa, Michael Zink, and Ramesh K Sitaraman. Optimizing the video transcoding workflow in content delivery networks. In *Proceedings of the 6th ACM Multimedia Systems Conference*, pages 37–48. ACM, 2015.
12. Kapil Kumar. Drm on android. In *Proceedings of the Annual IEEE India Conference*, INDICON '17, pages 1–6, 2013.
13. Zhourong Miao and A. Ortega. Scalable proxy caching of video under storage constraints. *IEEE Journal on Selected Areas in Communications*, 20(7):1315–1327, Sep 2002.
14. D. A. Rodriguez-Silva, L. Adkinson-Orellana, F. J. Gonz'lez-Castaño, I. Armiño-Franco, and D. Gonz'lez-Martínez. Video surveillance based on cloud storage. pages 991–992, June 2012.

15. Prashant J Shenoy and Harrick M Vin. Efficient striping techniques for variable bit rate continuous media file servers. *Performance Evaluation*, 38(3):175–199, 1999.
16. FairPlay Streaming. https://developer.apple.com/streaming/fps/. Accessed May URL:.
17. T. Thomas, S. Emmanuel, A. V. Subramanyam, and M. S. Kankanhalli. Joint watermarking scheme for multiparty multilevel DRM architecture. *IEEE Transactions on Information Forensics and Security*, 4(4):758–767, Dec 2009.
18. Dapeng Wu, Y. T. Hou, Wenwu Zhu, Ya-Qin Zhang, and J. M. Peha. Streaming video over the internet: approaches and directions. *IEEE Transactions on Circuits and Systems for Video Technology*, 11(3):282–300, Mar 2001.
19. Wei Zhang, SS Cheung, and Minghua Chen. Hiding privacy information in video surveillance system. In *proceedings of the IEEE International Conference on Image Processing, ICIP 2005.*, volume 3, pages II–868, 2005.

Chapter 9
Prototype Implementation of the MSC Platform

9.1 Overview

In this chapter we describe a prototype implementation of the serverless MSC platform [3, 4, 10]. This platform allows users to define their own media processing functions. Such user-defined interactive processing tasks are processed using serverless computing cloud, as shown in Fig. 9.1.

MSC facilitates cost-efficient and QoS-aware interactive *live* or *on-demand* multimedia streaming using serverless cloud computing paradigm. MSC serves multiple service providers and different type of subscribers. It is designed to be extensible, meaning that the stream service provider will be able to introduce new services on the multimedia contents and streams. To keep the cost in check, the core architecture respects the QoS and cost constraints defined by the streaming service providers. To accommodate the large number of available services, each service is stored in the *service repository* where stream providers (and viewers) can cherry-pick which of these services they want to have available to them.

9.2 Serverless Computing Paradigm in Practice

The common practice to utilize serverless computing is to break the monolithic application into multiple micro-service [10] functions. Each user (in this case, the stream service provider) provides their executable functions and the conditions to trigger them (e.g., based on a timer or upon arrival of a web request). Once triggered, the task requests are formed, and it has to be completed in a timely manner. From the provider's perspective, a scheme to efficiently utilize cloud resources is based on a shared queue of arriving micro-service (henceforth, termed task) requests with a scheduler that allocates these task requests to a elastic pool of computing resources behind the scene. This shared computing resource approach reduces resource start-

© Springer Nature Switzerland AG 2021
M. A. Salehi, X. Li, *Multimedia Cloud Computing Systems*,
https://doi.org/10.1007/978-3-030-88451-2_9

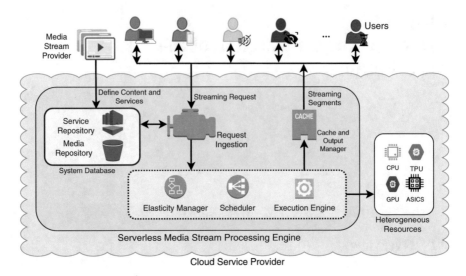

Fig. 9.1 Prototype implementation of the MSC platform

up overhead and amortizes the spare reserve of the computing resources. The service requests often have individual deadlines that failure to meet them compromises the Quality of Service (QoS) expected by the viewers.

The abstraction from user-managed resource allocation also allows the scheduler to utilize heterogeneous computing resources. Different task types from various users have different affinities (i.e., matching) with heterogeneous machines that are available in cloud data centers. Furthermore, each of these task types can be consistently heterogeneous within itself. For instance, it takes a longer time to change the resolution of a high bit-rate video, compared to the time of a lower bit-rate one.

9.3   A Use Case for the MSC Platform

In the prototype implementation of the MSC platform, we define two types of users in the system, namely the **stream service providers** and **application developers** who host their own media streaming front-end websites or applications. These types of companies or advanced users define their available services, media content and billing policy to serve their **viewers**. The viewers issue request to stream multimedia contents and are allowed by the stream providers to generate content (live or upload) and cherry-pick their media processing service functions. For more information, please refer back to Chap. 3.

In a given use case, the viewer requests the media through their stream service provider's application or web site. Each request generally leads to generating multiple *processing tasks* in the system, each of which has it own specific deadline. The MSC platform receives and must schedule tasks from multiple viewers of several stream providers, such that their QoS requirements and budget constraints are fulfilled. In addition, the MSC platform must allow the stream providers to introduce new services and new contents as well as making changes to their settings without any interruption of other stream service providers.

9.4   Characteristics of Multimedia Stream Processing

As described in Chap. 3, there are certain specifications that are common across the media processing functions supported by the MSC platform:

1. Each Multimedia streaming request generates multiple **independent** tasks [6].
2. Each of the task is tied to at least one media segment.
3. Most media segments are cache-able, yet the content variability is too high to cache every content [1, 2], and therefore, require on-demand processing [12].
4. The early segments of most media streams have high urgency, as they are required shortly after the request. The urgency of later segments are lowered, as the system have more time to prepared them ahead of the presentation time [8]. Thus, a special-purpose scheduler can significantly reduce the deadline violations.
5. Media processing functions can be broadly categorized into task types based on their main processing frameworks (e.g., media transcoding using FFmpeg [13] and object detection using YOLO framework).
6. Multimedia processing functions benefit from being executed on heterogeneous computing resources.

In MSC, a task is defined as a pair of object (i.e., media segment) and the action (a.k.a. a function call, with its parameters). Both components of the tasks' (media segment and function call) arrival pattern are not completely random. When a media segment is requested, there is a high probability that the next media segments within the sequence of media stream will be requested. Similarly, a user generally have their favourite or preferred set of functions that would have to apply to all their media streams. Therefore, the task arrival rate and pattern in MSC tends to change slowly between the time windows. In other words, the recent history of resource usage can help predict the demand in the near future.

9.5   Architecture of the MSC Prototype Implementation

Operating over a serverless computing platform as shown in Fig. 9.2, MSC has a shared scheduling queue to serve tasks from multiple users on the shared resource pool. On top of the scheduling and processing systems, there are multiple

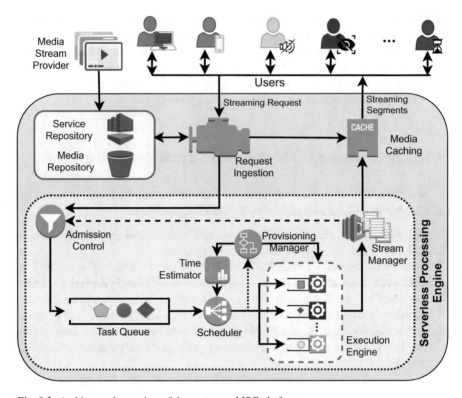

Fig. 9.2 Architectural overview of the prototype MSC platform

components including Media and Service Repository, Admission Control, Time Estimator, Scheduler, Stream Merger, Stream Caching, Provisioning Manager and Request Ingestion. On top of the system, there are different types of users with diverse service requirements. For instance, a blind user may need extra explanation on each video page and a deaf viewer needs a service to dynamically create subtitle for each video frame. Another user of the system is Media Stream Provider who can add content or services to the MSC repository. In the rest of this section, we go into detail of each component of MSC.

9.5.1 Media Repository

Media Repository contains a copy of each media segment available on the platform (excluding live media streaming content). Those media segments are usually stored in a high definition (HD) format suitable to be reprocessed to other specifications. Whenever a media stream request is received, the media repository notify the media segment specifications to the request ingestion. Then, once the task is assigned to one of the Task Execution Units, a copy of the original media segment is then transferred to the Task Execution Unit, waiting to be processed. Media Repository can be augmented with content deduplication and approximate storage features, as discussed in Chap. 6.

To help manage the growing library of media repository, MSC stores media's metadata in a data-structure separate from the media segments for quick access. Such metadata are accessible by the scheduler module to makes its scheduling decisions. In addition to the common predefined data fields (such as resolution, bit-rate, codec), MSC allows extra customized data fields to be stored as dictionary along side other data. An example use-case of extra information is to help providers categorize their content to be available only for a specific set of users (e.g., premium users or only users over specified age).

In the case where MSC is deployed in a distributed or federated manner (similar to those discussed in Chap. 7), Media Repository of each MSC node can store just a subset of the entire media library expected to be used in such location, rather than the full repository. A request for a content that does not exist in such a location will result in the Media Repository to fetch the missing segments from other nearby MSC nodes.

9.5.2   Service Repository

Service repository manages the types of processing that the MSC can perform. In MSC, a new stream processing service can be dynamically defined by the users (e.g., stream service provider or even the end users). Traditionally, each serverless function is a stateless standalone function that is initiated to execute one task (then terminate). However, due to the nature of media processing that can have a large framework dependency footprint, MSC also allows frequently used functions to be offered in the form of a durable container. That is, each container is kept alive to serve multiple instance of a specific set of task types (that share the same processing framework). Doing so, MSC can significantly reduce the overhead of loading large functions that are used repeatedly. We later experiment this overhead in Sect. 9.6.2.

9.5.3   Request Ingestion

Request ingestion handles all processing requests being made by viewers. Upon an arrival of user request, the request ingestion validates the user accessibility of the content (including user billing balance availability). Then, each one of the streaming request generates multiple tasks that can be processed in parallel. In essence, the request ingestion component converts the user request to tasks for the MSC to handle with defined deadline. For most media streaming, each request has the individual deadline as the presentation time of the media segment [9].

In certain cases where the specified media with exact specifications are already cached, the content is then sent directly to the user without reprocessing.

9.5.4 Task Admission Control

Admission control is the front gate of the task queue (queue for tasks waiting to be scheduled by the scheduler) and it is in charge of assigning a priority level and a certain internal metadata to each media segment based on their level of urgency. Furthermore, it can be extended to perform other functions such as deduplicating or merging the arriving task to an existing one in the system, as discussed in Chap. 6.

Each of the processing task is an association between (a) the pre-split media segment required by the media stream. We pre-split the media in such a way that it allows them to be parallel processed independently; (b) processing service available in the *Service Repository*; and (c) processing specification and metadata. Note that a certain function may require more than one pre-split media segment at a time. For example, a sound mixer function may require vocal media segment, music segment and effect segment to combine them in a user-defined volume settings before streaming to the end user.

9.5.5 Task Queue

In MSC, Task is defined as a pair of object (i.e., media segment) and the action (a.k.a., function call, with its parameters). The task is formally defined as $Tq = \{(s_x y, f_i) | Tq \subset S x F\}$ where $S = \{s_{xy} | x \in \forall Media I D, y \in Segment I D\}$ and $F = \{f_i | \forall f_i \in Service Repository\}$. In addition, tasks in the system are categorized in four states for the scheduling purpose. They are *Unmapped* Task—which means they are not mapped to be executed on a computing unit, *Pending* Task (mapped and waiting to be executed on a computing unit, *Running* Task on each computing unit and finally, *Completed* Task which complete its execution from the computing unit. Only tasks in the unmapped stage reside in the central task queue. Tasks in other states are dispatched to the assigned computing node.

9.5.6 Task Scheduler

MSC takes scheduler logic as a modular plug-and-play component. We implemented a few example schedulers including the ones discussed in Sect. 5.5.1. To deploy them in MSC, several restriction must be enforced on each scheduler to fit the system: First, not all Task Execution Units can process any given task type. This is due to the nature of heterogeneous task and computing resources along with service container availability. Second, even the Task Execution Units capable of processing the task type can get too busy to be considered as a candidate (i.e., their waiting queue is too long). Third, the scheduling decisions must comply with billing policy that is defined with stream service provider.

9.5.7 Task Execution Time Estimator

Time Estimator predicts task execution time (and completion time) of each request on each Task Execution Unit. For the balance of usability and prediction accuracy, the Time Estimator model execution time follows a normal distribution. Hence, the result of timing predictions has a mean and standard deviation component. However, the class can be overwritten to predict the execution time in more complicated ways, e.g., with Probability Mass Function (PMF) or Probability Density Function (PDF) as necessary.

We prototyped three implementations of the Time Estimator in the MSC. In an implementation called profile mode, the Time Estimator reads the pre-defined table for the expected execution time of each media segment, with the specified processing service on the specified Task Execution Unit type. This mode is highly deterministic and is primary suitable for testing and simulating the Scheduler.

In another implementation called learn-mode, Time Estimator accumulates historical data from prior task executions to form knowledge for estimating each task type of the later occurrences. Unlike profile mode, the Time Estimator in this mode does not attempt to discriminate the estimation data between different media segments. In other words, a task that involves the same operation on the same Task Execution Unit yields the same Time Estimation, regardless of involved media segments. This mode is useful when a high task type variation is expected and there is no complete execution time profile available. Finally, a third configuration of Time Estimator called hybrid-mode. In this mode, it uses data in the predefined table as in profile mode when there is a estimation profile available. For those that do not have a predefined estimation profile available, it predicts using the learning-mode logic.

9.5.8 Execution Engine

Execution Engine consists of scalable pool of Task Execution Units. We define a Task Execution Unit as the most granular computing resource in the view of the scheduler. It must have its own machine queue that the scheduler can assign task to. Once started, each Task Execution Unit in the Execution Engine listens to its machine queue for tasks assigned from the scheduler. The machine queue is vital for efficient usage of processing power by minimizing the resource idle time between the scheduling events. Upon task arrival to machine task queue, the Task Execution Unit fetches the corresponding media (such as video segment) ahead of its turn to execution. All machine queues are managed largely in a FCFS manner for tasks with normal priority. However, a task with a high priority can skip the line for urgent execution.

9.5.8.1 Heterogeneity Within the Execution Engine

A Function Execution Unit in the MSC platform can be launched as a Bare-Metal machine, a VM, or a container. In this prototype, we focus on using containers as the default function execution units because it has lower overhead than a virtual machine while still providing some isolation and portability. Within the container platform, there are still two types of function execution scheme: (a) launch as a *ephemeral* container on-demand, or (b) pre-allocate them *durable* container(s).

In the first configuration (top configuration in Fig. 9.3), each container platform (e.g., Docker platform) has a task queue outside of the function containers. Upon receiving a task request, a function container is created to serve such task before terminating once the task is completed. This execution model allows multiple functions to time-share the computing resources. Launching functions as ephemeral containers is a vital approach to support a large function repository within a limited memory space. However, this type of Task Execution Unit imposes significant overhead of repeatedly launch and terminate function containers. The repeated overhead can compose of (a) fetching a container from repository, (b) starting the container (c) forward and initialize the task (including video segment) from the shared queue into the container.

The second configuration of the function execution unit has a scheduling queue and the functional code self-contained inside each container. Such that, each container has its own task queue that is accessible from the main task scheduler, without utilizing task queue of the container platform first. Each container is created

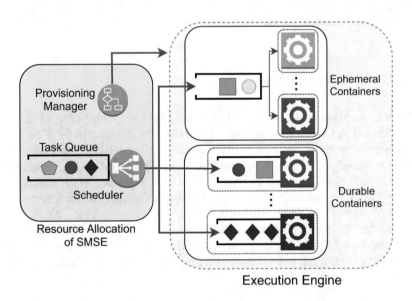

Fig. 9.3 A simplified example of the provisioning manager controlling function containers in two configurations. The top one has centralized machine queue which create a ephemeral container for each task. The later configuration creates durable containers to serve their targeted task types

to serve multiple tasks of a specific set of functions. We call function executed in this manner a *durable* container.

Executing tasks in this durable container configuration reduce the overhead of repeatedly launch and terminating containers as well as less data forwarding overhead versus the ephemeral one. However, it is wasteful on the memory to keep functions available when there is no task to utilize the container. Therefore, a provisioner to minimize idle durable container is required. We evaluate the overhead of durable containers against the ephemeral ones in Sect. 9.6.2.2.

9.5.9 Provisioning Manager and Elasticity Manager

In a large function repository, the usage frequency of each function vary, with only a small portion of the functions used frequently and the rest are rarely accessed. Therefore, expanding the execution unit's memory to keep them all available for rapid activation does not make sense economically. It is of a paramount importance to select which functions to provision them the dedicated resource for rapid execution, in contrast to other functions that are made available upon request. Additionally, each popular function can be so popular that a single function execution unit (i.e., container) cannot cope with its usage. Such that, it can be more beneficial for the duplicated execution unit of popular functions than to use such resource for a less popular function. To enable this, Function Provisioning Manager monitors and adjusts available function instance inside each computing host. Specifically, which function (container) and how many of its worker instances to keep ready in the host to serve the upcoming tasks.

While Function Provisioning Manager handles function deployment, Elasticity Manager manages scaling in and out of the computing resources. Like that, it retrieves more computing hosts (physical and virtual machines) upon the increase in workload and reduces it when the workload stress reduces. In the case that MSC is deployed on top of a public serverless cloud that cannot control the actual provisioning, MSC's Provisioning Manager operates in an alternative mode where it adjusts the appropriate budget limit to the serverless platform usage, leaving the actual resource management works to the serverless platform.

9.5.10 Stream Manager

Stream Manager resides near the end of the processing pipeline. It keeps track of all requested media segments of all users and making sure all segments are processed properly and in a timely manner. In the case that a certain segment is missing, Stream Manager can request the Admission Control to resend the processing request of the segment in an urgent priority. Stream Manager also allows the multi-stage (i.e., workflow) tasks to be performed in the system. When the Stream Manager detect a task that needs to be processed further with a different service function to reach the viewer's specification, it generates the new task accordingly.

9.5.11   Media Caching

The last stage before the media stream reaches the viewer is the Media Caching component. The Media Caching manages the streaming channel (direct streaming, or through CD [11]) and billing is charged at this stage. The caching system can determine the hotness [2] (i.e., popularity) of each segment. Media segments that are predicted to be requested again in the near future can be cached for reusing in a local caching server or on CDN [12].

9.6   Performance Evaluation

9.6.1   Experimental Setup

The experiments are organized in two parts. The first two experiments focus on evaluating the function deployment configurations. The rest of the experiments, evaluate MSC as a whole system with different scheduling policies.

The media repository we used for evaluation includes a set of videos. Videos in the repository set are diverse both in terms of the content types and length. The length of the videos in the repository varies in the range of [10, 220] seconds splitting into 5–110 video segments. The benchmark videos are publicly available for reproducibility purposes.[1] The processing services in the experiment includes: reducing resolution, adjusting bit rate, and adjusting frame rate. In each case, two conversion parameters are examined. For example, frame rate is changed from 60 fps down to either 30 or 24 fps.

To evaluate the system under various workload intensities, user requests are profiled to request for [1500, 3000] media segment processing tasks within a fixed time interval. Other than the first two experiments, all functions are deployed as warm start functions. Processing tasks arrive to the system in a group of up to 20 consecutive segments at a time. To accurately profile common workload arrival pattern observed in the real video steaming systems, each workload repeatedly toggle their arrival rate between base period and high load period where the arrival rate is increased by twofold. Each base period is approximately three times longer than the high load period.

---

[1] https://github.com/hpcclab/videostreamingBenchmark.

9.6.2 Evaluating Task Execution Unit Configurations

In this part, we compare the start-up overhead of various deployment schemes of the Task Execution Unit. In MSC, the Task Execution Unit can be deployed in various ways including on bare-metal, VMs, or on a container. To cope with the ever-changing demand of each function, the number of Task Execution Units of each function is periodically adjusted. Therefore, a low start-up overhead of the resource can help to keep up with the surge in demand without resorting to a high number of spare resources.

9.6.2.1 Evaluating Startup Latency of Task Execution Units

Figure 9.4 shows the start-up latency of three Task Execution Unit deployments: bare-metal, container, and VM. We evaluate the start up latency of three function sizes. A small function has a function code that compile to 200 MB container Image. A medium function requires multiple video processing dependencies make the total function container 400 MB. Finally, a large function require 600 MB of space.

The latency of starting VMs in our set-up is far beyond other schemes at over 12 s in all the configurations. Therefore, we leave their data out of the chart for the clarity of other configurations. Performance wise, starting a Task Execution Unit on bare-metal has the least start-up overhead. However, such configuration lack isolation and scaling flexibility. A Function Execution Unit running on a bare-metal can potentially interfere with others, particularly, because each function has its own

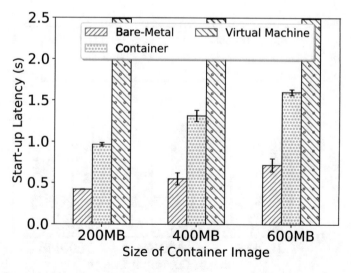

Fig. 9.4 Comparing the start-up latency of three Task Execution Unit deployments: bare-metal, container and virtual machine. X-axis shows the size of the functioning program code. Y-axis shows the time in seconds to start all the Task Execution Units indicated in X-axis

software dependency that conflicts with others. Deploying the Task Execution Unit in a container eliminates such a downside, while imposing a minimal overhead.

9.6.2.2   Evaluating the Ephemeral Container Versus Durable Container

In this part, we evaluate the overhead of using containers for task processing as ephemeral containers and durable containers as proposed in Sect. 9.5.2. We experiment with the same three function sizes as the previous experiment.

Figure 9.5 shows the round trip time from assigning one to four tasks to getting the processing result back from the Task Execution Units. A durable function takes more time to initialize before running the first task. This extra overhead is due to initialization of the message queue registration with the scheduler. However, following tasks (reusing the durable container) experience a shorter execution time than running it with ephemeral function container. Therefore, it is advisable to allocate frequently used functions as durable containers.

9.6.3   Evaluating Scheduling Policy

In this part, we evaluate the perceived QoS [5, 7] of the users in the system with three scheduling policies, namely QoS Aware (termed Priority in the Figure), First-Come-First-Serve (FCFS), and Earliest-Deadline-First (EDF). The task executions run on eight concurrent durable containers. Figure 9.6 shows the deadline miss-

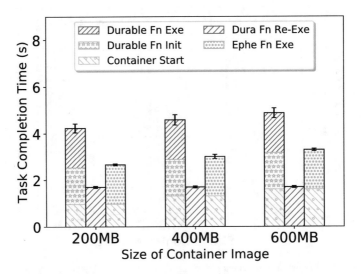

Fig. 9.5 Comparing the execution time of tasks in three various sizes executed on durable function and ephemeral function

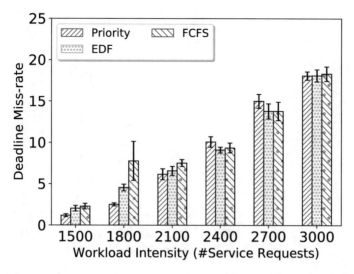

Fig. 9.6 Comparing the deadline miss-rate of system with various workload intensity with various scheduling policies

rate as the workload intensity increases. We found that the deadline miss-rate of three scheduling policies is not significantly different from each other. Therefore, we measure other factors in addition to the deadline miss-rate, namely: start-up delays and fairness.

To evaluate the streaming start-up delay, we measure the end-to-end time from when the stream request arrives in the system to the time that the first segment is delivered to the viewer. Figure 9.7 shows the start-up delay of systems with different task scheduling policies across various workload intensities. Note that all these workload intensities are causing oversubscription in the system. Specifically, even at 1500 tasks arrival during the time window, the system already misses a few percentages of task deadlines (see Fig. 9.6). By the nature of how each policy operates, the QoS-Aware (priority) scheduling policy yields the lowest start-up delay by far. This is because the priority-based scheduling policy prioritizes the first few segments of each video stream over the later ones. Therefore, this policy likely results in the lowest waiting time for each streaming.

9.6.3.1   Evaluating Fairness Across Users

In this part, we assume each user to request exactly one media stream. Recalling that deadline miss-rate are similar between each of the scheduling policy, the variance of deadline miss-rate across different streams can indicate unfairness. Specifically, stream with a high deadline miss-rate get unfair treatment compare to another stream that has a lower deadline miss-rate. Based on the result in Fig. 9.8, QoS-Aware (priority) scheduling is also the fairest scheduling policy. It makes sure that each

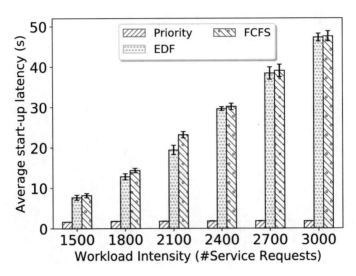

Fig. 9.7 Comparing the start-up delay of the first video segment of each stream between the systems with different scheduling policy

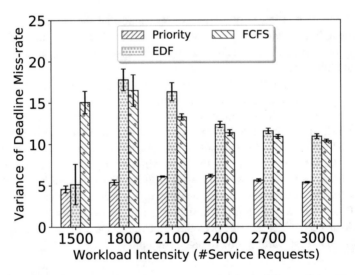

Fig. 9.8 Comparing the fairness among users as a result of scheduling policies. Vertical axis shows the suffering variation of each user measured by variance of deadline miss-rate across video streams

user can get their first few media segments in a timely manner. Then, if the system cannot keep up with the workload intensity, all the streams suffer equally.

9.7 Summary

In this chapter, we designed a prototype implementation of MSC to enables interactive streaming services on serverless cloud in a cost-efficient manner. The architecture is designed to be modular and extensible for future alterations.

The platform allows stream service provider to define their own functions while offering tools and services to aids efficient use of resources to serve media streaming related tasks. By deploying multiple MSC across many serverless computing clouds in different locations, the MSC allows small to achieve efficient and low latency interactive streaming in a cost-effective manner.

References

1. Mahmoud Darwich, Ege Beyazit, Mohsen Amini Salehi, and Magdy Bayoumi. Cost efficient repository management for cloud-based on-demand video streaming. In *Proceedings of the 5th IEEE International Conference on Mobile Cloud Computing, Services, and Engineering*, pages 39–44, Apr. 2017.
2. Mahmoud Darwich, Mohsen Amini Salehi, Ege Beyazit, and Magdy Bayoumi. Cost-efficient cloud-based video streaming through measuring hotness. *The Computer Journal*, Jun. 2018.
3. Simon Eismann, Joel Scheuner, Erwin van Eyk, Maximilian Schwinger, Johannes Grohmann, Nikolas Herbst, Cristina Abad, and Alexandru Iosup. Serverless applications: Why, when, and how? *IEEE Software*, 2020.
4. Simon Eismann, Joel Scheuner, Erwin van Eyk, Maximilian Schwinger, Johannes Grohmann, Nikolas Herbst, Cristina L Abad, and Alexandru Iosup. A review of serverless use cases and their characteristics. *arXiv preprint arXiv:2008.11110*, 2020.
5. Matin Hosseini, Mohsen Amini Salehi, and Raju Gottumukkala. Enabling interactive video streaming for public safety monitoring through batch scheduling. In *Accepted in the 19th IEEE International Conference on High Performance Computing and Communications*, Dec. 2017.
6. Fareed Jokhio, Tewodros Deneke, Sébastien Lafond, and Johan Lilius. Analysis of video segmentation for spatial resolution reduction video transcoding. In *Proceedings of IEEE International Symposium on Intelligent Signal Processing and Communications Systems (ISPACS)*, pages 1–6, 2011.
7. Fareed Jokhio, Tewodros Deneke, Sébastien Lafond, and Johan Lilius. Analysis of video segmentation for spatial resolution reduction video transcoding. In *Proceedings of the 19th International Symposium on Intelligent Signal Processing and Communications Systems*, ISPACS '11, pages 1–6, Dec. 2011.
8. Xiangbo Li, Mohsen Amini Salehi, Magdy Bayoumi, and Rajikumar Buyya. CVSS: A Cost-Efficient and QoS-Aware Video Streaming Using Cloud Services. In *Proceedings of the 16th IEEE/ACM International Symposium on Cluster, Cloud, and Grid Computing*, CCGrid '16, May 2016.

9. Xiangbo Li, Mohsen Amini Salehi, and Magdy Bayoumi. VLSC: Video Live Streaming Using Cloud Services. In *Proceedings of the 6th IEEE International Conference on Big Data and Cloud Computing Conference*, BDCloud '16, pages 595–600, Oct. 2016.

10. Wes Lloyd, Shruti Ramesh, Swetha Chinthalapati, Lan Ly, and Shrideep Pallickara. Serverless computing: An investigation of factors influencing microservice performance. In *Proceedings of the 2018 IEEE International Conference on Cloud Engineering*, IC2E '18, pages 159–169, Apr. 2018.

11. P. A. L. Rego, M. S. Bonfim, M. D. Ortiz, J. M. Bezerra, D. R. Campelo, and J. N. de Souza. An OpenFlow-Based Elastic Solution for Cloud-CDN Video Streaming Service. In *Proceedings of IEEE Global Communications Conference (GLOBECOM)*, pages 1–7, Dec 2015.

12. Vaughan Veillon, Chavit Denninnart, and Mohsen Amini Salehi. F-FDN: Federation of fog computing systems for low latency video streaming. In *Proceedings of the 3rd IEEE International Conference on Fog and Edge Computing*, ICFEC '19, pages 1–9, May 2019.

13. H. Zeng, Z. Zhang, and L. Shi. Research and implementation of video codec based on FFmpeg. In *Proceedings of 2nd International Conference on Network and Information Systems for Computers (ICNISC)*, pages 184–188, April 2016.

Chapter 10
Future of Multimedia Streaming and Cloud Technology

10.1 Overview

Multimedia streaming is one of the most prevalent and resource-hungry Internet-based services that will shape up the future of human's lifestyle. Considering the new variations of multimedia streaming, such as 360-degree video and AR/VR streaming, maintaining a high QoE and uninterrupted streaming experience is a key. This process is dependent on several other technologies—from content production technologies at the source to processing them on the cloud and playing them on a widely variety of display devices at the destination.

In this chapter, we discuss the future of Cloud-based multimedia streaming and the areas that are intact or require further exploration by researchers and practitioners. In the rest of this chapter, we discuss several of these areas that we believe addressing them will impact in the future of multimedia streaming and/or special-purpose clouds.

10.2 Application-Specific Integrated Circuits (ASICs) in Domain-Specific Clouds

Current cloud-based multimedia stream providers predominantly utilize homogeneous cloud services (e.g., in form of homogeneous VMs) for stream processing [11, 12]. However, clouds providers are increasingly becoming heterogeneous [13] and use specialized computing resources. In addition to using accelerators such as GPUs and FPGAs, Application Specific Integrated Circuits (ASICs) are becoming popular. For instance, machines built only for transcoding from a certain source and destination codec. This is in addition to conventional heterogeneity in cloud machine types that are offered in cloud providers such as Amazon and Microsoft Azure [13] that offer CPU-optimized, Memory-optimized, and IO-optimized. Heterogeneity

© Springer Nature Switzerland AG 2021
M. A. Salehi, X. Li, *Multimedia Cloud Computing Systems*,
https://doi.org/10.1007/978-3-030-88451-2_10

may also refer to the reliability of the provisioned services. For instance, cloud providers offer *spot* and *reserved* compute services that cost remarkably lower than the normal compute services [9]. The heterogeneity is not limited to compute services and are extended to heterogeneous storage services (e.g., SSD, HDD, and tape-based storage services).

Specifically, elastic resource provisioning methods in conventional cloud systems determine *when* and *how many* resources to be provisioned. By considering heterogeneity, a third dimension has appeared: *what type* of resources should be provisioned? The more specific questions that must be addressed are: how can we harness cloud services to offer video streaming with QoE considerations and with the minimum incurred the cost for the video stream provider? How can we learn the affinity (i.e., the match) of a user-defined function with the heterogeneous services? How can we strike a balance between the incurred cost of heterogeneous services and the performance offered? and finally, how should the heterogeneity of the allocated resources be modified (i.e., reconfigured) with respect to the type and rate of arriving video streaming requests?

10.3   Efficient Scheduling of Functions on Heterogeneous Machines

Once a set of potentially heterogeneous machines are allocated to the worker containers of a given function, the next issue is to schedule the segments (tasks) of different users, such that their QoEs (deadlines) are met.Scheduling decisions on heterogeneous machines are made in consultation with a matrix that includes the execution time information of that task type on different machine types [19]. In particular, the execution time information of segment m for task type i on machine type j, denoted as m_{ij}, is inferred based on the historic execution time information of task type i on machine type j, plus the characteristics of s (e.g., its data size). The challenge is that for newly-defined functions, there is not such historic execution information. Lack of such information causes uninformed scheduling decisions and becomes an impediment in achieving the scheduling goals.

Transfer learning is a technique to reuse the knowledge gained while solving one problem and applying it to a different but related problem [21]. Accordingly, to address this challenge, transfer learning can be employed to predict the execution time of a new task type on a given machine type based on the trained networks of other task types on the same machine type (i.e., based on entries of the same column in the matrix). Methods are required to measure the similarity between the new task type and each one of the existing task types. For that purpose, each task type can be represented as a vector in the space defined by dependencies and libraries of that task type and then the distance between the two vectors can be found. Then, the weighted average similarity of the new task type with other task types is calculated to infer the execution time of the new task type on that machine type. Once enough execution time information for the new task type is collected, a model specific to that task type can be trained to infer its execution time independent from other task types.

Although a point-estimate machine learning model that operates based on historical execution time information and characteristics of the arriving task can provide an idea about the execution time of the task on that machine type, it ignores the uncertainties present in the prediction. That is, the real execution time might be different than the estimation. The uncertainty is higher for the predictions made by the transfer learning [27]. If the uncertainty in the prediction is not captured, it perturbs the scheduling decisions. To make the scheduling robust against the uncertainty, machine learning models (e.g., based on the Gaussian Process [8]) can be utilized that consider uncertainties and output the posterior probability distribution of the execution time of the task without demanding significant training data. Using the execution time distribution, the scheduler can calculate the probability of on-time completion for each task by convolving the execution time distribution of tasks ahead of it [5]. The task should be assigned to the machine that offers the highest chance of success.

10.4 Supporting Both Live and On-Demand Multimedia Streaming on the Same Underlying Resources

Live and VOD streaming are structurally similar, thus, have similar computational demands. However, processing them is not entirely the same. In particular, live-streaming tasks have a hard deadline and have to be dropped if they miss their deadline [11] whereas VOD tasks have a soft deadline and can tolerate deadline violations. Accordingly, in VOD, upon violating deadlines for a segment, the deadlines of all segments behind it in the same stream should be updated. That is, VOD tasks have dynamic deadlines which is not the case for live streaming. In addition, there is no historic computational information for live-streaming tasks to predict the execution time of new arriving tasks. This is not the case for VOD tasks.

Based on these differences, stream providers currently utilize different streaming engines and even different resources/racks for processing and providing the live and VOD services [10, 11]. The question is that how can we have an integrated streaming engine that can accommodate both of the streaming types simultaneously on a single set of allocated resources? How will this affect the scheduling and processing time estimation of the streaming engine?

10.5   Blockchain Technology for Multimedia Streaming

The idea of blockchain is to create a secure peer-to-peer communication through a distributed ledger (database). In this method, every network node owns a copy of the blockchain, and every copy includes the full history of all recorded transactions. All nodes must agree on a transaction before it is placed in the blockchain.

The idea has rapidly got adopted and is being extensively developed in various domains to improve traceability and auditability [2]. We envisage that this technology will have a great impact in the multimedia streaming industry. Some of the applications can be as follows: White-listing, which means keeping a list of legitimate publishers or distributors; Identity Management: the ability to perform identity management in a decentralized manner.

Blockchain technology provides more controls and opportunities to content producers/publishers. In fact, the current multimedia streaming industry is driven by quality expected and algorithms embedded in the streaming service providers. For instance, ordinary people cannot be publishers on Netflix. Even in the case of YouTube that enables ordinary users to publish content, the search and prioritization algorithms are driven by YouTube and not by the publisher. These limitations are removed in blockchain and publishers have more freedom in exposing their generated content. The secure distribution network of blockchain can be also useful for current streaming service providers (e.g., Netflix). They can use the network to securely maintain multiple versions of videos near viewers and distribute them with low latency and at the meantime reduce their cloud storage costs.

10.6   Reuse and Approximate Computing of Functions in Multimedia Clouds and Other Domain-Specific Clouds

Previous studies show that streaming requests have spatiotemporal patterns [25]. That is, there is a considerable chance for a multimedia content to be streamed by similar/compatible services/functions. For instance, in an online education system consider two scenarios: *First*, students playback the same videos during the exam week; *Second*, consider two viewers who need to view the same content on dissimilar display devices. They both have to call the change resolution function, but with different arguments (e.g., distinct resolutions). The first instance creates *identical* tasks in the system that can fully reuse computation, whereas the latter one creates *similar* tasks that share *part* of their computation (to decode the same content), while each task has its individual part (to encode to different resolutions).

Reusing computation via function aggregation (a.k.a. merging), if applied intelligently, can reduce the makespan time and achieve cost- (and energy-) efficiency. It can also mitigate the load, when the system is oversubscribed and there is a higher chance of finding similarity. The challenge in this part is to detect identical and similar functions and aggregate them before execution (while pending). In particular, our early observations indicate that not all merging cases are necessarily worthwhile performing. In fact, merging tasks increases both the execution time and uncertainty of the merged task, hence, can potentially hurt the QoS of other tasks. Accordingly, two problems are posed: (a) How to maximize the chance of finding mergeable functions? (b) For a given merging case, how to know its gain and side-effects prior to performing it?

Current reusing approaches operate based on caching [4, 26]. However, caching is limited in reusing identical tasks that are already completed [26] and cannot capture partial reusing [18]. Moreover, live-streaming tasks naturally cannot be cached, but can benefit from our reusing mechanism. The reusing mechanism can operates within the Admission Control module of the MSC that detects identical or similar functions calls upon invocation. In addition to detecting partially overlapping functions, the reusing mechanism should measure the benefit and side-effects of any given merging case and determine if it is worthwhile to perform it.

Compromising the QoS of a few tasks can potentially enhance the likelihood of merging and improve the overall QoS and this should be considered in the research on this topic. The likelihood of merging functions can increase by leveraging the spatiotemporal patterns in the streaming requests [3, 24]. In particular, deferring of a task (request) can increase the likelihood of receiving similar tasks and achieving task merging. The question is that, for a given streaming task, how long it should be deferred to maximize the chance of merging with other tasks without missing its QoS constraint? This question can be answered by taking the popularity of function calls of a content into consideration [14, 22, 23]. To maximize the likelihood of reusing for a popular request, it is worthwhile to defer its execution to the extent possible, i.e., before endangering its deadline. Conversely, for unpopular requests, it is unlikely to receive similar ones, hence, there is no advantage in deferring them. To defer popular tasks to the extent possible, one can define a *Latest Start Time (LST)* as the latest time a popular task can start its execution without missing its deadline. LST can be calculated based on the worst-case analysis of the tasks' stochastic completion time.

10.7 Machine Learning for Multimedia Processing

Methods based on modern machine learning (ML) and deep neural networks (DNN) are widely usable in multimedia stream processing and have brought previously unforeseen capabilities. In particular, they can be used in the functions developed by the stream providers in the MSC platform to offer novel services, such as dynamic content rating of the multimedia contents, object- and motion-detection, dynamic language translation, face detection, text detection, among many others.

Provided that Convolutional Neural Networks (CNNs) offer superior performance when applied to the computer vision and image processing, they can be employed for the basic live and on-demand streaming services offered to viewers in MSC. Specifically, CNN-based methods are used for video compression (encoding/decoding), transcoding, and enhancement imply multiple predictions, e.g., intra- and inter-frame prediction [17] to improve them and produce smaller size videos without a major loss on the video quality. In general, deeper (hence, more complicated) CNNs can offer a more accurate processing and capture more complex patterns in the input multimedia content. For instance, ResNet [7], as a widely used network model in video processing, includes more than 100 layers. This complex structure often makes it difficult to achieve the real-time QoE for the streaming. Moreover, current ML and DNN models predominantly have a black box nature and are in lack of transparency.

One such experience appeared in the development of the Versatile Video Coding (VVC) standard [17], the successor of HEVC, that can reduce the bit-rate by 50% without affecting the video quality. Although DNN methods can theoretically be used to further improve VVC, the complexity of these methods is the main impediment of such improvement. As such, DNN solutions cannot be blindly employed in production. For effective usage of DNN methods in multimedia streaming further research needs to be undertaken in the following areas: (a) They have to be interpretable (i.e., properly explained and understood) to reduce the chance of unexpected outcomes. In other words, transparent DNNs will make it possible to build up trust with these methods as we can see what is happening in the network. (b) They have to be less complex and simplified to make them usable for real-time use cases in multimedia streaming.

10.8 Avoiding Bias in MSC and Other Domain-Specific Clouds

Different forms of bias and unfairness exist in the computing world and cloud computing as well. This is because human is directly involved in all phases of developing a software solution—from the requirement analysis to the development and testing. As such, the inherent bias in the human's mind can be (is) either consciously or unconsciously reflected in the solutions they develop [6]. This includes various forms of biases, from gender and ethnicity bias to culture, language, geography, and even biases related to physical challenges [20]. For instance, a video suggestion service that operates based on the gender and navigates the minds of people to certain topics suffers from the gender bias (or age bias when it is applied to kids). Excluding certain languages in a translation service of MSC is considered as a form of language bias. One example of the ethnic bias can appear in a face detection service that is more sensitive to detecting people of a certain ethnicity or skin color. An example of the culture bias can occur in an automatic content rating service of MSC that considers certain contents as appropriate for kids, while it is deemed inappropriate in the culture of some viewers. A geographical bias can be caused by the MSC platform when the QoE of streaming in a certain jurisdiction(s) is lower than others.

Accordingly, we argue that one aspect that requires specific attention and research in the next generation of cloud computing systems is to provide bias-free and human-centric solutions. In particular, dealing with the challenge of how to incorporate diverse viewers' demands (e.g., gender, age, culture, language, etc.) in the developed services. Similarly, how to achieve fairness in streaming for people located in different areas. Other related challenges can be human-centric distribution of compute and data in edge systems of MSC? How to perform caching and low-latency based on human-centric factors rather than being only cost oriented? Importantly, investigations are needed in domain-specific clouds to support human-centric feedback and service providers (or developers) can understand these issues.

10.9 Dependability of Cloud-Based Multimedia Streaming

Reliability and dependability of a multimedia streaming service is one of the main advantages of MSC and other domain-specific cloud systems. Reliability is measured based on the tolerance of the streaming services against possible failures and uncertainties. MSC offers its streaming services under a certain Service Level Agreement (SLA) with the stream providers. SLA explains the availability of services and the latency of accessing them. A multimedia streaming engine translates the SLA terms to its Service Level Objectives (SLO) [15] and attempts to respect them even in the presence of failures. Fault tolerance is defined against two types of failures as follows:

- **Fault tolerance of cloud services.** Availability of Cloud services (e.g., processing, content delivery, and storage) is critical for streaming providers. To maintain the availability, upon failure in a server, its workload has to be migrated to another server to keep the streaming service uninterrupted. Service fault tolerance has been widely studied in cloud computing and solutions for that mainly include redundancy of cloud services and data checkpointing [1, 16].
- **Fault tolerance in multimedia processing.** Some streaming tasks may fail during the processing. Multimedia streaming engines should include policies to cope with the failure of streaming tasks being processed. The policies can re-dispatch the failed task for on-demand streaming or ignore it for live-streaming.

Currently, there is not any failure-aware solution tailored for multimedia streaming. Given the specific characteristics of video streaming services, in terms of large data-size, expensive computation, and unique QoE expectations, it will be necessary to explore failure-aware solutions for reliable multimedia streaming services.

References

1. Anju Bala and Inderveer Chana. Fault tolerance-challenges, techniques and implementation in cloud computing. *International Journal of Scientific and Research Publications (IJSRP)*, 9(1):1694–0814, June 2012.

2. Rajkumar Buyya, Satish Narayana Srirama, Giuliano Casale, Rodrigo Calheiros, Yogesh Simmhan, Blesson Varghese, Erol Gelenbe, Bahman Javadi, Luis Miguel Vaquero, Marco AS Netto, et al. A manifesto for future generation cloud computing: Research directions for the next decade. *ACM Computing Survey*, Aug. 2018.

3. U. Drolia, K. Guo, J. Tan, R. Gandhi, and P. Narasimhan. Cachier: Edge-caching for recognition applications. In *Proceedings of the 37th IEEE International Conference on Distributed Computing Systems (ICDCS)*, pages 276–286, June 2017.

4. Brad Fitzpatrick. Distributed Caching with Memcached. *Linux journal*, 2004(124):5–11, Aug 2004.

5. James Gentry, Chavit Denninnart, and Mohsen Amini Salehi. Robust dynamic resource allocation via probabilistic task pruning in heterogeneous computing systems. In *Proceedings of the 33rd IEEE International Parallel & Distributed Processing Symposium (IPDPS '19)*, May. 2019.

6. John Grundy. Human-centric software engineering for next generation cloud- and edge-based smart living applications. In *Proceedings of the 20th IEEE/ACM International Symposium on Cluster, Cloud and Internet Computing (CCGRID)*, pages 1–10, May 2020.

7. Kaiming He, Xiangyu Zhang, Shaoqing Ren, and Jian Sun. Deep residual learning for image recognition. In *Proceedings of the IEEE conference on computer vision and pattern recognition*, pages 770–778, 2016.

8. L. Hewing, J. Kabzan, and M. N. Zeilinger. Cautious model predictive control using gaussian process regression. *IEEE Transactions on Control Systems Technology*, pages 1–8, 2019.

9. Dinesh Kumar, Gaurav Baranwal, Zahid Raza, and Deo Prakash Vidyarthi. A survey on spot pricing in cloud computing. *Journal of Network and Systems Management*, 26(4):809–856, Oct 2018.

10. Xiangbo Li, Mohsen Amini Salehi, and Magdy Bayoumi. High perform on-demand video transcoding using cloud services. In *Proceedings of the 16th ACM/IEEE International Conference on Cluster Cloud and Grid Computing*, CCGrid '16, May.

11. Xiangbo Li, Mohsen Amini Salehi, and Magdy Bayoumi. VLSC:Video Live Streaming Using Cloud Services. In *Proceedings of the 6th IEEE International Conference on Big Data and Cloud Computing Conference*, BDCloud '16, Oct. 2016.

12. Xiangbo Li, Mohsen Amini Salehi, Magdy Bayoumi, and Rajkumar Buyya. CVSS: A Cost-Efficient and QoS-Aware Video Streaming Using Cloud Services. In *Proceedings of the 16th ACM/IEEE International Conference on Cluster Cloud and Grid Computing*, CCGrid '16, May 2016.

13. Xiangbo Li, Mohsen Amini Salehi, Magdy Bayoumi, Nian-Feng Tzeng, and Rajkumar Buyya. Cost-efficient and robust on-demand video transcoding using heterogeneous cloud services. *IEEE Transactions on Parallel and Distributed Systems (TPDS)*, 29(3):556–571, 2018.

14. Yao-Chung Lin, Chao Chen, Balu Adsumilli, Anil Kokaram, and Steve Benting. Geo-popularity assisted optimized transcoding for large scale adaptive streaming. In *Applications of Digital Image Processing XLI*, volume 10752. International Society for Optics and Photonics, 2018.

15. Guoxin Liu, Haiying Shen, and Haoyu Wang. An economical and SLO-guaranteed cloud storage service across multiple cloud service providers. *IEEE Transactions on Parallel and Distributed Systems*, 28(9):2440–2453, 2017.

16. Sheheryar Malik and Fabrice Huet. Adaptive fault tolerance in real time cloud computing. In *Proceedings of the 2011 IEEE World Congress on Services*, SERVICES '11, pages 280–287, Jul. 2011.

17. Luka Murn, Marc Gorriz Blanch, Maria Santamaria, Fiona Rivera, and Marta Mrak. Towards transparent application of machine learning in video processing, 2021.

18. Rajesh Nishtala, Hans Fugal, Steven Grimm, Marc Kwiatkowski, Herman Lee, Harry C. Li, Ryan McElroy, Mike Paleczny, Daniel Peek, Paul Saab, David Stafford, Tony Tung, and Venkateshwaran Venkataramani. Scaling Memcache at Facebook. In *Proceedings of the 10th USENIX Conference on Networked Systems Design and Implementation*, NSDI '13, pages 385–398, Apr 2013.

19. Mohsen Amini Salehi, Jay Smith, Anthony A. Maciejewski, Howard Jay Siegel, Edwin K. P. Chong, Jonathan Apodaca, Luis D. Briceno, Timothy Renner, Vladimir Shestak, Joshua Ladd, Andrew Sutton, David Janovy, Sudha Govindasamy, Amin Alqudah, Rinku Dewri, and Puneet Prakash. Stochastic-based robust dynamic resource allocation for independent tasks in a heterogeneous computing system. *in Journal of Parallel and Distributed Computing (JPDC)*, 97(C), Nov. 2016.

20. Md. Shamsujjoha, John Grundy, Li Li, Hourieh Khalajzadeh, and Qinghua Lu. Human-centric issues in ehealth app development and usage: A preliminary assessment. In *Proceedings of the IEEE International Conference on Software Analysis, Evolution and Reengineering (SANER)*, pages 506–510, 2021.

21. Chuanqi Tan, Fuchun Sun, Tao Kong, Wenchang Zhang, Chao Yang, and Chunfang Liu. A survey on deep transfer learning. In *International conference on artificial neural networks*, pages 270–279, 2018.

22. Linpeng Tang, Qi Huang, Amit Puntambekar, Ymir Vigfusson, Wyatt Lloyd, and Kai Li. Popularity prediction of facebook videos for higher quality streaming. In *Proceedings of the USENIX Conference on Usenix Annual Technical Conference*, USENIX ATC '17, pages 111–123, 2017.

23. Jiqiang Wu, Yipeng Zhou, Dah Ming Chiu, and Zirong Zhu. Modeling dynamics of online video popularity. *IEEE Transactions on Multimedia*, 18(9):1882–1895, Sep. 2016.

24. Shanhe Yi, Cheng Li, and Qun Li. A survey of fog computing: Concepts, applications and issues. In *Proceedings of the Workshop on Mobile Big Data*, Mobidata '15, pages 37–42, 2015.

25. Hongliang Yu, Dongdong Zheng, Ben Y Zhao, and Weimin Zheng. Understanding user behavior in large-scale video-on-demand systems. In *ACM SIGOPS Operating Systems Review*, volume 40, pages 333–344, 2006.

26. Hao Zhang, Bogdan Marius Tudor, Gang Chen, and Beng Chin Ooi. Efficient In-memory Data Management: An Analysis. *Proceedings of the VLDB Endowment*, 7(10):833–836, Jun 2014.

27. Jing Zhang, Wanqing Li, Philip Ogunbona, and Dong Xu. Recent advances in transfer learning for cross-dataset visual recognition: A problem-oriented perspective. *ACM Computing Surveys*, 52(1), Feb. 2019.

Correction to: Multimedia Cloud Computing Systems

Correction to:
M. A. Salehi, X. Li,
Multimedia Cloud Computing Systems
https://doi.org/10.1007/978-3-030-88451-2

The book was inadvertently published with an incorrect affiliation for one of the author Xiangbo Li as "Brightcove, Scottsdale AZ, USA". It has been updated as "Twitch Interactive Inc., San Francisco, CA, USA"

The updated online version of this book can be found at
https://doi.org/10.1007/978-3-030-88451-2

Printed in the United States
by Baker & Taylor Publisher Services